Better Homes and Gardens®

QUILT-LOVERS' FAVORITES™

FROM AMERICAN PATCHWORK & QUILTING®

Better Homes and Gardens® Creative Collection™
Des Moines, Iowa

VOLUME 6

Better Homes and Gardens®

QUILT-LOVERS' FAVORITES™

FROM AMERICAN PATCHWORK & QUILTING®

Printing Number and Year: 5 4 3 2 1 04 03 02 01

ISSN: 1532-8848 ISBN: 0-696-22871-8

For book editorial questions, write:
Better Homes and Gardens Quilt-Lovers' Favorites • *1716 Locust St., Des Moines, IA 50309-3023*

TREASURED QUILTS

Welcome to Quilt-Lovers' Favorites™, *Volume 6, the latest book from the staff of* American Patchwork & Quilting® *magazine. We're sure you'll be inspired by the wealth of styles, sizes, and colors of the projects found in these pages. The book contains 15 of the quilts most often requested by readers of* American Patchwork & Quilting. *We took a fresh look at these time-tested classics, then created over 30 all-new projects based on each quilt's blocks, units, borders, or appliqué shapes.*

So whether you're looking for a quick gift to make in a weekend or an heirloom bed quilt that generations will cherish, we have you covered with dozens of ideas from wall hangings to pillows to wearables. For even more versatility, charts of optional sizes will let you alter quilt dimensions quickly and easily.

To ensure your success with whatever project you choose, we've included step-by-step instructions, full-size patterns, and Quilter's Schoolhouse—a reference guide on quiltmaking. In addition, full-color photographs, illustrations, and color options no doubt will spark your imagination. Just turn the pages and let the quiltmaking begin!

Heidi Kaisand

Executive Editor, American Patchwork & Quilting

TABLE *of* CONTENTS

TIME AND AGAIN

QUICK-TO-CUT CLASSICS

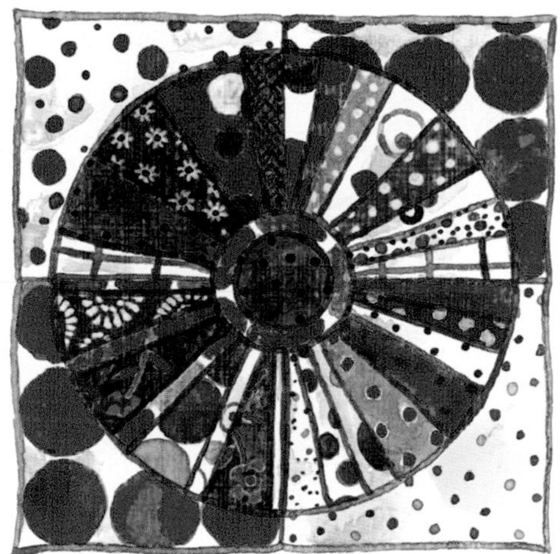

BOLD AND SASSY

TALL TIMBERS

ALWAYS APPLIQUÉ

TIME AND AGAIN

In an effort to preserve the past, we often seek to exactly replicate antique pieces. But well-loved quilt patterns can offer new surprises. Use the elegant "Fleur-de-Lis" appliqués in a graphic bed quilt, integrate the cheerful "Sailor's Voyage" sashing into a flannel throw, and reconfigure the dainty "Seven Sisters" diamond pieces into a scarf embellishment. Take another look at old favorites and delight in new discoveries.

FLEUR-DE-*Lis*

Collector Terry Ferrell purchased this appliqué quilt at an auction in Illinois in the late 1960s. The vivid green fabric indicates the quilt probably was made in the 1870s or '80s. It has the unusual configuration of 12 full blocks and four half blocks.

Materials

5 yards of solid green for appliqués

7 yards of solid ecru for appliqué foundations, border, and binding

5 yards of backing fabric

81×90" of quilt batting

Freezer paper

Finished quilt top: 75×84"
Finished block: 18" square

Quantities are for 44/45"-wide, 100% cotton fabrics. All measurements include a ¼" seam allowance. Sew with right sides together unless otherwise stated.

Designer Notes

The appliquéd fleur-de-lis motif in the antique quilt shown *opposite* was created with multiple pieces. To make it easier to position, this re-creation uses a one-piece fleur-de-lis.

These instructions are for needle-turn appliqué, an effective method for appliquéing small areas like those on this quilt. For best results, use small, sharp scissors for snipping the tiny inner areas of both paper and fabric.

Cut the Fabrics

To make the best use of your fabrics, cut the pieces in the order that follows. The patterns are found on *Pattern Sheet 2*. To make a template of Pattern B, follow the instructions in Quilter's Schoolhouse, which begins on *page 150*. Remember to add a 3⁄16" seam allowance when cutting out the B leaf appliqués.

Cut the border strips lengthwise (parallel to the selvage). The border strip measurements are mathematically correct. You may wish to cut your strips longer than specified to allow for possible sewing differences.

From solid green, cut:

- 1—15×42" rectangle, cutting it into enough 1½"-wide bias strips to total 360" in length for vine (For specific instructions, see Cutting Bias Strips in Quilter's Schoolhouse.)
- 12—18½" squares for fleur-de-lis appliqués
- 4—9½×18½" rectangles for fleur-de-lis appliqués
- 275 of Pattern B

continued

From solid ecru, cut:

- 2—6½×84½" border strips
- 2—6½×63½" border strips
- 9—2½×42" binding strips
- 12—20½" squares for appliqué foundations
- 4—10½×20½" rectangles for appliqué foundations

From freezer paper, cut:

- 14—18" squares

Prepare the Fabrics

1. Fold one solid green 18½" square in half, making a 9¼×18½" rectangle (see Diagram 1). Fold the rectangle in half, making a 9¼" square. Then fold the square in half diagonally, bringing together the folded edges, to make a triangle; press well to create precise placement lines. Repeat with the remaining green 18½" squares and the solid ecru 20½" squares.

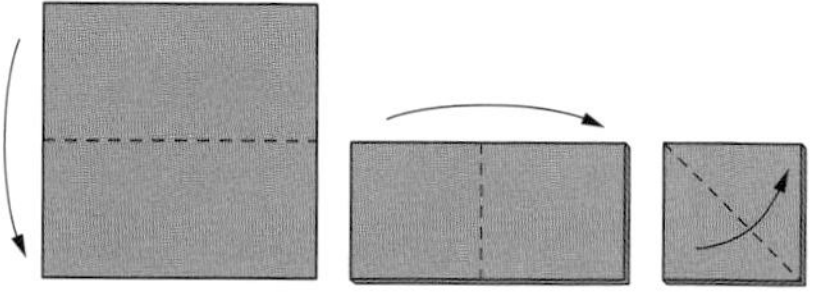

Diagram 1

2. Referring to Diagram 2, fold one solid green 9½×18½" rectangle in half, making a 9½×9¼" rectangle. Then fold the rectangle in half diagonally, leaving a ¼" seam allowance at the bottom, to make a triangle; press well. Repeat with the remaining green 9½×18½" rectangles and the solid ecru 10½×20½" rectangles.

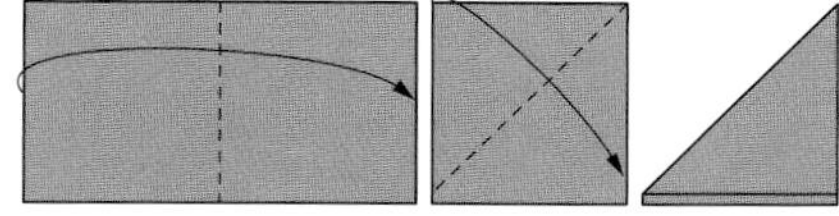

Diagram 2

Make the Freezer-Paper Templates

1. Fold each freezer-paper 18" square, shiny side in, in the same manner described in Prepare the Fabrics, Step 1, sharply creasing each fold. Staple the folds together in a corner of each folded triangle to keep them stable.

2. Align the dashed line of Pattern A with the diagonal fold of a folded freezer-paper triangle. Securely tape or glue the pattern in place.

3. Carefully cut out the design, including the inside open spaces, to make a fleur-de-lis freezer-paper template.

4. Repeat steps 2 and 3 to make a total of 14 fleur-de-lis freezer-paper templates.

Appliqué the Blocks

1. Unfold one solid green 18½" square and one solid ecru 20½" square. Place the solid green square atop the solid ecru square with the right sides of both squares facing up. Carefully align the creases. Pin the squares together along the vertical and horizontal creases.

2. Carefully unfold one fleur-de-lis freezer-paper template. Position the freezer paper on the pinned solid green square, matching the diagonal creases on the template to those on the fabric. Using a hot, dry iron, press the freezer paper to the solid green square. Trace the outline of the pattern with a light-color fabric marker. You'll need to see these marks throughout the appliqué process. Be sure that every part of the design has been traced, then remove the freezer paper. Baste inside each fleur-de-lis shape.

3. Cut a scant ⅛" outside the drawn lines of the appliqué design, cutting a small portion at a time (2" to 3"). Appliqué with green thread and small blind stitches, turning under the edges with your needle as you work. To turn tight inside curves, clip into the seam allowance up to the drawn line. When the appliqué is complete, with the solid green appliqué in the center, trim the solid ecru foundation to measure 18½" square, including the seam allowances, to finish an appliquéd block.

4. Repeat steps 1 through 3 to make a total of 12 appliquéd blocks.

5. Cut the two remaining fleur-de-lis freezer-paper templates in half along the vertical fold line to make a total of four half templates.

6. Unfold a solid green 9½×18½" rectangle and a solid ecru 10½×20½" rectangle. Pin the solid green rectangle atop the solid ecru rectangle with creases aligned and right sides up.

7. Position a half template on the pinned solid green rectangle, matching diagonal creases and leaving a ¼" seam allowance at the bottom. Press the freezer-paper half template to the rectangle. Trace and appliqué the design as before (see Diagram 3). Trim the top and side edges to measure 9½×18½", including the seam allowances, to finish an appliquéd half block.

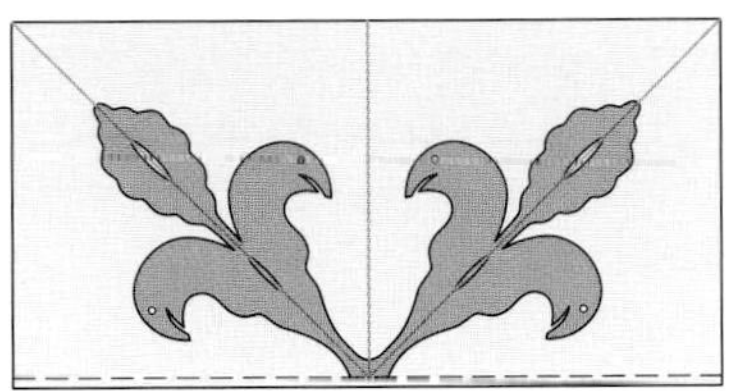

Diagram 3

8. Repeat steps 6 and 7 to make a total of four appliquéd half blocks.

Assemble the Quilt Center

1. Referring to the photograph *opposite*, lay out the appliquéd blocks and half blocks in four rows.

2. Sew together the blocks in each row. Press the seam allowances in one direction, alternating the direction with each row. Then join the rows to make the quilt center. Press the seam allowances in one direction. The pieced quilt center should measure 63½×72½", including the seam allowances.

Add and Appliqué the Border

1. Sew the solid ecru 6½×63½" border strips to the short edges of the pieced quilt center. Press the seam allowances toward the border. Then join the solid ecru 6½×84½" border strips to the long edges of the pieced quilt center to complete the quilt top. Press the seam allowances toward the border.

2. Piece the solid green 1½"-wide bias strips to make a 360"-long strip. Fold the green 360"-long bias strip in half lengthwise with the wrong side inside; press. Stitch ¼" from the long edges (see the Bias Strip Diagram *right*). Trim the seam allowance to ⅛". Refold the strip, centering the seam in the back, to make the vine appliqué; press.

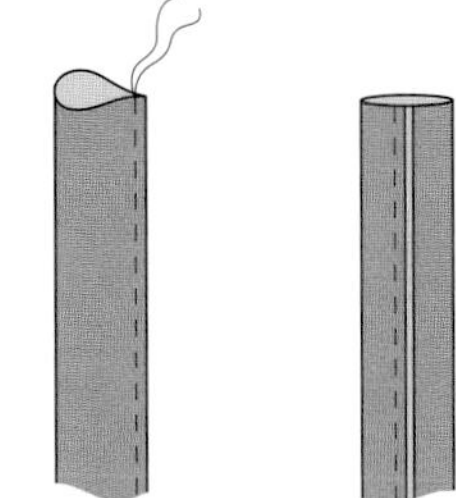

Bias Strip Diagram

3. Prepare the B leaf appliqué pieces by pressing under the ³⁄₁₆" seam allowances.

continued

4. Referring to the photograph on *page 10*, arrange the vine and leaf appliqués on the border, spacing the leaves 1¾" to 2" apart. Baste the pieces in place.

5. Using green thread, appliqué the vine and leaves to the border.

Complete the Quilt

1. Layer the quilt top, batting, and backing according to the instructions in Quilter's Schoolhouse, which begins on *page 150*.

2. Quilt as desired. The antique quilt shown was hand-quilted in the ditch around all the appliqués. Echo-quilting appears between the branches of each fleur-de-lis appliqué, and diagonal lines fill the quilt center.

3. Use the solid ecru 2½×42" strips to bind the quilt according to the instructions in Quilter's Schoolhouse.

Fleur-de-Lis *optional sizes*

If you'd like to make this quilt in a size other than for a throw, use the information *below*. The solid ecru yardage requirements are for cutting binding strips the length of the fabric, instead of across the fabric width.

Alternate quilt sizes	Wall	Full/Queen	King
Number of blocks	4	20	25
Number of blocks wide by long	2×2	4×5	5×5
Finished size	48" square	84×102"	102" square
Yardage requirements			
Solid green	2¼ yards	6½ yards	7⅞ yards
Solid ecru	3 yards	8⅞ yards	10¾ yards
Backing	3 yards	7½ yards	9 yards
Batting	54" square	90×108"	108" square

APPLIQUÉD PILLOW

A quarter of the original appliqué pattern gracefully adorns a decorative pillow.

Materials

¼ yard of dark blue print for fleur-de-lis appliqués

1 yard of blue-and-ivory floral for appliqué foundation and pillow back

⅓ yard of blue-and-ivory print for covered cording

18×32" rectangle of muslin for lining

18×32" of quilt batting

Lightweight fusible web

2¾ yards of ¼"-diameter cording

28×14" pillow form

Finished pillow: 28×14"

Cut the Fabrics

To make the best use of your fabrics, cut the pieces in the order that follows. This project uses "Fleur-de-Lis" Pattern A, which is on *Pattern Sheet 2*.

To use fusible web for appliquéing, as was done in this project, follow these steps.

1. Fold an 8½×11" sheet of paper in half vertically, making a 4¼×11" rectangle. Trace Pattern A onto the paper and cut out to make a full Pattern A. Lay the fusible web, paper side up, over the full pattern. With a pencil, trace the pattern three times, leaving ½" between tracings. Cut out each fusible-web shape roughly ¼" outside the traced lines.

2. Following the manufacturer's instructions, press the fusible-web shapes onto the back of the dark blue print; let cool. Cut out the fabric shapes on the drawn lines, including the inside open spaces. Peel off the paper backings.

From blue-and-ivory floral, cut:
- 1—18×32" rectangle for appliqué foundation
- 1—14½×28½" rectangle for pillow back

From blue-and-ivory print, cut:
- 1—11×20" rectangle, cutting it into enough 1½"-wide bias strips to total 100" in length; piece it into a 1½×94" strip (For specific instructions, see Cutting Bias Strips in Quilter's Schoolhouse, which begins on *page 150*.)

Appliqué the Pillow Top

Referring to the photograph *above* for placement, position the three dark blue print A fleur-de-lis appliqués on the blue-and-ivory floral 18×32" appliqué foundation. Fuse in place. Using a machine blanket stitch, appliqué the three fleur-de-lis shapes to the foundation to make the pillow top.

Complete the Pillow

1. Layer the pillow top, batting, and 18×32" muslin lining rectangle according to the instructions in Quilter's Schoolhouse, which begins on *page 150*. Quilt as desired. Center the design and trim the quilted pillow top to 28½×14½", including the seam allowances.

2. Cover a 94" length of cording with the pieced blue-and-ivory print 1½×94" bias strip (see Covered Cording in Quilter's Schoolhouse for instructions).

3. Aligning raw edges and using a machine cording foot, stitch the covered cording to the pillow top.

4. With right sides together, sew together the pillow top and the blue-and-ivory floral 28½×14½" rectangle, leaving an opening, to make a pillow cover. Turn the pillow cover right side out; insert the pillow form through the opening. Whipstitch the opening closed.

MULTICOLOR BED QUILT

Bright appliqué vines climb this striking gray-and-black quilt.

Cut the Fabrics

To make the best use of your fabrics, cut the pieces in the order that follows. Cut the appliqué foundations lengthwise (parallel to the selvage). This project uses "Fleur-de-Lis" Pattern B and two additional leaf patterns (C and D), which are on *Pattern Sheet 2.*

To use fusible web for appliquéing, as was done in this project, follow these steps.

1. Lay the fusible web, paper side up, over the patterns. With a pencil, trace each pattern the number of times indicated, leaving ½" between tracings. Cut out each fusible-web shape roughly ¼" outside the traced lines.

2. Following the manufacturer's instructions, press the fusible-web shapes onto the backs of the designated fabrics; let cool. Cut out the fabric shapes on the drawn lines. Peel off the paper backings.

From black print, cut:
- 4—13×90½" rectangles for appliqué foundations

From dark gray print, cut:
- 3—13×90½" rectangles for appliqué foundations

From multicolor print, cut:
- 1—30×42" rectangle, cutting it into enough 1½"-wide bias strips to total 735" in length for vines (For specific instructions, see Quilter's Schoolhouse, which begins on *page 150.*)

From assorted orange, pink, and purple prints, cut:
- 43 of Pattern B
- 36 of Pattern C
- 80 of Pattern D

From assorted blue, green, and teal prints, cut:
- 16 of Pattern B
- 35 of Pattern C
- 50 of Pattern D

Materials

5¼ yards of black print for appliqué foundations

2⅔ yards of dark gray print for appliqué foundations

⅞ yard of multicolor print for vine appliqués

¾ yard total of assorted orange, pink, and purple prints for leaf appliqués

⅝ yard total of assorted blue, green, and teal prints for leaf appliqués

¾ yard of multicolor stripe for binding

7⅞ yards of backing fabric

94×96" of quilt batting

Lightweight fusible web

Finished quilt top: 87½×90"

From multicolor stripe, cut:

- 9—2½×42" binding strips

Appliqué and Assemble the Quilt Top

1. Referring to Add and Appliqué the Border on *page 11,* Step 2, prepare seven multicolor print 105"-long vine strips.

2. Referring to the photograph *below* for placement, position a vine strip in a wavy line down the center of a black print 13×90½" appliqué foundation; baste. Using a narrow machine zigzag stitch, appliqué the vine in place. Repeat to appliqué a vine strip to each black print and dark gray print 13×90½" appliqué foundation.

3. Randomly position the assorted orange, pink, and purple print B, C, and D leaves along the vines on the four black print appliqué foundations, grouping some in sets of five to form flowers; fuse in place. Using a machine zigzag or decorative stitch, appliqué the leaves in place. Repeat to appliqué the assorted blue, green, and teal print leaves along the vines on the dark gray print appliqué foundations.

4. Referring to the photograph *below,* lay out the black print and dark gray print appliqué foundations; sew together to make the quilt top. Press the seam allowances in one direction.

Complete the Quilt

1. Layer the quilt top, batting, and backing according to the instructions in Quilter's Schoolhouse, which begins on *page 150.*

2. Quilt as desired. Mabeth Oxenreider machine-quilted around the vines and leaves and stitched rows of wavy lines in between the vines.

3. Use the multicolor stripe 2½×42" strips to bind the quilt according to the instructions in Quilter's Schoolhouse.

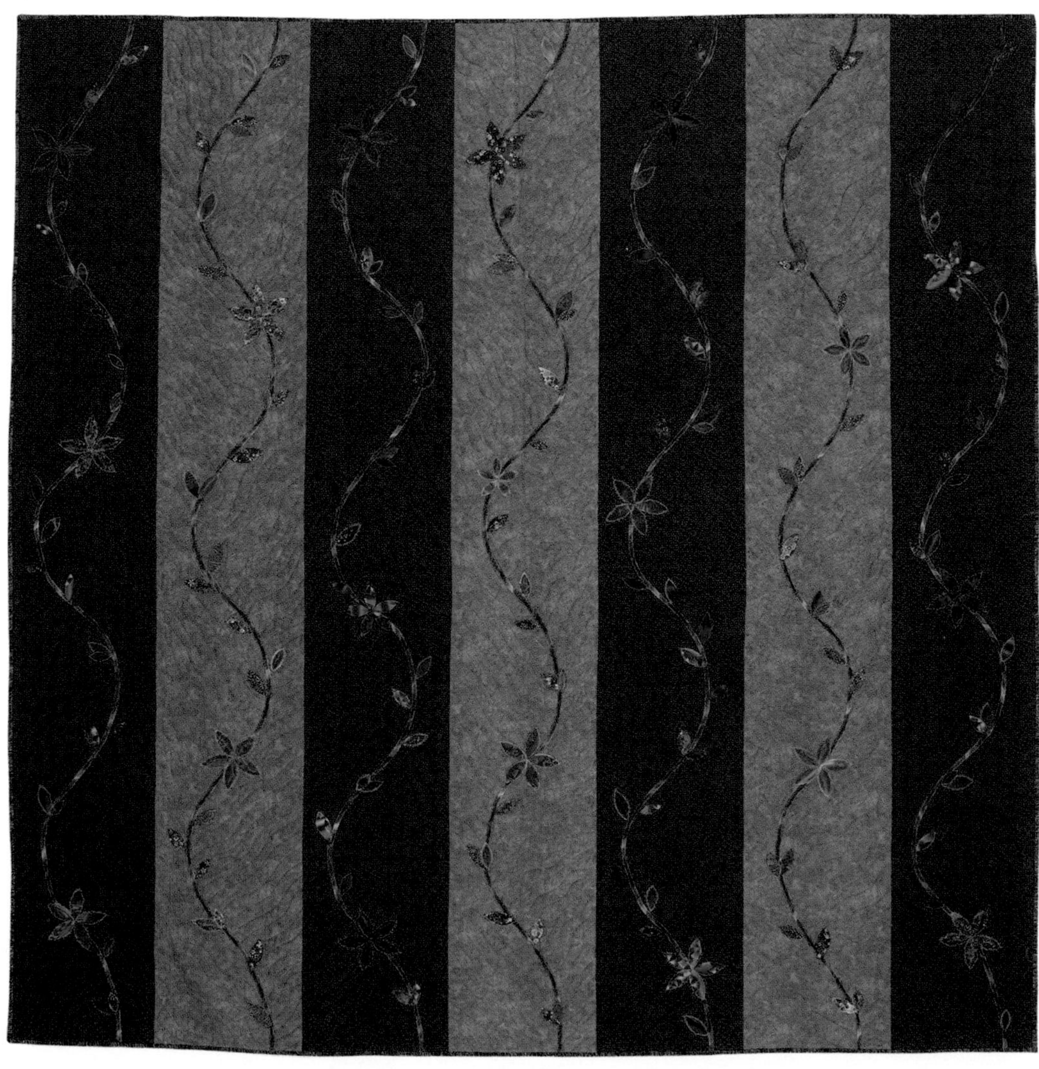

SAILOR'S *Voyage*

Containing a variation of the classic Sailor's Joy block, this vintage scrappy quilt from collector Libby Lowe is a rare find. A wine-red print frames graphic block centers that appear to be swirling in a green sea.

Materials

3 yards total of assorted blue prints for blocks

3 yards total of assorted pink-and-gray prints for blocks

3¾ yards of green print for blocks and sashing squares

3⅞ yards of wine-red print for sashing

⅞ yard of pink print for binding

8⅔ yards of backing fabric

104" square of quilt batting

Finished quilt top: 98" square
Finished block: 14½" square

Quantities are for 44/45"-wide, 100% cotton fabrics. All measurements include a ¼" seam allowance. Sew with right sides together unless otherwise stated.

Cut the Fabrics

To make the best use of your fabrics, cut the pieces in the order that follows.

The patterns are on *Pattern Sheet 1*. To make templates of the patterns, follow the instructions in Quilter's Schoolhouse, which begins on *page 150*. Be sure to transfer the dots and center points marked on the patterns to the templates, then to the fabric pieces. The dots are the matching points and are needed to set in seams. Using the templates' center points for placement, clip a small notch in the center of each curved edge's seam allowance.

From assorted blue prints, cut:
- 100 *each* of patterns A and B (25 sets of four matching A pieces and four matching B pieces)

From assorted pink-and-gray prints, cut:
- 100 *each* of patterns A and B (25 sets of four matching A pieces and four matching B pieces)

From green print, cut:
- 25—7¼" squares, cutting each diagonally twice in an X for a total of 100 triangles
- 136—4¾" squares

From wine-red print, cut:
- 60—4¾×15" sashing rectangles

From pink print, cut:
- 10—2½×42" binding strips

continued

Assemble the Blocks

The following instructions yield one block. Repeat the instructions to make a total of 25 blocks.

This block requires setting in seams. For specific instructions on setting in seams, see Quilter's Schoolhouse, which begins on *page 150.*

1. For one block, you'll need one blue print A/B set (four A pieces and four B pieces), one pink-and-gray print A/B set (four A pieces and four B pieces), four green print 4¾" squares, and four green print triangles.

2. Layer a blue print A piece atop a pink-and-gray print B piece. Pin together the curved edges, carefully aligning the centers and the matching points, using slender pins and picking up only a few threads at each position. Sew together the pieces to make a pieced diamond (see Diagram 1). Press the seam allowance toward the blue print piece. Repeat to make a total of four pieced diamonds.

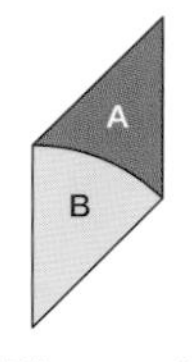

Diagram 1

3. Repeat Step 2 using the pink-and-gray print A pieces and blue print B pieces to make four pieced diamonds in the opposite colorway.

4. Pin together a Step 2 pieced diamond and a Step 3 pieced diamond, carefully aligning the seams (see Diagram 2). Join to make a diamond pair, making sure you don't stitch into the ¼" seam allowance and don't stretch the bias edges as you sew. Press the seam allowance open to reduce bulk. Join the remaining pieced diamonds in the same manner to make four diamond pairs.

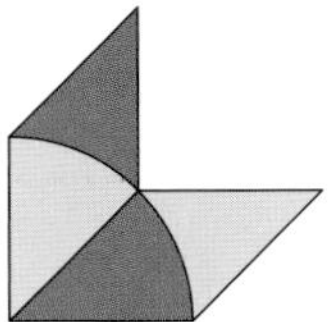
Diagram 2

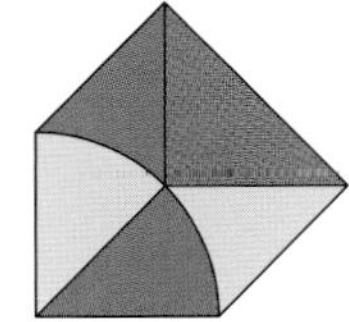
Diagram 3

5. Set a green print triangle into a diamond pair to make a diamond unit (see Diagram 3). To set in the triangle, pin one short edge of the triangle to one of the pieced diamond edges. Sew from the inside seam to the outside edge. Bring up the adjacent pieced diamond in the diamond pair and align it with the next edge of the green print triangle. Stitch from the inside seam to the outside edge. In the same manner, set a green print triangle into each of the remaining diamond pairs to make a total of four diamond units.

6. Sew together two diamond units (see Diagram 4), making sure you don't sew into the seam allowance. Press the seam allowance open. Then set in a green print 4¾" square to make a half block. Repeat to make a second half block.

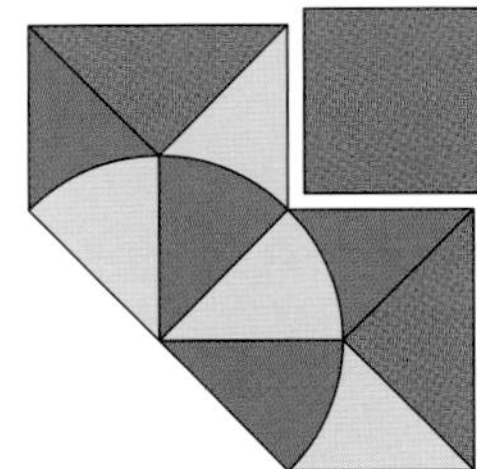
Diagram 4

7. Sew together the two half blocks (see Diagram 5), making sure not to sew into the ¼" seam allowance. Press the seam allowance open. Set in the remaining green print 4¾" squares to complete a Sailor's Voyage block. The pieced block should measure 15" square, including the seam allowances.

Quilt Assembly Diagram

Diagram 5

Assemble the Quilt Top

1. Referring to the Quilt Assembly Diagram, lay out the 25 Sailor's Voyage blocks, the 60 wine-red print 4¾×15" sashing rectangles, and the 36 remaining green print 4¾" squares in 11 horizontal rows.

2. Sew together the pieces in each row. Press the seam allowances toward the wine-red print rectangles. Then join the rows to complete the quilt top. Press the seam allowances in one direction. If desired, round the corners slightly as in the antique version of the quilt.

continued

Complete the Quilt

1. Layer the quilt top, batting, and backing according to the instructions in Quilter's Schoolhouse, which begins on *page 150.*

2. Quilt as desired. This antique quilt was hand-quilted with a classic fan pattern.

3. Use the pink print 2½×42" strips to bind the quilt according to the directions in Quilter's Schoolhouse.

optional colors

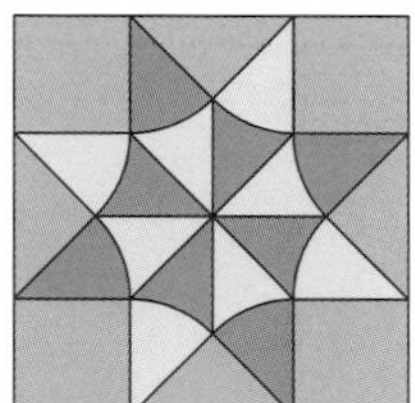

Quilt tester Laura Boehnke rotated the pieced diamonds 180° before sewing them into diamond pairs (see the diagram *left,* noting the curvature of the diamond seams). Laura's fabric choices impart a folk art feel to her three-block table runner, *below*.

Sailor's Voyage

optional sizes

If you'd like to make this quilt in a size other than for a queen bed, use the information *below*.

Alternate quilt sizes	Small Wall	Lap/Large Wall	Full
Number of blocks	4	9	20
Number of blocks wide by long	2×2	3×3	4×5
Finished size	41¾" square	60½" square	79¼×98"
Yardage requirements			
Total of assorted blue prints	¾ yard	1⅓ yards	2½ yards
Total of assorted pink-and-gray prints	¾ yard	1⅓ yards	2½ yards
Green print	1 yard	1¾ yards	3⅛ yards
Wine-red print	1⅓ yards	1¾ yards	3⅜ yards
Pink print	½ yard	⅝ yard	¾ yard
Backing	2⅔ yards	3¾ yards	7¼ yards
Batting	48" square	67" square	86×104"

DOTTY WALL HANGING

The center of the "Sailor's Voyage" block appears in intriguing combinations of pieced and layered appliqués in this playful wall hanging.

Materials

1 yard of white print for appliqué foundation

1¾ yards total of assorted bright prints for appliqués

⅜ yard of blue stripe for binding

1⅓ yards of backing fabric

40×46" rectangle of quilt batting

Finished quilt top: 34×40"

Cut the Fabrics

To make the best use of your fabrics, cut the pieces in the order that follows.

This project uses "Sailor's Voyage" Pattern B and three additional circle patterns (C, D, and E), which are on *Pattern Sheet 1*. To make templates of patterns B–E, follow the instructions in Quilter's Schoolhouse, which begins on *page 150*. Remember to add a $\frac{3}{16}$" seam allowance when cutting out the C, D, and E circle appliqués.

From white print, cut:
- 1—34½×40½" rectangle for appliqué foundation

From assorted bright prints, cut:
- 56 of Pattern B (14 sets of 4 matching B pieces)
- 3 of Pattern C
- 9 of Pattern D
- 27 of Pattern E

From blue stripe, cut:
- 4—2½×42" binding strips

Assemble the Pieced Circles

1. To make one pieced circle, you'll need two sets of four matching B pieces each.

2. Referring to Diagram 6, pair a B piece from each bright print and sew together to make a quarter circle. Repeat to make a total of four matching quarter circles.

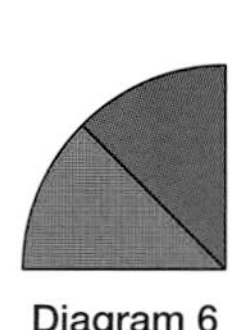

Diagram 6

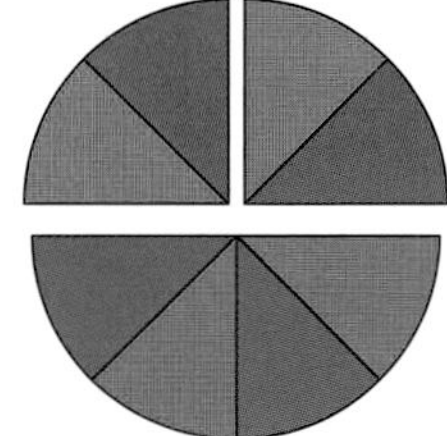

Diagram 7

3. Lay out the four quarter circles in pairs. Join the pairs to make two half circles (see Diagram 7), then join the half circles to make a pieced circle.

4. Repeat steps 1 through 3 to make a total of seven pieced circles.

continued

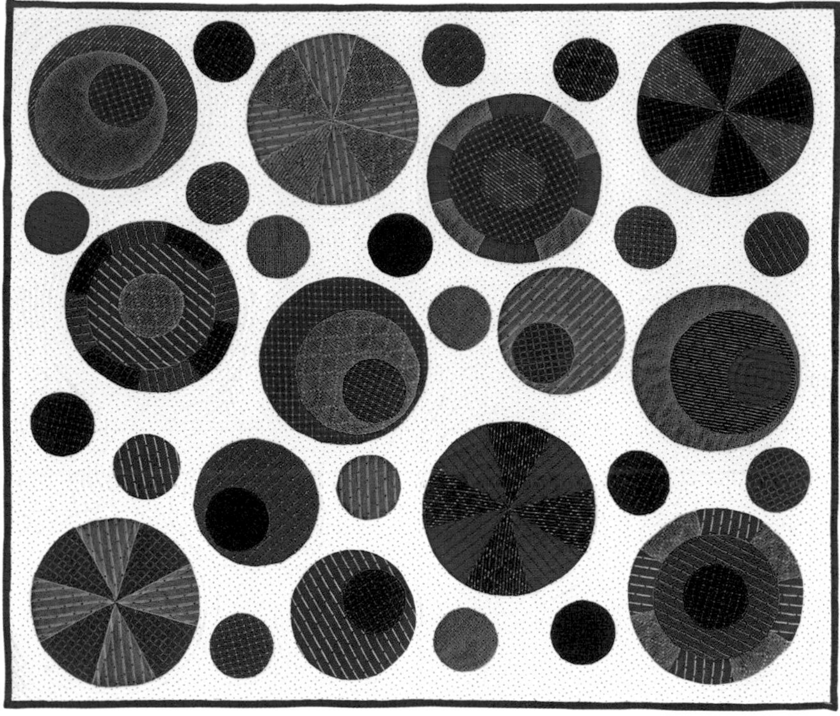

Appliqué the Quilt Top

1. Press under the 3⁄16" seam allowance on each of the assorted bright print C, D, and E circles. Then press under the ¼" seam allowance on each of the pieced circles.

2. Referring to the photograph *left,* arrange the prepared circles on the white print 34½×40½" appliqué foundation. When you are pleased with the arrangement, baste the circles in place.

3. Using monofilament thread and working from the bottom layer to the top, machine-blanket-stitch the pieces in place to complete the quilt top.

Complete the Quilt

1. Layer the quilt top, batting, and backing according to the instructions in Quilter's Schoolhouse, which begins on *page 150.*

2. Quilt as desired. Mabeth Oxenreider echo-quilted around each circle to create a ripple effect. She stitched spiral designs inside some of the circle appliqués and stitched large zigzags, outline quilting, or echo quilting inside some of the B pieces in the pieced circles.

3. Use the blue stripe 2½×42" strips to bind the quilt according to the instructions in Quilter's Schoolhouse.

LARGE-PRINT THROW

This cozy flannel throw gets its interest not from piecing, but from the large-scale florals used in the solid blocks.

Materials

3—1-yard pieces of assorted florals

⅝ yard of green polka dot for sashing squares

2¼ yards of brown stripe for sashing

⅔ yard of blue polka dot for binding

4⅞ yards of backing fabric

Finished quilt top: 60½×79¼"

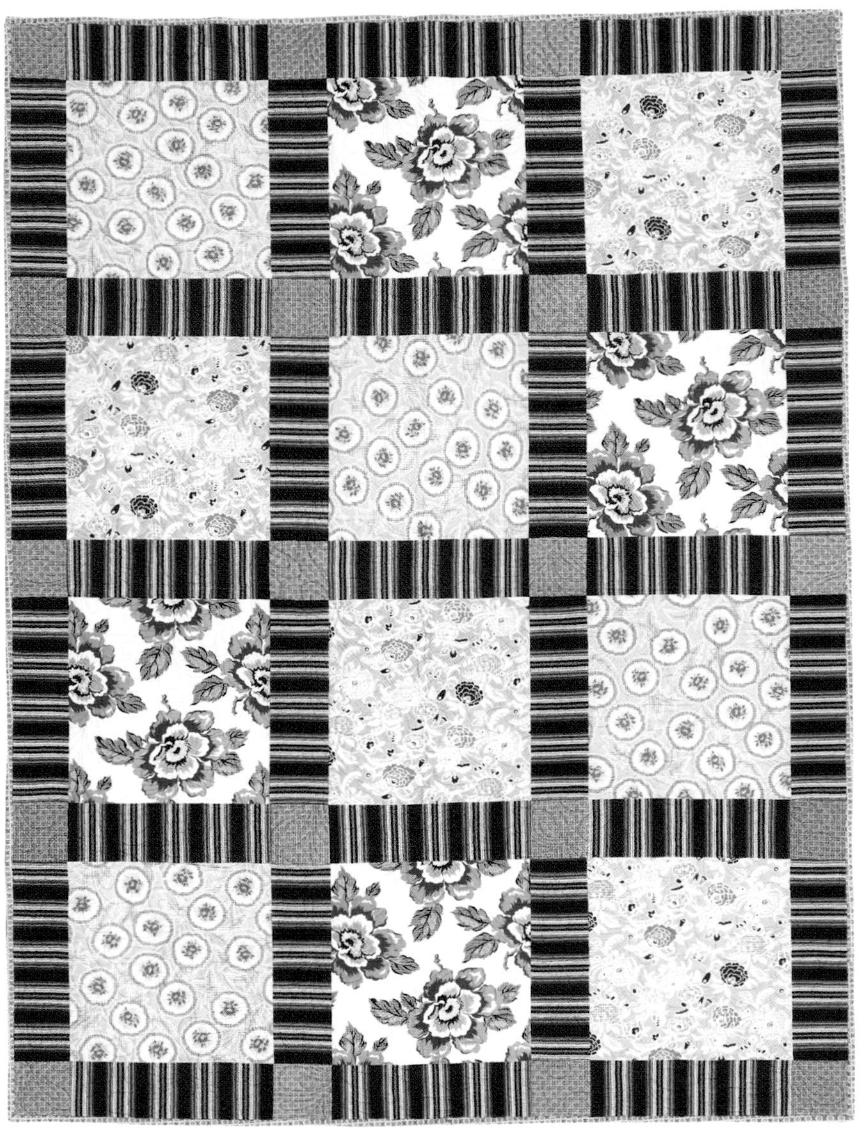

Cut the Fabrics

To make the best use of your fabrics, cut the pieces in the order that follows.

From *each* floral, cut:
- 4—15" squares

From green polka dot, cut:
- 20—4¾" sashing squares

From brown stripe, cut:
- 31—4¾×15" sashing rectangles

From blue polka dot, cut:
- 8—2½×42" binding strips

Assemble the Quilt Top

1. Referring to the photograph *above,* lay out the 12 floral 15" squares, the 31 brown stripe 4¾×15" sashing rectangles, and the 20 green polka-dot 4¾" sashing squares in nine horizontal rows.

2. Sew together the pieces in each row. Press the seam allowances toward the sashing rectangles. Then join the rows to complete the quilt top. Press the seam allowances in one direction.

Complete the Quilt

1. Layer the quilt top, batting, and backing according to the instructions in Quilter's Schoolhouse, which begins on *page 150.*

2. Quilt as desired. The featured throw was machine-quilted with an allover large floral design inspired by the floral fabrics.

3. Use the blue polka-dot 2½×42" strips to bind the quilt according to the instructions in Quilter's Schoolhouse.

SEVEN *Sisters*

The Seven Sisters block was popular before the turn of the 20th century and during the Great Depression, when challenging hand-piecing patterns were in vogue. Use hand piecing or precise machine piecing to set in the many seams on this block, which was named after a constellation.

Materials

3⅛ yards of muslin for blocks and binding

3 yards of solid gold for border and setting triangles

1⅞ yards total of assorted dark prints for blocks

1⅞ yards total of assorted medium prints for blocks

5⅛ yards of backing fabric

75×91" of quilt batting

Finished quilt top: 68½×85¹⁄₁₆"
Finished block: 12½×14⅜"

Quantities are for 44/45"-wide, 100% cotton fabrics. All measurements include a ¼" seam allowance. Sew with right sides together unless otherwise stated.

Select the Fabrics

In the original quilt, prints of many different colors and values were used to piece the seven stars in each of the Seven Sisters blocks; however, each block can be viewed as just three fabrics—a dark print, a medium print, and muslin (see Diagram 1 on *page 27*). Change your prints from block to block, but keep the same overall color scheme. To tie the colorful blocks together, select a fabric for the setting pieces that unites all the colors.

Note that we have slightly changed the block layout from that of the original quilt. Half blocks, rather than partial blocks, are used at the ends of the vertical rows. This produces a more proportional lap-size design instead of the long and narrow shape of the original quilt.

Cut the Fabrics

To make the best use of your fabrics, cut the pieces in the order that follows. Cut the border strips lengthwise (parallel to the selvage). The border strip measurements are mathematically correct. You may wish to cut your strips longer than specified to allow for possible sewing differences.

The patterns are on *Pattern Sheet 2*. To make templates of the patterns, follow the instructions in

continued

Quilter's Schoolhouse, which begins on *page 150*. Be sure to transfer the dots marked on the patterns to the templates, then to the fabric pieces. The dots are the matching points and are needed to set in seams.

From muslin, cut:

- 8—2½×42" binding strips
- 510 of Pattern A
- 170 of Pattern B

From solid gold, cut:

- 2—3½×82" border strips
- 2—3½×69" border strips
- 50 of Pattern C
- 5 *each* of patterns D and D reversed

Cut and Assemble the Blocks

We recommend hand-piecing the blocks because of the many 60° diamonds that must be set in. For specific instructions on setting in seams, see Quilter's Schoolhouse, which begins on *page 150*. Hand-stitching from dot to dot on the sewing lines means the seam allowances are not sewn down so you can choose the direction to press the seam allowances after you've pieced the *entire* block. Carefully machine-piecing from dot to dot also provides this option.

As you piece the blocks, finger-press the seam allowances in your desired direction to help keep your work smooth. Press the completed blocks with an iron, pressing the seam allowances in directions that allow them to lie as flat as possible or that will enable you to quilt the block as desired without stitching through seam allowances.

The following instructions yield one Seven Sisters block. Repeat the cutting and assembly steps to make a total of 25 blocks.

From assorted dark prints, cut:
- 21 of Pattern A

From assorted medium prints, cut:
- 21 of Pattern A

1. Referring to Diagram 1, lay out the 21 dark print A diamonds, 21 medium print A diamonds, 18 muslin A diamonds, and six muslin B pieces.

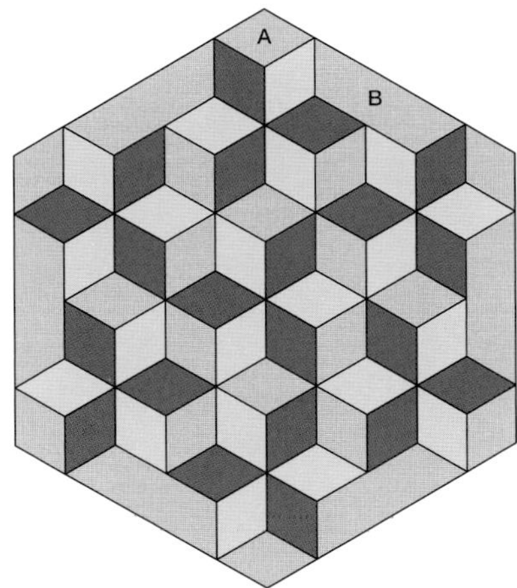

Diagram 1

2. Referring to Diagram 2, sew together the dark and medium print A diamonds in sets of six to form seven stars. First sew the diamonds together in pairs. Then join the pairs, setting in seams where necessary.

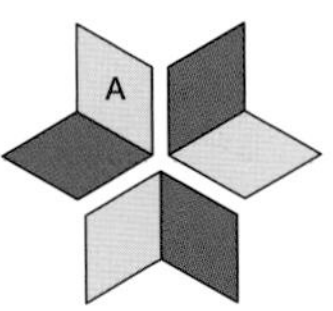

Diagram 2

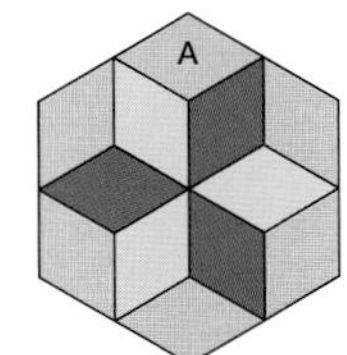

Diagram 3

3. Referring to Diagram 3, set six muslin A diamonds in a star unit to make a center star unit.

4. Referring to Diagram 4, add the remaining stars and muslin A diamonds to the center star unit. Set in the muslin B pieces and A diamonds around the outer edge to make a Seven Sisters block.

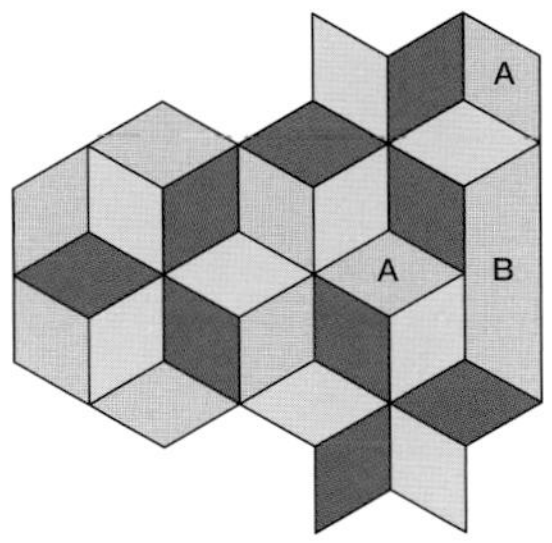

Diagram 4

Cut and Assemble the Half Blocks

The following instructions yield a half block. Repeat the cutting and assembly steps to make a total of five half blocks.

From assorted dark prints, cut:
- 14 of Pattern A

From assorted medium prints, cut:
- 14 of Pattern A

1. Referring to Diagram 5, lay out the 14 dark print A diamonds, 14 medium print A diamonds, 12 muslin A diamonds, and four muslin B pieces.

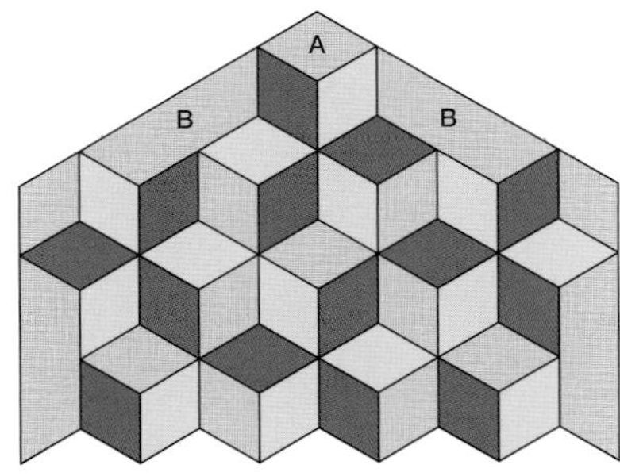

Diagram 5

2. Join the pieces, setting in seams where necessary, to make a half block. (The uneven patchwork edge will be trimmed off later.)

Assemble the Quilt Top

1. Referring to the Quilt Assembly Diagram on *page 28,* lay out the 25 Seven Sisters blocks, the five half blocks, the 50 solid gold C triangles, the five solid gold D triangles, and the five solid gold D reversed triangles in five vertical rows.

2. Sew together the pieces in each row, pressing the seam allowances toward the C and D triangles.

3. Join the vertical rows to make the quilt center. Press the seam allowances in one direction.

continued

Add the Border

1. Sew the solid gold 3½×82" border strips to the long edges of the pieced quilt center; the border strip ends will extend slightly past the edges of the quilt. Press the seam allowances toward the border.

2. Use a ruler and quilter's pencil to mark a line on the right side of the top and bottom edges for trimming the half blocks and side border strips even with the other rows; do not trim them yet.

3. Add the solid gold 3½×69" strips to the top and bottom edges of the quilt center. Press all seam allowances toward the border. Trim the excess from the half blocks and side border strips to complete the quilt top.

Complete the Quilt

1. Layer the quilt top, batting, and backing according to the instructions in Quilter's Schoolhouse, which begins on *page 150*. Quilt as desired.

2. Use the muslin 2½×42" strips to bind the quilt according to the instructions in Quilter's Schoolhouse.

Quilt Assembly Diagram

BORDERED SCARF

Stitch the diamond shapes in a straight setting to create a fetching line of trim.

Materials

1 yard of tan silk for scarf

Scraps of assorted dark prints for pieced borders

½ yard of beaded fringe

Finished scarf: 8×52"

Cut the Fabrics

To make the best use of your fabrics, cut the pieces in the order that follows. This project uses "Seven Sisters" Pattern A, which is on *Pattern Sheet 2*. To make a template of Pattern A, follow the instructions in Quilter's Schoolhouse, which begins on *page 150*.

From tan silk, cut:

- 3—8½×42" rectangles
- 2—2¼×8½" rectangles
- 2—1½×8½" rectangles

From assorted dark prints, cut:

- 28 of Pattern A

Assemble the Scarf

1. Referring to Diagram 6, lay out seven assorted dark print A diamonds in a row. Sew together the diamonds; press the seam allowances in one direction. Center and trim the row to 1¾×8½" to make a pieced border strip A. Repeat to make a second pieced border strip A.

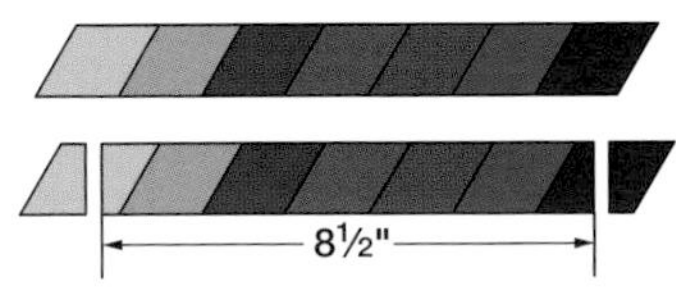

Diagram 6

2. Repeat Step 1 using the remaining assorted dark print A diamonds, laying them so the diagonal seams will run in the opposite direction, to make a total of two of pieced border strip B.

3. Referring to Diagram 7, lay out one tan silk 1½×8½" rectangle, one tan silk 2¼×8½" rectangle, and one each of pieced border strips A and B. Join the pieces to make an end unit; press the seam allowances toward the pieced border strips. The pieced end unit should measure 5¾×8½", including seam allowances. Repeat to make a second end unit.

Diagram 7

4. Sew the end units to the short edges of a tan silk 8½×42" rectangle to make the scarf front (see the photograph on *page 30*). The scarf front should measure 8½×52½", including the seam allowances.

5. Cut and piece the remaining tan silk 8½×42" rectangles to make an 8½×52½" scarf back.

continued

6. Cut the beaded trim into two 8½" lengths. Baste one trim piece to the right side of each end of the scarf front (see Diagram 8).

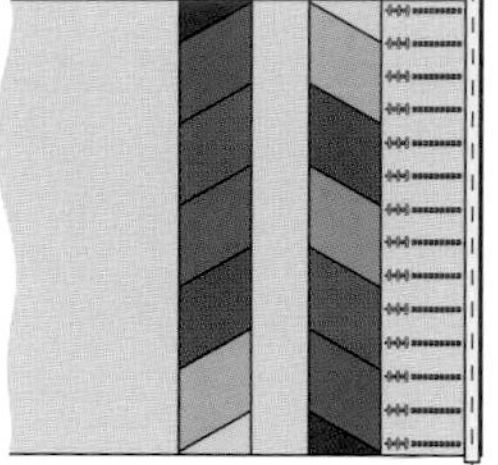

Diagram 8

7. Pin the scarf front to the scarf back, sandwiching the beaded trim inside. Sew around all four edges, leaving a 4" opening. Turn right side out through the opening and slipstitch the opening closed. Stitch in the ditch along each border strip edge to complete the scarf.

MINI TABLE MAT

Create a finished project from a single block by putting a border around this hexagonal piece.

Materials

Scraps of assorted dark and medium prints for block

⅛ yard of white print for block

⅜ yard of navy blue print for border and binding

⅝ yard of backing fabric

21" square of quilt batting

Finished table mat: 16⅝×14½"

Cut the Fabrics

To make the best use of your fabrics, cut the pieces in the order that follows. This project uses the "Seven Sisters" patterns, which are on *Pattern Sheet 2.* To make templates of the patterns, follow the instructions in Quilter's Schoolhouse, which begins on *page 150.*

From assorted dark prints, cut:

- 21 of Pattern A (7 sets of 3 matching diamonds)

From assorted medium prints, cut:

- 21 of Pattern A (7 sets of 3 matching diamonds)

From white print, cut:

- 6 of Pattern B
- 18 of Pattern A

From navy blue print, cut:

- 2—2½×42" binding strips
- 6—1½×11" border strips

Assemble the Quilt Top

1. Referring to Cut and Assemble the Blocks on *page 26*, use the dark print A diamonds, the medium print A diamonds, and the white print A diamonds and B pieces to make one Seven Sisters block.

2. Sew navy blue print 1½×11" border strips to every other edge of the pieced Seven Sisters block (see Diagram 9). Press the seam allowances toward the border. Trim each strip even with the block edges.

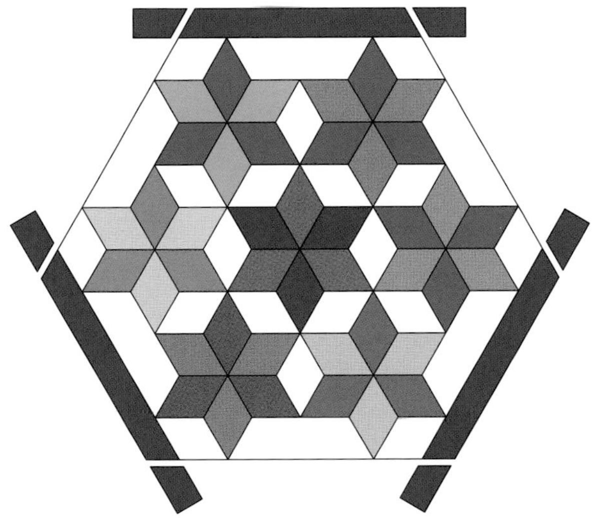

Diagram 9

3. Sew the remaining navy blue print 1½×11" border strips to the three remaining edges of the block to complete the quilt top; press as before. Trim the last three strips even with the edges of the first three strips.

Complete the Quilt

1. Layer the quilt top, batting, and backing according to the instructions in Quilter's Schoolhouse, which begins on *page 150*.

2. Quilt as desired. The featured quilt was hand-quilted in the ditch of each star and ¼" from the edge of the block in the border.

3. Use the navy blue print 2½×42" strips to bind the quilt according to the instructions in Quilter's Schoolhouse.

QUICK-TO-CUT CLASSICS

Explore the diversity of projects made with rotary-cut pieces. From the subtle pattern in "Diamonds Are Forever" to the whirl of motion in "Pink Spring Fling" or the traditional motifs in "Simple Tribute," you can find a rotary-cut quilt to suit anyone's taste. Accuracy as well as speed are the benefits of using this cutting method.

PINK *Spring Fling*

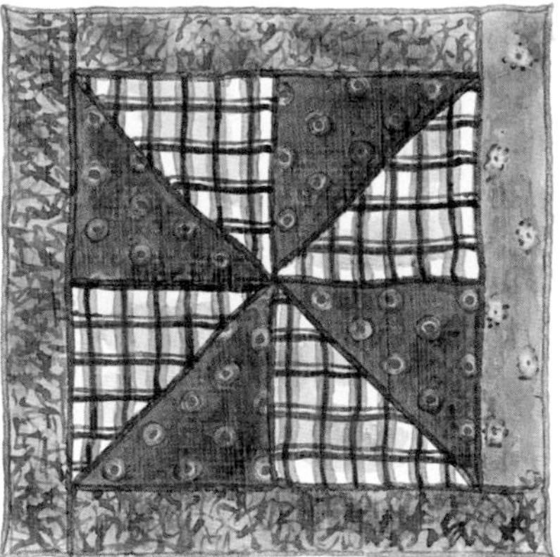

A photograph of an antique quilt prompted Georgia quilter Lila Scott to gather years of scraps into this quilt full of motion. While a pair of blocks swirl in the center, pieced blocks in the outer border add to the movement.

Materials

2¼ yards total of assorted light prints in blue, pink, green, purple, tan, and yellow for blocks and outer border

3⅛ yards total of assorted medium and dark prints in blue, pink, green, and purple for blocks and outer border

1⅜ yards of pale pink print for inner border

½ yard of dark blue print for binding

3⅛ yards of backing fabric

56×66" of quilt batting

Finished quilt top: 50×60"
Finished Pinwheel block: 4" square
Finished Square-in-a-Square block: 4" square
Finished border block: 5" square

Quantities are for 44/45" wide, 100% cotton fabrics. All measurements include a ¼" seam allowance. Sew with right sides together unless otherwise stated.

Designer Notes

"I saw an old quilt top for sale several years ago that I loved but could not afford," designer Lila Scott says. "I took a picture of it and knew that someday I would make my version of the lovely old scrappy quilt top."

She purposefully chose "humble" fabrics so that none would scream for attention, adding a few splashes of yellow for sparkle.

"I wanted the quilt to be seen and not the fabrics used to make it," she says. "I also wanted to maintain the pink and blue feel of the original quilt top, so I only used other colors sparingly. They all appear in the outside border."

Cut and Assemble the Pinwheel Blocks

Lila made her Pinwheel blocks of dark or medium blues with light blues or pinks. She splashed in a few other colors here and there to give the blocks a little zest.

The following instructions are to make one Pinwheel block. Repeat the cutting and assembly steps to make a total of 50 Pinwheel blocks.

continued

From one light print, cut:

- 2—2⅜" squares

From one medium or dark print, cut:

- 2—2⅜" squares

From a different light, medium, or dark print, cut:

- 1—1×4½" rectangle
- 2—1×4" rectangles
- 1—1×3½" rectangle

1. Use a quilter's pencil to mark a diagonal line on the wrong side of each light print 2⅜" square. (To prevent the fabric from stretching as you draw the lines, place 220-grit sandpaper under the squares.)

2. Layer each marked light print 2⅜" square with a medium or dark print 2⅜" square. Sew each pair together with two seams, stitching ¼" on each side of the drawn line (see Diagram 1).

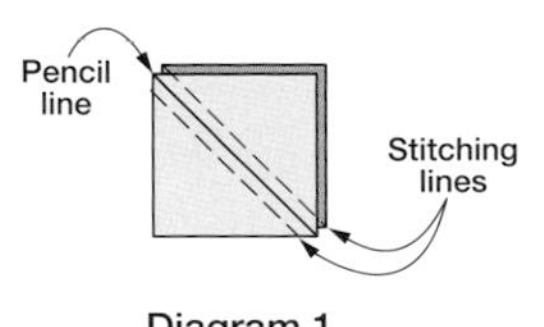

Diagram 1

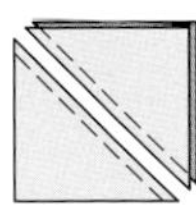
Diagram 2

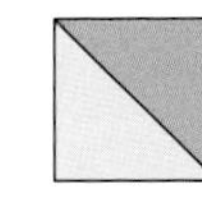
Diagram 3

3. Cut each pair apart on the drawn line to make two triangle units each (see Diagram 2). Press the triangle units open, pressing the seam allowances toward the darker triangles, to make a total of four triangle-squares (see Diagram 3). Each triangle-square should measure 2" square, including the seam allowances.

4. Referring to Diagram 4, sew together the four triangle-squares in pairs. Press the seam allowances in opposite directions. Then join the pairs to make a pinwheel unit. Press the seam allowances in one direction. The pinwheel unit should measure 3½" square, including the seam allowances.

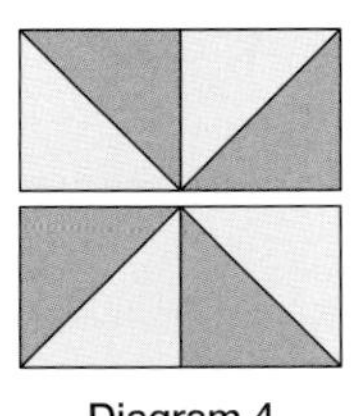
Diagram 4

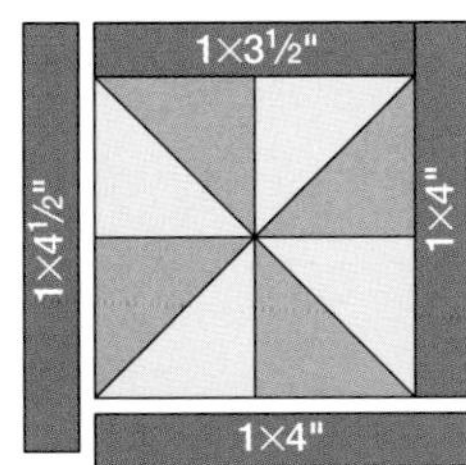

Diagram 5

5. Referring to Diagram 5, sew the 1×3½" rectangle to one edge of the pinwheel unit; press the seam allowance toward the rectangle. Working clockwise, add a 1×4" rectangle to the adjacent edge; press. Repeat to add the remaining rectangles as shown to make a Pinwheel block. The Pinwheel block should measure 4½" square, including the seam allowances.

Cut and Assemble the Square-in-a-Square Blocks

Lila incorporated more medium and dark prints into these blocks to offer contrast with the Pinwheel blocks.

The following instructions are to make one Square-in-a-Square block. Repeat the cutting and assembly steps to make a total of 49 Square-in-a-Square blocks.

From one light print, cut:
- 2—1½" squares

From one medium or dark print, cut:
- 2—1½" squares

From a second light, medium, or dark print, cut:
- 2—2¼" squares, cutting each in half diagonally for a total of 4 small triangles

From a third light, medium, or dark print, cut:
- 2—2⅞" squares, cutting each in half diagonally for a total of 4 large triangles

1. Pair the two light print 1½" squares with the two medium or dark print 1½" squares (see Diagram 6); sew together. Press the seam allowances toward the darker squares. Join the pairs to make a Four-Patch unit. Press the seam allowance in one direction. The Four-Patch unit should measure 2½" square, including the seam allowances.

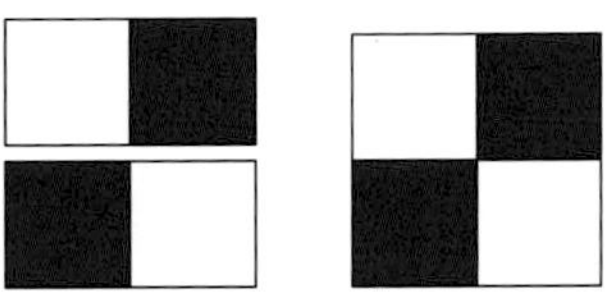
Diagram 6

2. Sew small triangles to opposite edges of the Four-Patch unit (see Diagram 7). Press the seam allowances toward the triangles. Then add small triangles to the remaining edges and press the seam allowances toward the triangles.

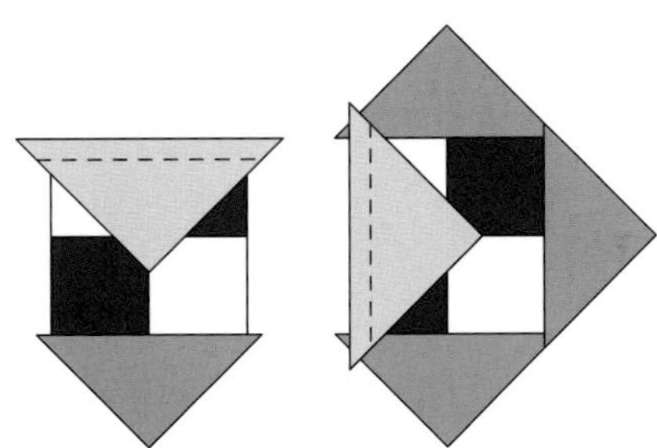
Diagram 7

3. Sew large triangles to opposite edges of the Step 2 unit; press the seam allowances toward the large triangles. Then add large triangles to the remaining edges, and press the seam allowances toward the large triangles to make a Square-in-a-Square block (see Diagram 8). The block should measure 4½" square, including the seam allowances.

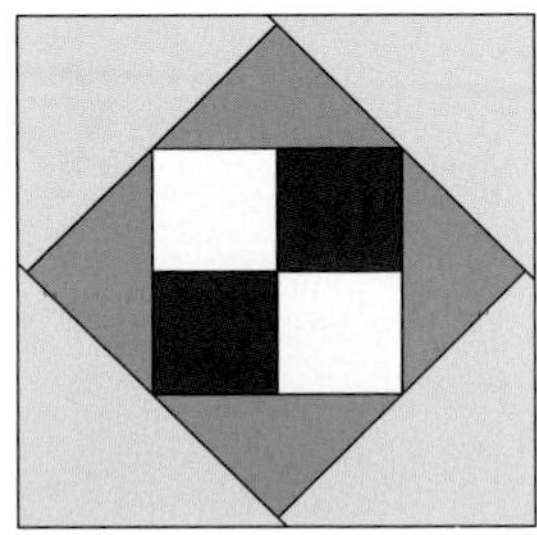
Diagram 8

continued

Assemble the Quilt Center

1. Referring to the Quilt Assembly Diagram, lay out the 50 Pinwheel blocks and the 49 Square-in-a-Square blocks in 11 horizontal rows, alternating the blocks.

2. Sew together the blocks in each row. Press the seam allowances in one direction, alternating the direction with each row. Join the rows to complete the quilt center. Press the seam allowances in one direction. The pieced quilt center should measure 36½×44½", including the seam allowances.

Cut and Add the Inner Border

Cut the border strips the length of the fabric (parallel to the selvage). Note that the inner border strips are cut in different widths to accommodate the pieced border.

From pale pink print, cut:

- 2—2½×44½" inner border strips
- 2—3½×40½" inner border strips

1. Sew the long inner border strips to the long edges of the quilt center. Press the seam allowances toward the border.

2. Sew the short inner border strips to the remaining edges of the quilt center. Press the seam allowances toward the border. The pieced quilt center should now measure 40½×50½", including the seam allowances.

Cut and Assemble the Border Blocks

For the border blocks, Lila chose strong colors for the large triangles and light, soft prints for the small triangles that serve as the backgrounds. The dark squares offer continuous movement around the outside of the quilt.

The following instructions are to make one border block. Repeat the cutting and assembly steps to make a total of 40 pieced border blocks.

From one light print, cut:

- 3—2⅛" squares, cutting each in half diagonally for a total of 6 small triangles

From one medium or dark print, cut:

- 1—4⅝" square, cutting it in half diagonally for a total of 2 large triangles

From a different dark print, cut:

- 4—1¾" squares

1. Stitch a light print small triangle to each dark print 1¾" square (see Diagram 9). Press the seam allowances toward the dark print squares.

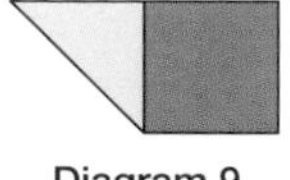

Diagram 9

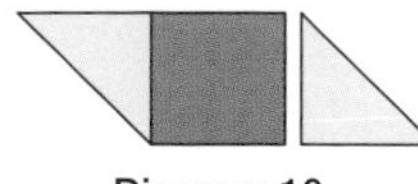

Diagram 10

2. Sew a second light print small triangle to the opposite edge of two of the Step 1 units (see Diagram 10). Press the seam allowances toward the squares.

3. Referring to Diagram 11, lay out two Step 1 units and two Step 2 units in a diagonal row; sew together. Press the seam allowances in one direction.

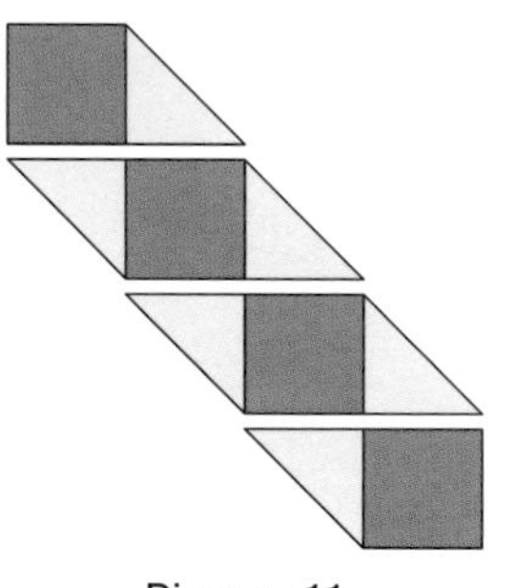

Diagram 11

Diagram 12

4. Sew a medium or dark print large triangle to each long edge of the Step 3 unit to make a border block (see Diagram 12). Press the seam allowances toward the large triangles. The pieced border block should measure 5½" square, including the seam allowances.

Add the Outer Border

1. Referring to the Quilt Assembly Diagram and the photograph on *page 36* for placement, lay out four rows of 10 border blocks each; sew together each row to make four pieced outer border strips. Press the seam allowances in one direction. The pieced border strips should each measure 5½×50½", including the seam allowances.

2. Sew a pieced border strip to each long edge of the pieced quilt center. Press the seam allowances toward the inner border. Sew the remaining pieced border strips to the remaining edges of the quilt center to complete the quilt top. Press the seam allowances toward the inner border.

Complete the Quilt

From dark blue print, cut:

- 6—2½x42" binding strips

1. Layer the quilt top, batting, and backing according to the instructions in Quilter's Schoolhouse, which begins on *page 150*. Quilt as desired.

2. Use the dark blue print 2½x42" strips to bind the quilt according to the instructions in Quilter's Schoolhouse.

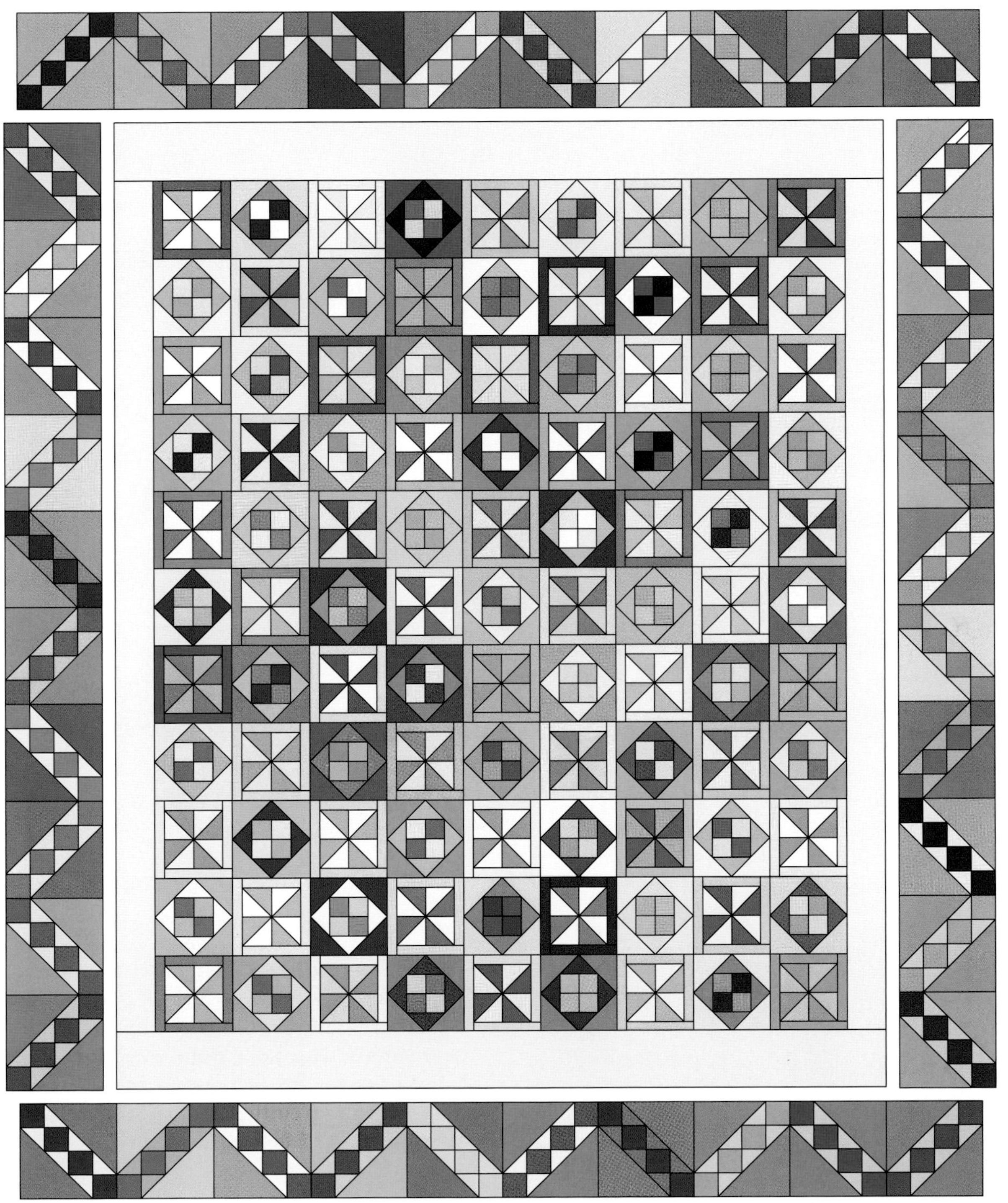

Quilt Assembly Diagram

BIG-PATCH BED QUILT

A smattering of Square-in-a-Square blocks adds visual interest to a simple, scrappy quilt.

Materials

8½ yards total of assorted prints in gold, rust, blue, brown, tan, and green for blocks

⅞ yard of blue print for binding

7⅞ yards of backing fabric

94×102" of quilt batting

Finished quilt top: 88×96"

Cut and Assemble the Blocks

The pieced blocks in the bed quilt are created by adding two rounds of setting triangles to the Square-in-a-Square block from "Pink Spring Fling."

The following instructions are to make one block. Repeat the cutting and assembly steps to make a total of 12 blocks.

From one assorted print, cut:
- 2—1½" squares

From a second assorted print, cut:
- 2—1½" squares

From a third assorted print, cut:
- 2—2¼" squares, cutting each in half diagonally for a total of 4 small triangles

From a fourth assorted print, cut:
- 2—2⅞" squares, cutting each in half diagonally for a total of 4 large triangles

From a fifth assorted print, cut:
- 2—3¾" squares, cutting each in half diagonally for a total of 4 small setting triangles

From a sixth assorted print, cut:
- 2—4⅞" squares, cutting each in half diagonally for a total of 4 large setting triangles

1. Referring to Cut and Assemble the Square-in-a-Square Blocks on *page 37*, use the four assorted print 1½" squares, the assorted print small triangles, and the assorted print large triangles to make a Square-in-a-Square block.

2. Sew small setting triangles to opposite edges of the Square-in-a-Square block; press the seam allowances toward the setting triangles. Then add the remaining small setting triangles to the remaining edges and press the seam allowances toward the setting triangles.

3. In the same manner, add the four large setting triangles to the Step 2 unit to complete a pieced block (see Diagram 13). The pieced block should measure 8½" square, including the seam allowances.

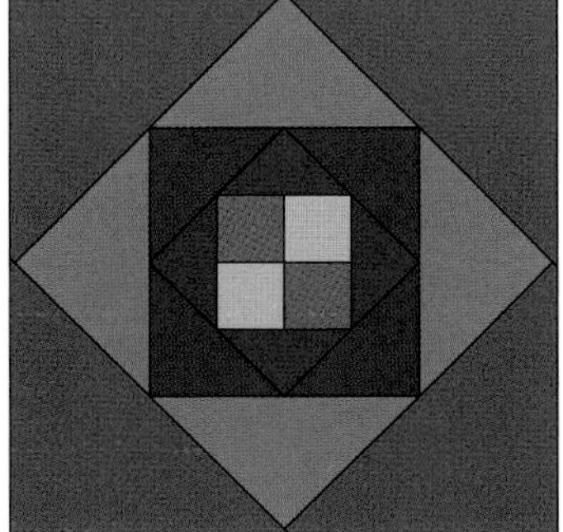

Diagram 13

Cut and Assemble the Quilt Top

From assorted gold, rust, blue, brown, tan, and green prints, cut:
- 120—8½" squares

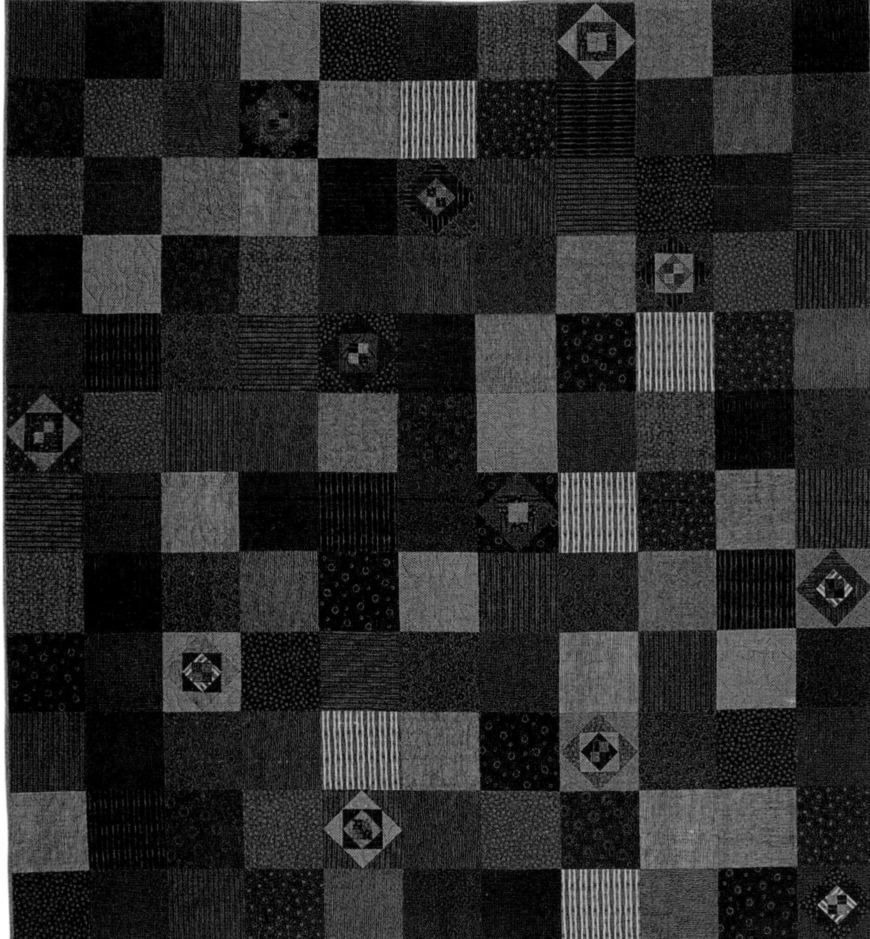

1. Referring to the photograph *above* for placement, lay out the 120 assorted print 8½" squares and the 12 pieced blocks in 12 horizontal rows.

2. Sew together the blocks in each row. Press the seam allowances in one direction, alternating the direction with each row. Then join the rows to complete the quilt top. Press the seam allowances in one direction.

Complete the Quilt

From blue print, cut:
- 10—2½×42" binding strips

1. Layer the quilt top, batting, and backing according to the instructions in Quilter's Schoolhouse, which begins on *page 150*. Quilt as desired.

2. Use the blue print 2½×42" strips to bind the quilt according to the instructions in Quilter's Schoolhouse.

PICNIC TABLE RUNNER

Crisp colors and fresh whites spin across this table runner, which is perfect for draping over a patio table set for an outdoor feast.

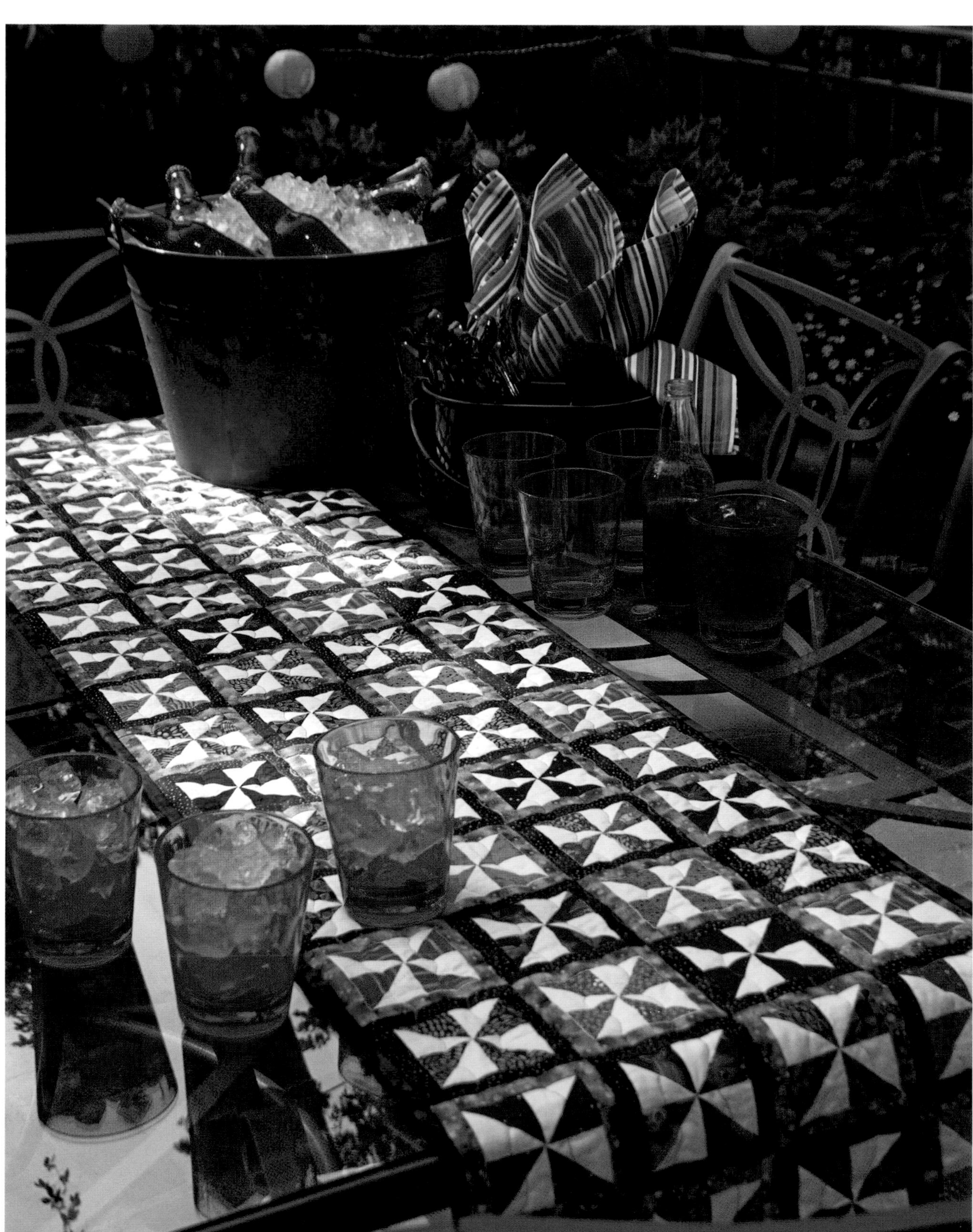

Materials

1 yard total of assorted red, orange, and yellow prints for blocks

1 yard of white print for blocks

¾ yard of blue print for blocks

¾ yard of dark blue print for blocks

½ yard of mottled dark blue for binding

1⅞ yards of backing fabric

22×94" of quilt batting

Finished table runner: 16×88"

Cut the Fabrics

To make the best use of your fabrics, cut the pieces in the order that follows.

From assorted red, orange, and yellow prints, cut:
- 88 sets of 2 matching 2⅜" squares

From white print, cut:
- 176—2⅜" squares

From blue print, cut:
- 44—1×4½" rectangles
- 88—1×4" rectangles
- 44—1×3½" rectangles

From dark blue print, cut:
- 44—1×4½" rectangles
- 88—1×4" rectangles
- 44—1×3½" rectangles

From mottled dark blue, cut:
- 6—2½×42" binding strips

Assemble the Pinwheel Blocks

1. Referring to Cut and Assemble the Pinwheel Blocks on *page 35*, steps 1 through 4, use two matching red, orange, or yellow print 2⅜" squares and two white print 2⅜" squares to make a pinwheel unit. Repeat to make a total of 88 pinwheel units.

2. Referring to Cut and Assemble the Pinwheel Blocks, Step 5, add blue print 1×3½", 1×4", and 1×4½" rectangles to a pinwheel unit to make a blue Pinwheel block. Repeat to make a total of 44 blue Pinwheel blocks.

3. Repeat Step 2 using the dark blue print 1×3½", 1×4", and 1×4½" rectangles and the remaining pinwheel units to make a total of 44 dark blue Pinwheel blocks.

Assemble the Quilt Top

1. Referring to Diagram 14 and the photograph *opposite* for placement, lay out the 88 blocks in 22 horizontal rows, alternating the blue and dark blue Pinwheel blocks.

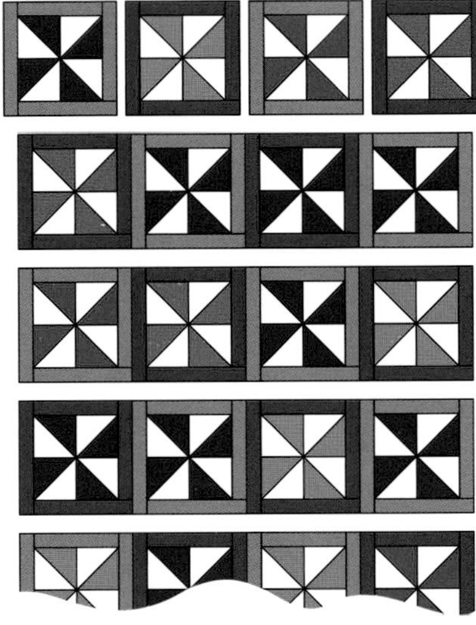

Diagram 14

2. Sew together the blocks in each row. Press the seam allowances in one direction, alternating the direction with each row. Then join the rows to complete the quilt top. Press the seam allowances in one direction.

Complete the Quilt

1. Layer the quilt top, batting, and backing according to the instructions in Quilter's Schoolhouse, which begins on *page 150*.

2. Quilt as desired. The quilt shown was machine-quilted in parallel wavy lines with variegated thread.

3. Use the mottled dark blue 2½×42" strips to bind the quilt according to the instructions in Quilter's Schoolhouse.

Twisted Wire
Ranch

DIAMONDS ARE *Forever*

Squares and triangle-squares join forces to create the diamond pattern that appears on designer Sandy Gervais' warm and cozy quilt.

Materials

10½ yards total of assorted light and dark prints for blocks

⅞ yard of dark red print for binding

8½ yards of backing fabric

102" square of quilt batting

Finished quilt top: 96" square
Finished block: 12" square

Quantities are for 44/45"-wide, 100% cotton fabrics. All measurements include a ¼" seam allowance. Sew with right sides together unless otherwise stated.

Designer Notes

It's not the interplay between lights and darks that makes the diamond pattern emerge on Sandy Gervais' quilt. It is the diagonal seams in the triangle-squares.

"When I was working on this design, the people who saw it were quick to recognize that it didn't matter where you placed the light prints and dark prints," Sandy says. "It's all about piecing the blocks in a uniform way, then rotating them when you're combining the blocks to create the quilt top."

Cut the Fabrics

To make the best use of your fabrics, cut the pieces in the order that follows.

From assorted light and dark prints, cut:

- 512—3⅞" squares
- 512—3½" squares

From dark red print, cut:

- 10—2½×42" binding strips

Make the Triangle-Squares

1. Use a quilter's pencil to mark a diagonal line on the wrong side of half of the assorted print 3⅞" squares. (To prevent the fabric from stretching as you draw the lines, place 220-grit sandpaper under the squares.)

2. Layer each marked print square atop an unmarked print 3⅞" square. Sew each pair together with two seams, stitching ¼" on each side of the drawn line (see Diagram 1).

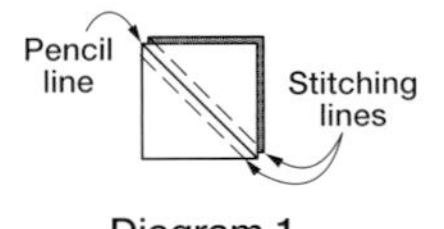

Diagram 1

To save time, chain-piece the layered squares. To chain-piece, machine-sew the pairs together one after the other without lifting the presser foot or clipping threads between pairs. First, sew along one side of the drawn lines, then turn the group of pairs

continued

around and sew along the other side of the lines (see Diagram 2). Clip the connecting threads between pairs.

3. Cut a pair apart on the drawn line to make two triangle units (see Diagram 3). Press the triangle units open to make two triangle-squares (see Diagram 4). Each triangle-square should measure 3½" square, including the seam allowances.

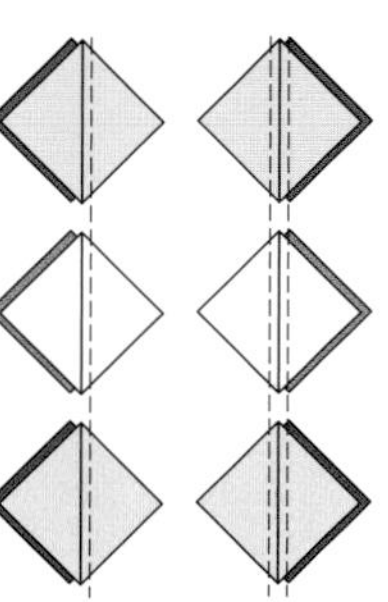

Diagram 2

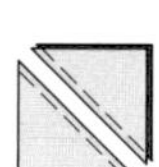

Diagram 3

Diagram 4

4. Repeat Step 3 to make a total of 512 triangle-squares.

Assemble the Blocks

1. Referring to Diagram 5 for placement, lay out eight assorted triangle-squares and eight assorted print 3½" squares in four rows, noting the direction of the triangle-squares' seams.

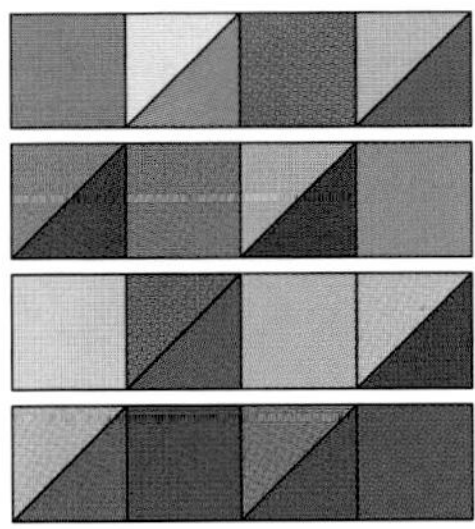

Diagram 5

2. Sew together the pieces in each row. Press the seam allowances toward the squares. Then join the rows to make a block. Press the seam allowances in one direction. The pieced block should measure 12½" square, including the seam allowances.

3. Repeat steps 1 and 2 to make a total of 64 blocks.

Assemble the Quilt Top

1. Referring to the photograph *opposite* and the Quilt Assembly Diagram, lay out the 64 blocks in eight horizontal rows, noting the direction of each block's diagonal seams. This rotation of the blocks makes the diamond pattern emerge in the completed quilt top.

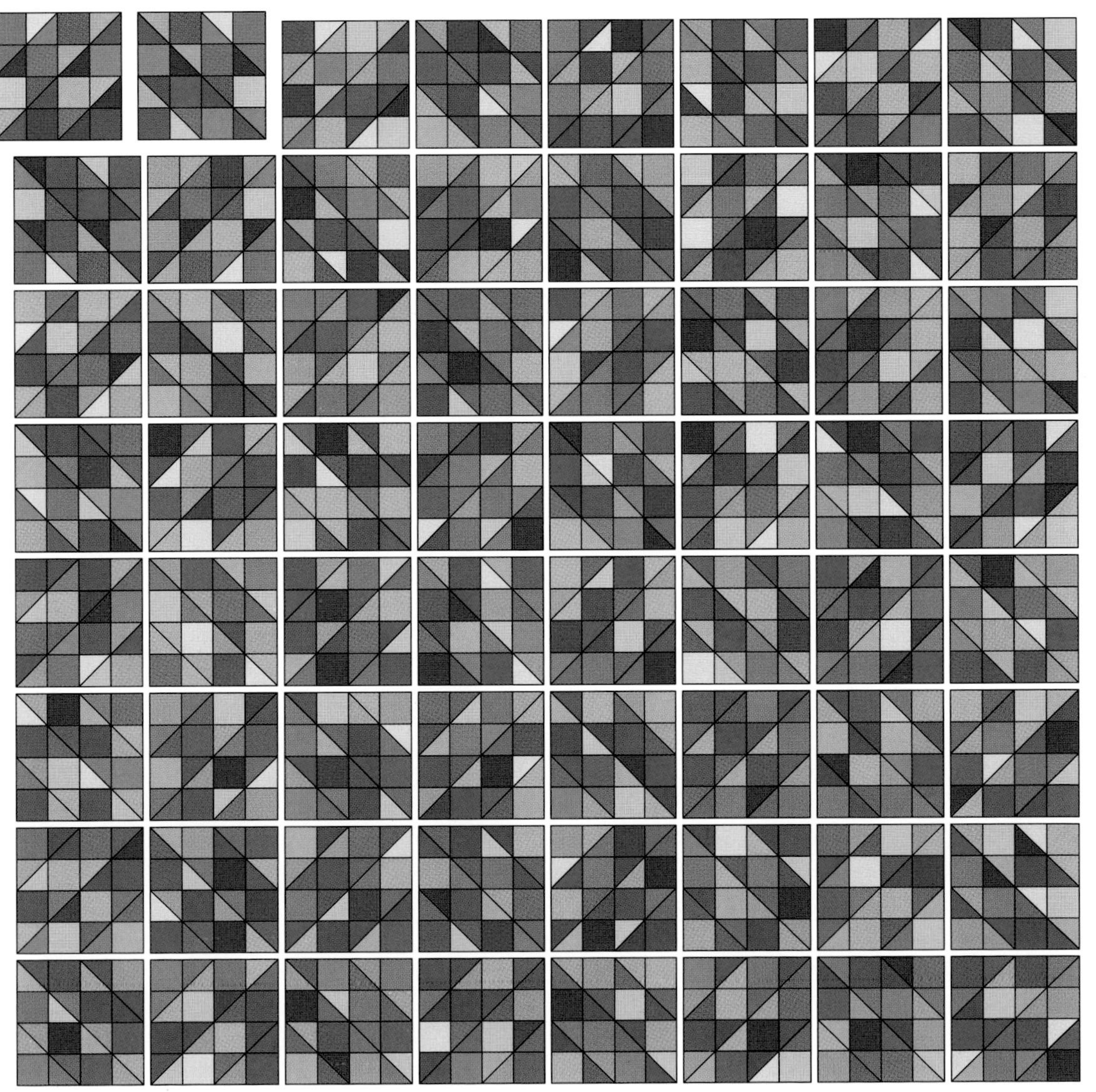

Quilt Assembly Diagram

continued

2. Sew together the blocks in each row. Press the seam allowances in one direction, alternating the direction with each row. Then join the rows to complete the quilt top. Press the seam allowances in one direction.

Complete the Quilt

1. Layer the quilt top, batting, and backing according to the instructions in Quilter's Schoolhouse, which begins on *page 150*.

2. Quilt as desired. The quilt shown was machine-quilted with diagonal lines in a diamond shape in each grouping of four blocks to further enhance the quilt top's diamond pattern (see Diagram 6).

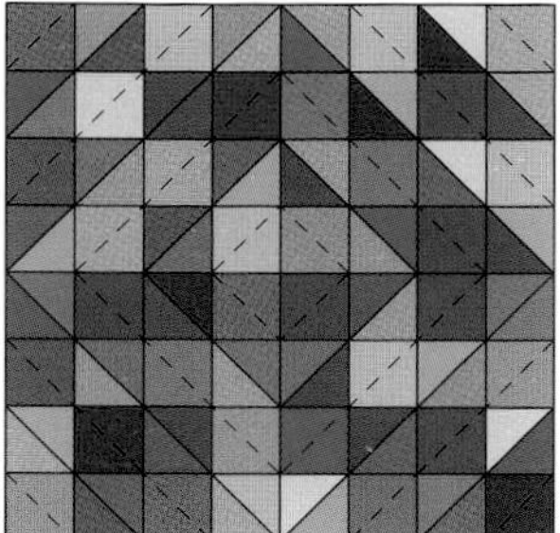

Diagram 6

3. Use the dark red print 2½×42" strips to bind the quilt according to the instructions in Quilter's Schoolhouse.

Diamonds Are Forever

optional sizes

If you'd like to make this quilt in a size other than for a double or queen bed, use the information *below*.

Alternate quilt sizes	Wall	Lap	Twin
Number of blocks	16	24	48
Number of blocks wide by long	4×4	4×6	6×8
Finished size	48" square	48×72"	72×96"
Yardage requirements			
Total of assorted light and dark prints	3 yards	4¼ yards	8 yards
Dark red print	½ yard	⅝ yard	¾ yard
Backing	3 yards	3 yards	5⅔ yards
Batting	54" square	54×78"	78×102"

optional colors

"I used a quilt program on my computer to play with color placement on my version of 'Diamonds Are Forever,'" quilt tester Laura Boehnke says. "I ended up with a scrappy three-color wall hanging."

Laura made each block with a combination of rust, tan, and green prints.

"By making distinct color changes on each half of the block, you can see the outline of the diamond shape in the piecing even more," Laura says.

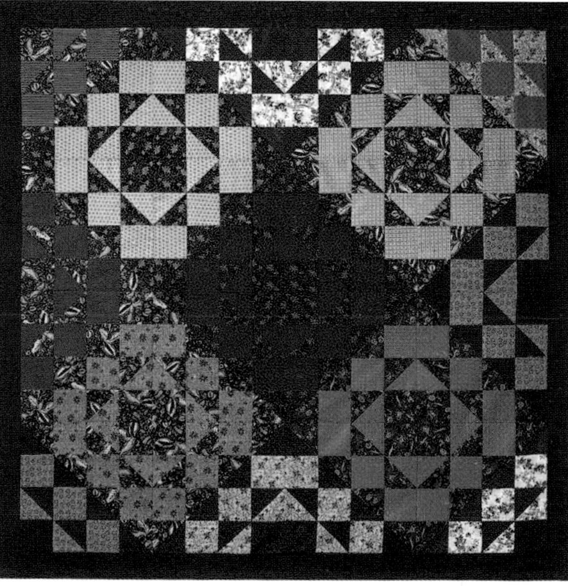

PASTEL BABY QUILT

Rotating the blocks in a different manner from the original quilt design results in a large X pattern rather than a diamond formation.

Materials

3 yards total of assorted pastel prints for blocks

½ yard of light purple print for binding

3 yards of backing fabric

54" square of quilt batting

Finished quilt top: 48" square

Cut the Fabrics

To make the best use of your fabrics, cut the pieces in the order that follows.

From assorted pastel prints, cut:

- 128—3⅞" squares
- 128—3½" squares

From light purple print, cut:

- 5—2½×42" binding strips

Assemble the Blocks

1. Referring to Make the Triangle-Squares on *page 45*, steps 1 through 3, use two assorted pastel print 3⅞" squares to make two triangle-squares. Repeat to make a total of 128 triangle-squares.

2. Referring to Assemble the Blocks on *page 47*, steps 1 and 2, use eight assorted pastel print 3½" squares and eight triangle-squares to make a block. Repeat to make a total of 16 blocks.

continued

Assemble the Quilt Top

1. Referring to the photograph *left* for placement, lay out the 16 blocks in four rows, noting the direction of each block's diagonal seams.

2. Sew together the blocks in each row. Press the seam allowances in one direction, alternating the direction with each row. Join the rows to make the quilt top. Press seam allowances in one direction.

Complete the Quilt

1. Layer the quilt top, batting, and backing according to the instructions in Quilter's Schoolhouse, which begins on *page 150*. Quilt as desired.

2. Use the light purple print 2½×42" strips to bind the quilt according to the instructions in Quilter's Schoolhouse.

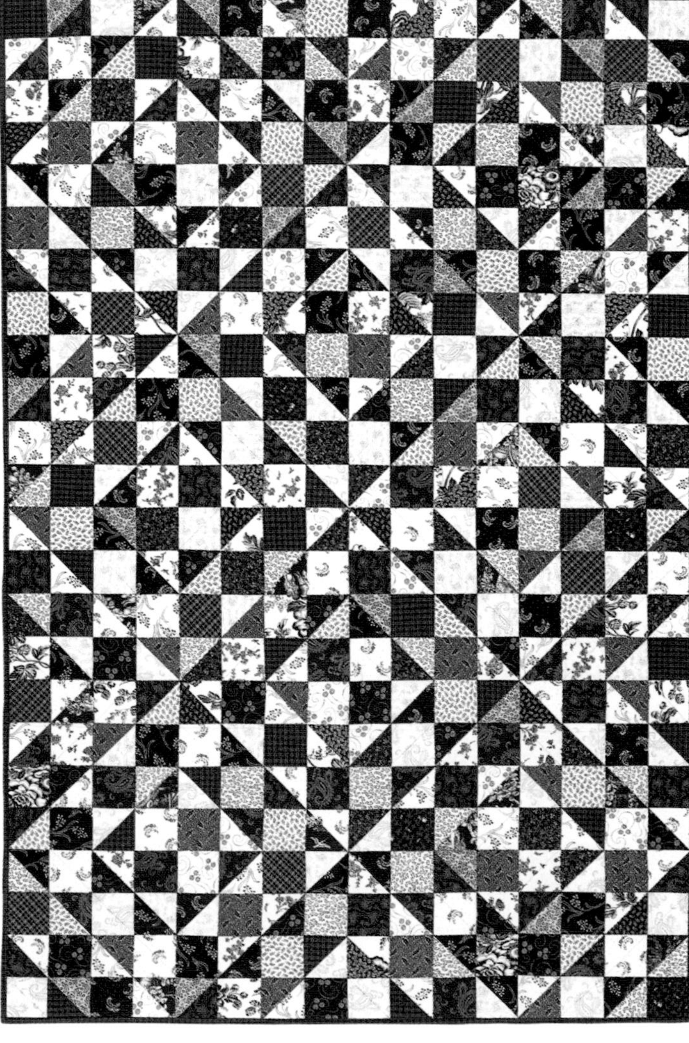

BLACK-AND-WHITE THROW

A deliberate placement of black and white fabrics makes the diamond pattern formed by the blocks more evident.

Materials

2¼ yards total of assorted white prints for blocks

2¼ yards total of assorted black prints for blocks

⅝ yard of black plaid for binding

3 yards of backing fabric

54×78" of quilt batting

Finished quilt top: 48×72"

Cut the Fabrics

To make the best use of your fabrics, cut the pieces in the order that follows.

From assorted white prints, cut:
- 96—3⅞" squares
- 96—3½" squares

From assorted black prints, cut:
- 96—3⅞" squares
- 96—3½" squares

From black plaid, cut:
- 7—2½×42" binding strips

Assemble the Blocks

1. Referring to Make the Triangle-Squares on *page 45*, steps 1 through 3, pair a white print 3⅞" square with a black print 3⅞" square to make two triangle-squares. Repeat to make a total of 192 triangle-squares.

2. Referring to Assemble the Blocks on *page 47*, steps 1 and 2, and Diagram 7, use four white 3½" squares, four black 3½" squares, and eight triangle-squares to make a block. Because this is a two-color quilt, careful placement of each piece is necessary to make the diamond pattern emerge in the completed quilt. Repeat to make a total of 24 blocks.

Diagram 7

Assemble the Quilt Top

1. Referring to the photograph *opposite,* lay out the 24 blocks in four vertical rows, carefully noting the direction of each block's diagonal seams.

2. Sew together the blocks in each row. Press the seam allowances in one direction, alternating the direction with each row. Then join the rows to complete the quilt top. Press the seam allowances in one direction.

Complete the Quilt

1. Layer the quilt top, batting, and backing according to the instructions in Quilter's Schoolhouse, which begins on *page 150*. Quilt as desired.

2. Use the black plaid 2½×42" strips to bind the quilt according to the instructions in Quilter's Schoolhouse.

Simple *Tribute*

Designer Alice Berg joins traditional favorite Log Cabin blocks with easy-to-piece star sashing for a patriotic quilt.

Materials

1 yard of gold print for blocks, sashing, and binding

1½ yards total of assorted light prints for blocks and sashing

1⅓ yards total of assorted red and blue prints for blocks

⅛ yard of dark red print for sashing

2 yards of dark blue stripe for sashing and border

3⅞ yards of backing fabric

69" square of quilt batting

Finished quilt top: 62¼" square
Finished block: 8" square

Quantities are for 44/45"-wide, 100% cotton fabrics. All measurements include a ¼" seam allowance. Sew with right sides together unless otherwise stated.

Designer Notes

"Making Log Cabin blocks has always been my way of testing my patchwork skills," designer Alice Berg says. "Since I'm ever in search of perfect piecing, this has been my practice block. I've tried many ways to make Log Cabin blocks, but for me, cutting the strips to the size needed for each log, combined with careful attention to my ¼" seam allowance, has proven to be the best way."

Cut the Fabrics

To make the best use of your fabrics, cut the pieces in the order that follows. Cut the border strips the length of the fabric (parallel to the selvage). The border measurements are mathematically correct. You may wish to cut your border strips longer than specified to allow for possible sewing differences.

From gold print, cut:
- 7—2½×42" binding strips
- 36—2½" squares
- 4—1¾" sashing squares
- 32—1⅛" squares

From assorted light prints, cut:
- 36—1½×8½" rectangles for position 12
- 36—1½×7½" rectangles for position 11
- 36—1½×6½" rectangles for position 8
- 36—1½×5½" rectangles for position 7
- 36—1½×4½" rectangles for position 4
- 36—1½×3½" rectangles for position 3

From one light print, cut:
- 9—1¾" sashing squares
- 72—1⅛" squares

continued

From assorted red or blue prints, cut:

- 36—1½x7½" rectangles for position 10
- 36—1½x6½" rectangles for position 9
- 36—1½x5½" rectangles for position 6
- 36—1½x4½" rectangles for position 5
- 36—1½x3½" rectangles for position 2
- 36—1½x2½" rectangles for position 1

From dark red print, cut:

- 12—1¾" sashing squares

From dark blue stripe, cut:

- 2—4½x62¾" border strips
- 2—4½x54¾" border strips
- 60—1¾x8½" sashing strips

Assemble the Log Cabin Blocks

1. Sew together a gold print 2½" square and a red or blue print position 1 rectangle to make a Log Cabin center (see Diagram 1). Press the seam allowance toward the red or blue print rectangle.

Diagram 1

2. Referring to Diagram 2, add a position 2 rectangle (in the same color as position 1) to the bottom edge of the Log Cabin center; press as before.

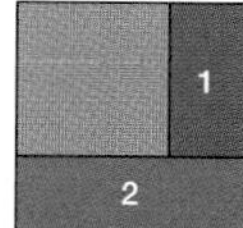

Diagram 2

3. Referring to Diagram 3, add a light print position 3 rectangle to the left edge of the Log Cabin center; press the seam allowance toward the light print rectangle.

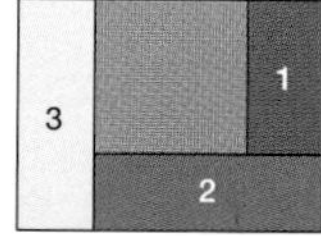

Diagram 3

4. Add a light print position 4 rectangle to the top edge of the Log Cabin center; press. Referring to Diagram 4, continue adding rectangles in numerical order to make a Log Cabin block. Always press the seam allowances toward the outside. The pieced Log Cabin block should measure 8½" square, including the seam allowances.

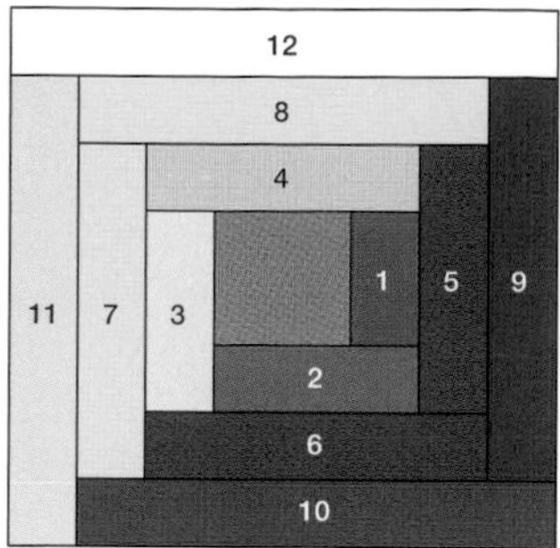

Diagram 4

5. Repeat steps 1 through 4 to make a total of 36 Log Cabin blocks.

Assemble the Sashing Units

1. For accurate sewing lines, use a quilter's pencil to mark a diagonal line on the wrong side of each light print 1⅛" square and each gold print 1⅛" square. (To prevent your fabric from stretching as you draw the lines, place 220-grit sandpaper under the squares.)

2. Layer a marked light print square with one end of a dark blue stripe 1¾x8½" sashing strip (see Diagram 5; note the direction of the drawn line). Stitch on the drawn line. Trim the excess fabric, leaving a ¼" seam allowance; press the attached triangle open. Repeat with a second marked light print 1⅛" square on the same end (see Diagram 5, again noting the position of the marked diagonal line) to make a light sashing unit.

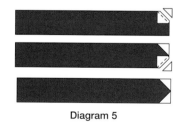

Diagram 5

3. Repeat Step 2 to make a total of 36 light sashing units.

4. Repeat Step 2 using the marked gold print 1⅛" squares to make a total of 16 gold sashing units.

Assemble the Quilt Center

1. Referring to the Quilt Assembly Diagram for placement, lay out the 36 Log Cabin blocks; the 36 light sashing units; the 16 gold sashing units; the remaining dark blue stripe 1¾×8½" sashing strips; and the four gold print, nine light print, and 12 dark red print 1¾" sashing squares in 11 horizontal rows. Note the placement of the sashing pieces necessary to create the pieced stars.

2. Sew together the pieces in each row. Press the seam allowances toward the sashing strips and sashing units. Then join the rows to make the quilt center. Press the seam allowances toward the sashing rows. The pieced quilt center should measure 54¾" square, including the seam allowances.

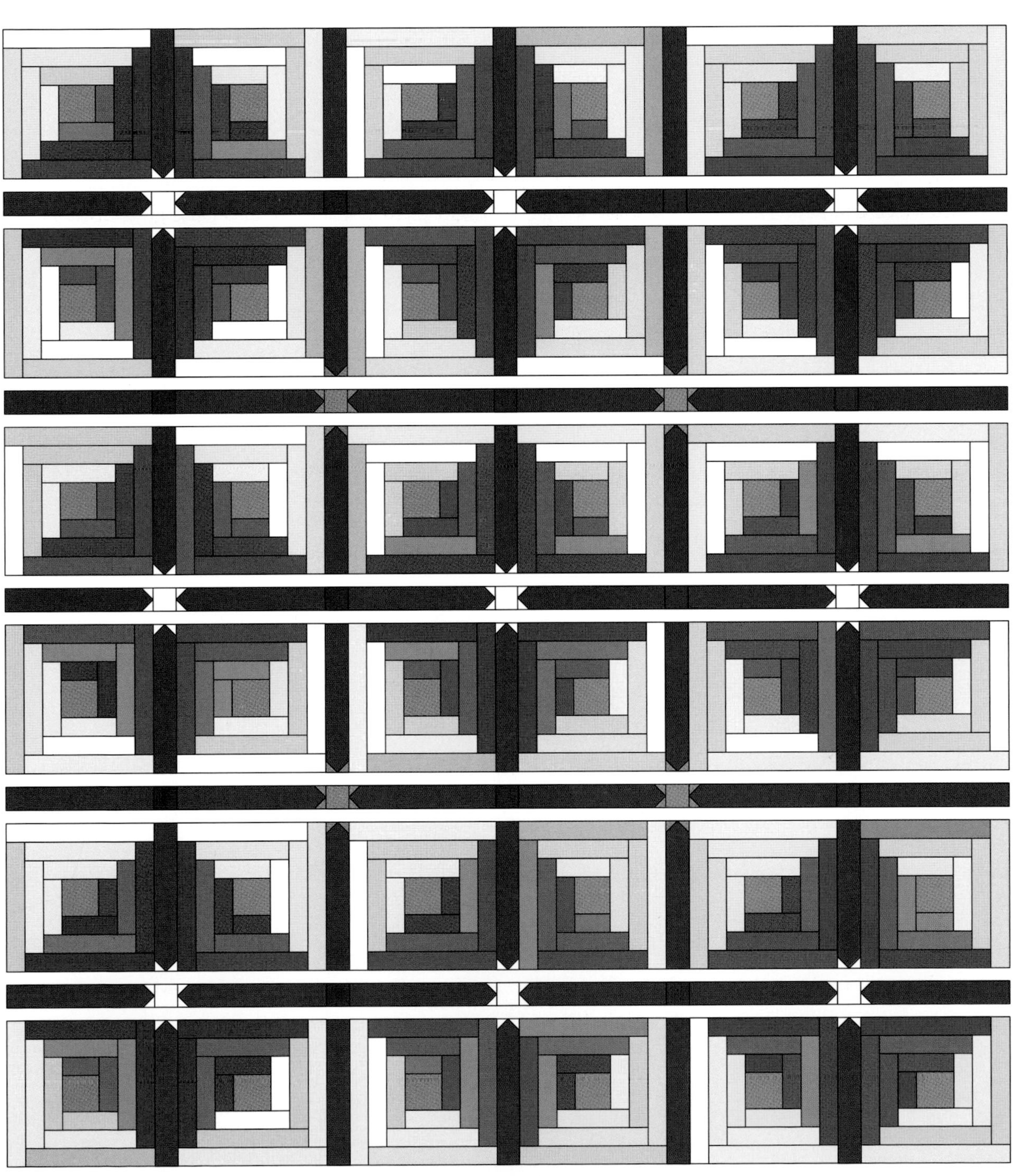

Quilt Assembly Diagram

continued

Add the Border

1. Sew the dark blue stripe 4½×54¾" border strips to opposite edges of the pieced quilt center. Press the seam allowances toward the border.

2. Sew the dark blue stripe 4½×62¾" border strips to the remaining edges of the pieced quilt center to complete the quilt top. Press the seam allowances toward the border.

Complete the Quilt

1. Layer the quilt top, batting, and backing according to the instructions in Quilter's Schoolhouse, which begins on *page 150.*

2. Quilt as desired. The featured quilt was hand-quilted with an X through the center of each gold square and a line down the middle of each rectangle in the Log Cabin blocks.

3. Use the gold print 2½×42" strips to bind the quilt according to the instructions in Quilter's Schoolhouse.

optional colors

Don't pass by this pattern if the patriotic look doesn't suit your style—simply try another color combination.

Quilt tester Laura Boehnke created her four-block rendition with homespuns and plaids in gold, rust, and green. She added additional star sashing around the outer edges of the blocks before adding the border.

The smaller size of Laura's "Simple Tribute" is perfect for a wall hanging or tabletop decoration.

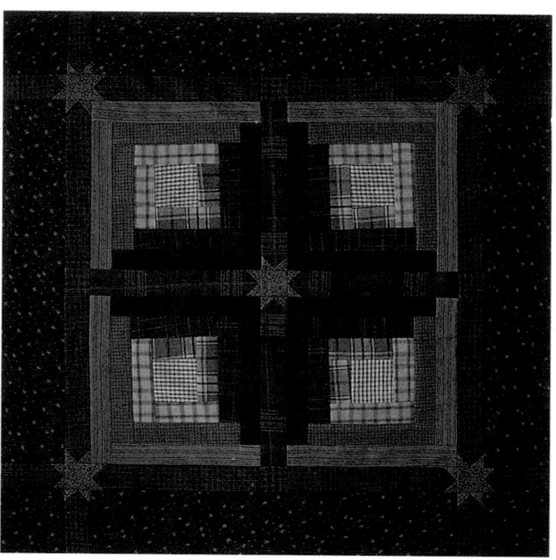

Simple Tribute

optional sizes

If you'd like to make this quilt in a size other than for a throw, use the information *below.*

Alternate quilt sizes	Twin	Full/Queen	King
Number of blocks	48	80	100
Number of blocks wide by long	6×8	8×10	10×10
Finished size	62¼×80¾"	80¾×99¼"	99¼" square
Yardage requirements			
Gold print	1⅛ yards	1⅓ yards	1⅝ yards
Total of assorted light prints	2¼ yards	3⅜ yards	4⅛ yards
Total of assorted red and blue prints	2 yards	3 yards	3½ yards
Dark red print	⅛ yard	⅛ yard	⅛ yard
Dark blue stripe	2¼ yards	3 yards	3½ yards
Backing	4⅞ yards	7¼ yards	8⅞ yards
Batting	69×87"	87×106"	106" square

LOG CABIN BED QUILT

A Streak of Lightning setting for Log Cabin blocks adds a powerful sense of movement and energy to this bed-size quilt.

Materials

⅝ yard of pink print for blocks and inner border

4 yards total of assorted light prints in tan and ecru for blocks

4⅞ yards total of assorted dark prints in green, rust, and brown for blocks

3½ yards of tan floral for outer border and binding

8½ yards of backing fabric

102" square of quilt batting

Finished quilt top: 96" square

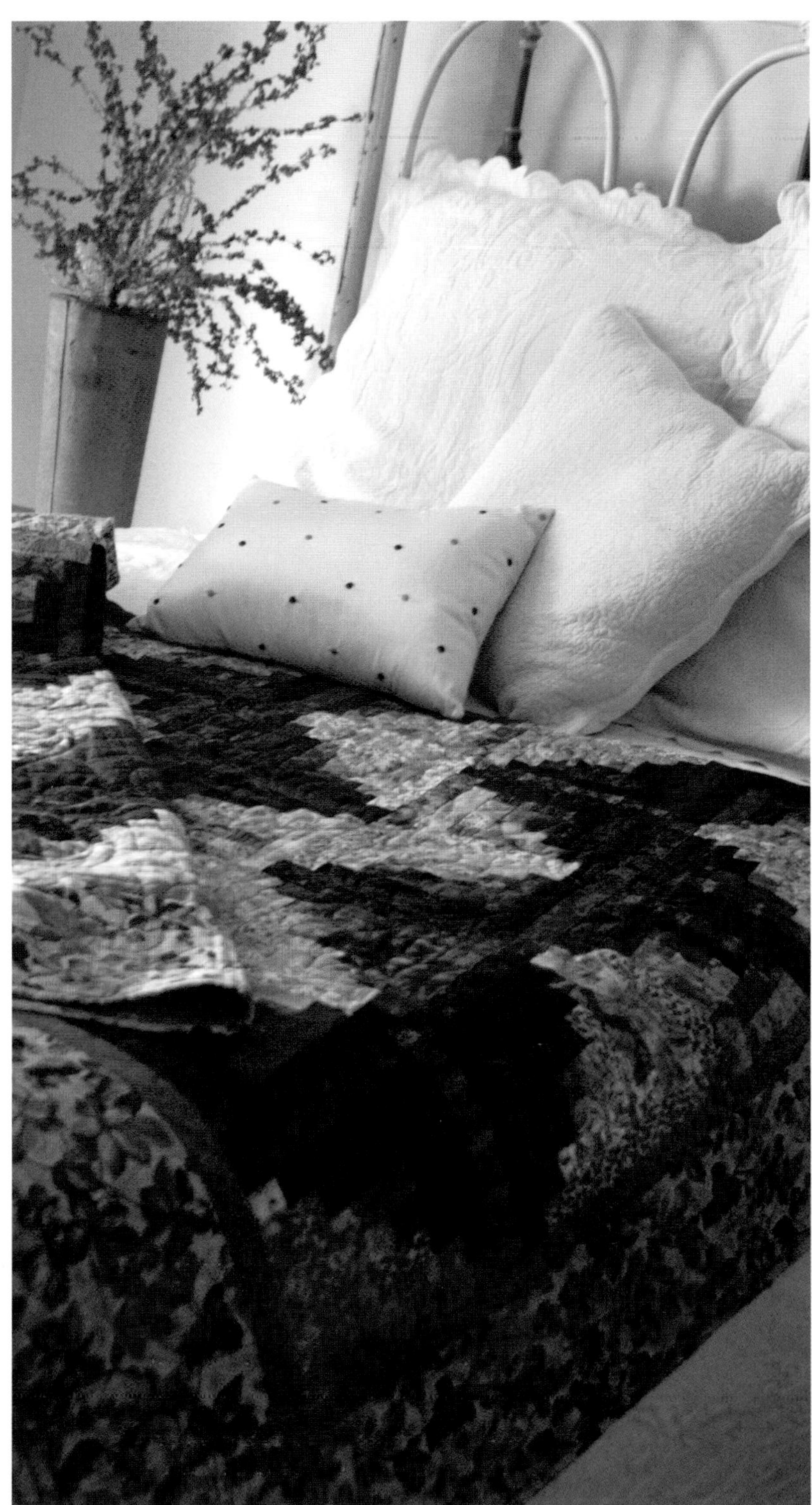

Cut the Fabrics

To make the best use of your fabrics, cut the pieces in the order that follows. Cut the outer border strips lengthwise (parallel to the selvage). The outer border strip measurements are mathematically correct. You may wish to cut your strips longer than specified to allow for possible sewing differences.

From pink print, cut:
- 8—1½×42" strips for inner border
- 100—1½" squares

From assorted light prints, cut:
- 100—1½×7½" rectangles for position 10
- 100—1½×6½" rectangles for position 9
- 100—1½×5½" rectangles for position 6
- 100—1½×4½" rectangles for position 5
- 100—1½×3½" rectangles for position 2
- 100—1½×2½" rectangles for position 1
- 100—1½" squares

From assorted dark prints, cut:
- 100—1½×8½" rectangles for position 12
- 100—1½×7½" rectangles for position 11
- 100—1½×6½" rectangles for position 8
- 100—1½×5½" rectangles for position 7
- 100—1½×4½" rectangles for position 4

continued

- 100—1½x3½" rectangles for position 3
- 100—1½x2½" rectangles

From tan floral, cut:
- 2—7½x96½" outer border strips
- 2—7½x82½" outer border strips
- 10—2½x42" binding strips

Assemble the Log Cabin Blocks

1. Sew together a pink print 1½" square and light print 1½" square. Press the seam allowance toward the pink print square. Then join a dark print 1½x2½" rectangle to the top edge of the joined squares to make a block center (see Diagram 6). Press the seam allowance toward the dark print rectangle. Repeat to make a total of 100 block centers.

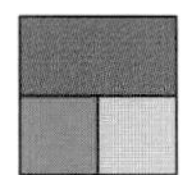

Diagram 6

2. Add a light print position 1 rectangle to the right edge of a block center. Press the seam allowance toward the light print rectangle. Then add a light print position 2 rectangle to the bottom edge of the block center; press as before.

3. Add a dark print position 3 rectangle to the left edge of the block center; press the seam allowance toward the dark print rectangle. Then add a dark print position 4 rectangle to the top edge of the block center; press as before.

4. Referring to Diagram 7, continue adding rectangles in numerical order to make a Log Cabin block. Always press the seam allowances toward the outside. The pieced Log Cabin block should measure 8½" square, including the seam allowances.

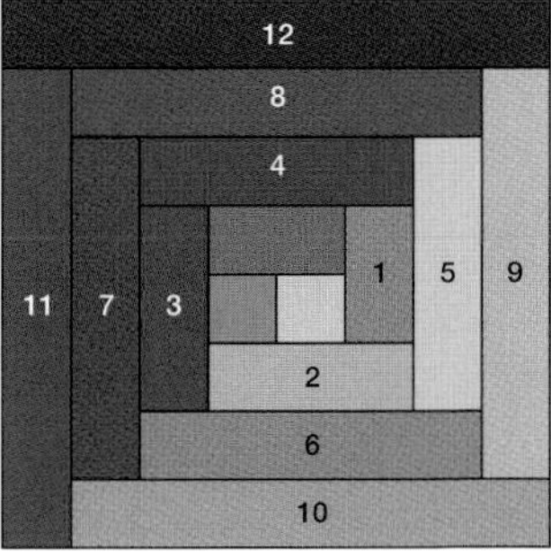

Diagram 7

5. Repeat steps 2 through 4 to make a total of 100 Log Cabin blocks.

Assemble the Quilt Center

1. Referring to the photograph *opposite* for placement, lay out the 100 Log Cabin blocks in 10 rows.

2. Sew together the blocks in each row. Press the seam allowances in one direction, alternating the direction with each row. Then join the rows to make the quilt center. Press the seam allowances in one direction. The pieced quilt center should measure 80½" square, including the seam allowances.

Add the Borders

1. Cut and piece the pink print 1½x42" strips to make the following:
- 2—1½x82½" inner border strips
- 2—1½x80½" inner border strips

2. Sew the short pink print inner border strips to opposite edges of the pieced quilt center. Then sew the long pink print inner border strips to the remaining edges of the pieced quilt center. Press all seam allowances toward the inner border.

3. Sew the tan floral 7½x82½" outer border strips to opposite edges of the pieced quilt center. Press the seam allowances toward the outer border.

4. Sew the tan floral 7½x96½" outer border strips to the remaining edges of the pieced quilt center to complete the quilt top. Press the seam allowances toward the outer border.

Complete the Quilt

1. Layer the quilt top, batting, and backing according to the instructions in Quilter's Schoolhouse, which begins on *page 150*. Quilt as desired.

2. Use the tan floral 2½x42" strips to bind the quilt according to the instructions in Quilter's Schoolhouse.

STARRY WALL HANGING

Increase the prominence of the sashing stars by reducing the block size and replacing the Log Cabin piecing with squares of print fabric.

Materials

¼ yard *each* of light gold and gold prints for sashing

1 yard of solid black for sashing and binding

⅛ yard of black floral for blocks

¼ yard total of assorted red prints for blocks

¼ yard total of assorted green prints for blocks

⅓ yard total of assorted purple prints for blocks

1⅛ yards of backing fabric

39" square of quilt batting

Finished quilt top: 32¾" square

Cut the Fabrics

To make the best use of your fabrics, cut the pieces in the order that follows.

From light gold print, cut:
- 12—1¾" sashing squares
- 96—1⅛" squares

From gold print, cut:
- 13—1¾" sashing squares
- 104—1⅛" squares

From solid black, cut:
- 4—2½×42" binding strips
- 112—1¾×3½" sashing strips
- 24—1¾" sashing squares

From black floral, cut:
- 10—3½" squares

From assorted red prints, cut:
- 15—3½" squares

From assorted green prints, cut:
- 14—3½" squares

From assorted purple prints, cut:
- 25—3½" squares

Assemble the Sashing Units

1. Referring to Assemble the Sashing Units on *page 54*, Step 1, mark a diagonal line on the wrong side of each light gold print and gold print 1⅛" square.

2. Referring to Assemble the Sashing Units, Step 2, and Diagram 8, use the marked light gold print 1⅛" squares and 48 solid black 1¾×3½" sashing strips to make a total of 48 light gold sashing units.

Diagram 8

3. Repeat Step 2 using the marked gold print 1⅛" squares and 52 solid black 1¾×3½" sashing strips to make a total of 52 gold sashing units.

Assemble the Quilt Top

1. Referring to the photograph *right* for placement, lay out the 64 total black floral, assorted red print, assorted green print, and assorted purple print 3½" squares; the 48 light gold sashing units; the 52 gold sashing units; the remaining solid black 1¾×3½" sashing strips; and the 49 total light gold print, gold print, and solid black 1¾" sashing squares in 15 horizontal rows. Carefully note the placement of the sashing pieces to create the pieced stars; make sure the light gold and gold sashing units adjoin their respective sashing squares.

2. Sew together the pieces in each row. Press the seam allowances toward the sashing strips and sashing units. Then join the rows to complete the quilt top. Press the seam allowances toward the sashing rows.

Complete the Quilt

1. Layer the quilt top, batting, and backing according to the instructions in Quilter's Schoolhouse, which begins on *page 150*.

2. Quilt as desired. The quilt shown was machine-quilted diagonally through each block, along the edges of the stars formed in the sashing.

3. Use the solid black 2½×42" strips to bind the quilt according to the instructions in Quilter's Schoolhouse.

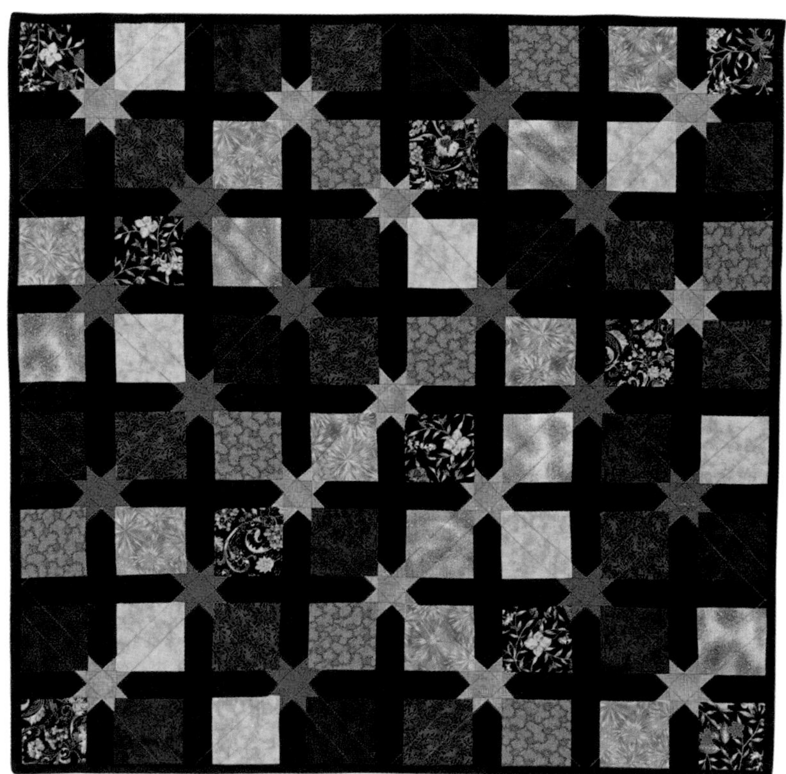

BOLD AND SASSY

Add excitement to your next project by using bright fabrics, or try one of the variations of the original projects in more subtle colors. The vibrant "Daisy Mania" takes a mellow turn in a square floor pillow and bed-size quilt. The contemporary "Slice and Dice" quilt turns into a two-color throw and an autumn table topper. And "Completely Dotty" spins onto a refreshing duvet cover and striped quilt. Surprise yourself with the fun of color experimentation.

DAISY *Mania*

Combine easy piecing and fusible appliqué for a fun and funky personalized quilt.

Materials

¾ yard of solid white for blocks

9—10½×42" strips and 16—8½×42" strips *or* 5½ yards total of assorted bright yellow, pink, green, orange, and teal prints and stripes for blocks and appliqués

1⅝ yards of pink floral for outer border

¾ yard of pink print for binding

6⅓ yards of backing fabric

76×106" of quilt batting

Lightweight fusible web

Finished quilt top: 70×100"
Finished blocks: 20×15"

Quantities are for 44/45"-wide, 100% cotton fabrics. All measurements include a ¼" seam allowance. Sew with right sides together unless otherwise stated.

Make the Initial Pattern

To personalize this quilt for the recipient, choose a font on your computer, type the desired letter, and enlarge it to approximately 8" wide to create a pattern for the initial.

Cut the Fabrics

To make the best use of your fabrics, cut the pieces in the order that follows.

The patterns are on *Pattern Sheet 2*. To use fusible web for appliquéing, as was done in this project, complete the following steps.

1. Lay fusible web, paper side up, over the patterns. Use a pencil to trace each pattern the number of times indicated, leaving ½" between tracings. Cut out each piece roughly ¼" outside the traced lines.

2. Following the manufacturer's instructions, press the fusible-web shapes onto the wrong side of the designated fabrics; let cool. Cut out the fabric shapes on the drawn lines. Peel off the paper backings.

From solid white, cut:
- 2—8½" squares
- 4—6½" squares
- 2—5½×6½" rectangles
- 1—3½×7½" rectangle
- 5—3½×6½" rectangles
- 1—3½×4½" rectangle
- 5—3½" squares

From assorted bright prints and stripes, cut:
- 9—10½" squares
- 7—8½" squares
- 5—6½" squares
- 9—5½×12½" rectangles
- 16—5½×6½" rectangles

continued

- 18—4½x6½" rectangles
- 17—3½x7½" rectangles
- 31—3½x6½" rectangles
- 17—3½x4½" rectangles
- 31—3½" squares
- 9—2½x10½" rectangles
- 9—2½x8½" rectangles
- 9—2½x6½" rectangles
- 9—2½x5½" rectangles
- 3 of the initial pattern
- 2 *each* of patterns A, I, and J
- 3 *each* of patterns F and G
- 10 *each* of patterns B and H
- 23 of Pattern C
- 6 of Pattern K
- 7 of Pattern D
- 33 of Pattern E

From pink floral, cut:
- 9—5½x42" strips for border

From pink print, cut:
- 9—2½x42" binding strips

Assemble Block A

1. Referring to Diagram 1 for placement, lay out the following solid white and assorted bright print and stripe pieces: one 8½" square, one 6½" square, two 3½" squares, one 5½x12½" rectangle, one 2½x8½" rectangle, two 5½x6½" rectangles, one 2½x6½" rectangle, one 2½x5½" rectangle, and two 3½x4½" rectangles.

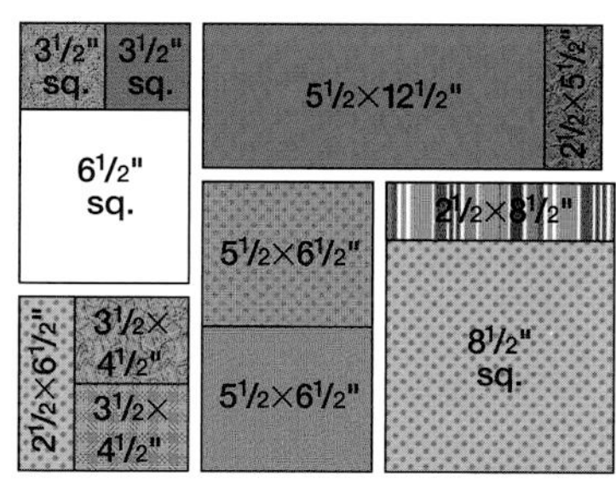

Diagram 1
Block A

2. Sew together the pieces in sections; press. Then join the sections to make a Block A; press. Pieced Block A should measure 20½x15½", including the seam allowances.

3. Repeat steps 1 and 2 to make a total of nine of Block A.

Assemble Block B

1. Referring to Diagram 2, lay out the following solid white and assorted bright print and stripe pieces: one 10½" square, two 3½" squares, one 2½x10½" rectangle, two 3½x7½" rectangles, two 4½x6½" rectangles, and four 3½x6½" rectangles.

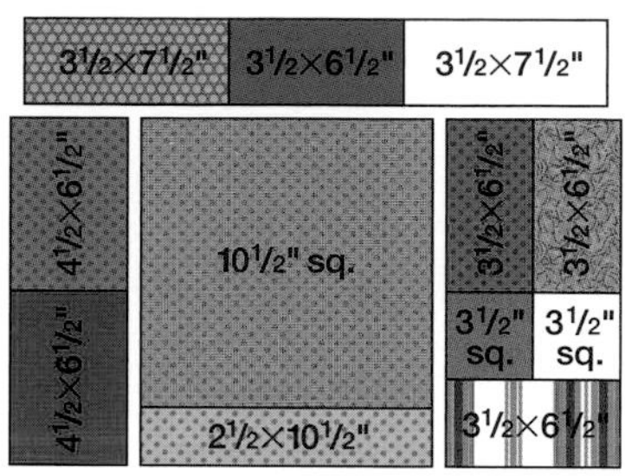

Diagram 2
Block B

2. Sew together the pieces in sections; press. Then join the sections to make a Block B; press. Pieced Block B should measure 20½x15½", including the seam allowances.

3. Repeat steps 1 and 2 to make a total of nine of Block B.

Appliqué and Assemble the Quilt Center

1. Referring to the photograph *opposite* and the Quilt Assembly Diagram on *page 68*, lay out the 18 blocks in three vertical rows, alternating blocks A and B. In the quilt shown, all three rows were laid out starting with a Block A, then the middle row was flipped (note the direction the arrows run in the Quilt Assembly Diagram). This kept the construction easy but broke up the repetition of the blocks.

2. Before sewing together the blocks, place all of the appliqué pieces, including the three initials, on the blocks to determine their appropriate locations. Refer to diagrams 3, 4, and 5 for placement of the large, medium, and small flower appliqué shapes.

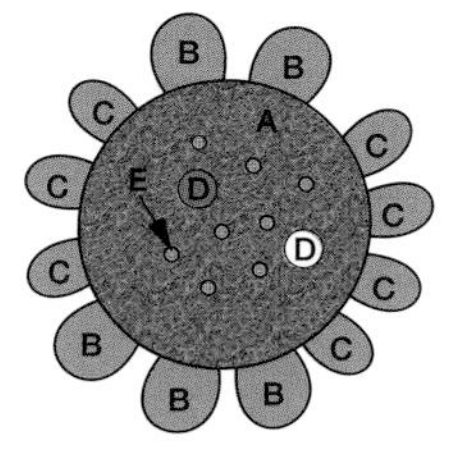

Diagram 3
Large Flower

Diagram 4
Medium Flower

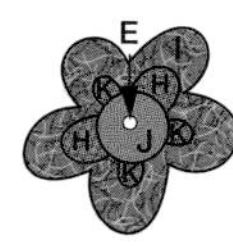

Diagram 5
Small Flower

3. When you're pleased with the arrangement of the appliqué shapes, fuse the pieces in place.

4. Using coordinating colors of thread and a small zigzag stitch, machine-stitch around each appliqué shape.

5. Sew together the blocks in each row. Press the seam allowances toward the B blocks. Then join the rows to make the quilt center. Press the seam allowances in one direction. The pieced quilt center should measure 60½×90½", including the seam allowances.

continued

Quilt Assembly Diagram

Add the Border

1. Cut and piece the pink floral 5½×42" strips to make the following:

- 2—5½×90½" border strips
- 2—5½×70½" border strips

2. Sew the long pink floral border strips to the long edges of the pieced quilt center. Press the seam allowances toward the border. Then join the short pink floral border strips to the remaining edges of the quilt center to complete the quilt top. Press the seam allowances toward the border.

Complete the Quilt

1. Layer the quilt top, batting, and backing according to the instructions in Quilter's Schoolhouse, which begins on *page 150*.

2. Quilt as desired. The quilt shown was machine-quilted all over with flowers and swirls. The appliqués were then echo-quilted to further enhance them.

3. Use the pink print 2½×42" strips to bind the quilt according to the instructions in Quilter's Schoolhouse.

optional colors

Quilt tester Laura Boehnke turned "Daisy Mania" into a boy's delight by using a variety of Western prints. She composed her six-block version without appliqués, making it a quick and easy option for a baby quilt.

"I think this is a great pattern to use with a large-motif conversation print," Laura says. "The largest pieces in each block are a great place to showcase a big print like these cowboys."

PIECED FLOOR CUSHION

Use home decorating fabrics to piece a pillow for extra seating during informal gatherings.

Materials

2⅞ yards total of assorted decorator fabrics in brown, blue, cream, and tan for blocks

1¼ yards of fleece

37×50" of extra-loft batting

23×23×5" piece of high-density foam

Heavy-duty spray adhesive

Upholstery or carpet thread

Ten 1"-diameter buttons to cover

Finished floor cushion: 24×24×6"

Quantities are for 52/54"-wide fabrics. Unless otherwise specified, all measurements include a ¼" seam allowance. Sew with right sides together unless otherwise stated.

From assorted decorator fabrics, cut:

- 4—10½" squares
- 5—8½" squares
- 5—6½" squares
- 5—5½x12½" rectangles
- 10—5½x6½" rectangles
- 8—4½x6½" rectangles
- 8—3½x7½" rectangles
- 16—3½x6½" rectangles
- 10—3½x4½" rectangles
- 18—3½" squares
- 4—2½x10½" rectangles
- 5—2½x8½" rectangles
- 5—2½x6½" rectangles
- 5—2½x5½" rectangles

From fleece, cut:

- 2—7×49" rectangles
- 2—25" squares

From extra-loft batting, cut:

- 2—23" squares
- 4—5×23" rectangles

Assemble the Blocks

1. Referring to Assemble Block A on *page 66,* steps 1 and 2, use the appropriate assorted decorator fabric pieces to make an A block. Repeat to make a total of five A blocks.

2. Referring to Assemble Block B on *page 66,* steps 1 and 2, use the appropriate assorted decorator fabric pieces to make a B block. Repeat to make a total of four B blocks.

continued

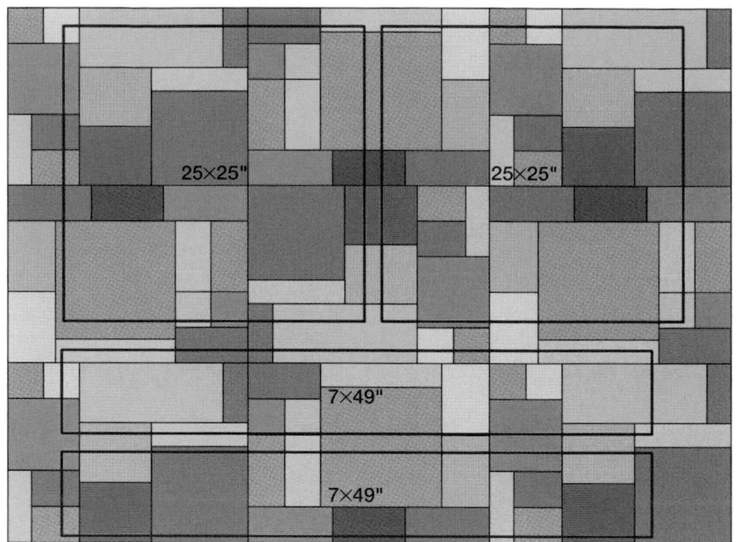

Cutting Diagram

Assemble the Cushion Pieces

1. Referring to the Cutting Diagram, lay out the nine pieced blocks in three rows, alternating blocks A and B. Note that in the featured project, the middle row was flipped to break up the repetition of the blocks.

2. Sew together the blocks in each row. Press the seam allowances toward the B blocks. Then join the rows to make the pieced fabric. Press the seam allowances in one direction. The pieced fabric should measure 60½×45½", including the seam allowances.

3. Referring to the Cutting Diagram, cut the pieced fabric to make the following:

- 2—7×49" rectangles for cushion gusset
- 2—25" squares for cushion top and bottom

4. Pair each cushion gusset, top, and bottom piece with corresponding-size fleece pieces. Baste each pair together, handling them gently to avoid fraying.

Prepare the Foam

Use heavy-duty spray adhesive to adhere the extra-loft batting 23" squares to the top and bottom of the high-density foam 23" square. Then adhere the extra-loft batting 5×23" rectangles around the sides of the high-density foam 23" square.

Assemble the Cushion

1. Using a ½" seam allowance, sew the fleece-lined gusset rectangles together along the short edges; finger-press the seams open.

2. Using a ½" seam allowance, sew one long edge of the pieced gusset to the fleece-lined cushion top, clipping the corners as necessary. Repeat to sew the remaining long edge of the pieced gusset to the fleece-lined cushion bottom, leaving one side open, to make the cushion cover. Turn the cushion cover right side out.

3. Insert the batting-covered high-density foam square into the cushion cover. Hand-sew the opening closed. *Note:* For easier insertion into the cushion cover, wrap the foam square in a large plastic bag, slip it in, and tear off the plastic bag to remove.

4. Flatten the edge along each side seam by pushing the batting-covered foam square away from the seam; pin. To create tufted edges, use a long running stitch and upholstery or carpet thread to hand-sew through both layers of each adjacent side edge, removing the pins as you sew.

5. Using a fabric-marking pen, make matching marks for the placement of five buttons on both sides of the cushion. Cover the buttons with scraps of assorted decorator fabrics. Using upholstery thread and a long needle, hand-sew the buttons on the cushion at each mark to complete the floor cushion.

ROMANTIC BED QUILT

Remove the appliqués and use pastel florals to make a quilt worthy of a tranquil retreat.

Choosing fabrics that are similar in value results in a subtle, color-wash effect.

continued

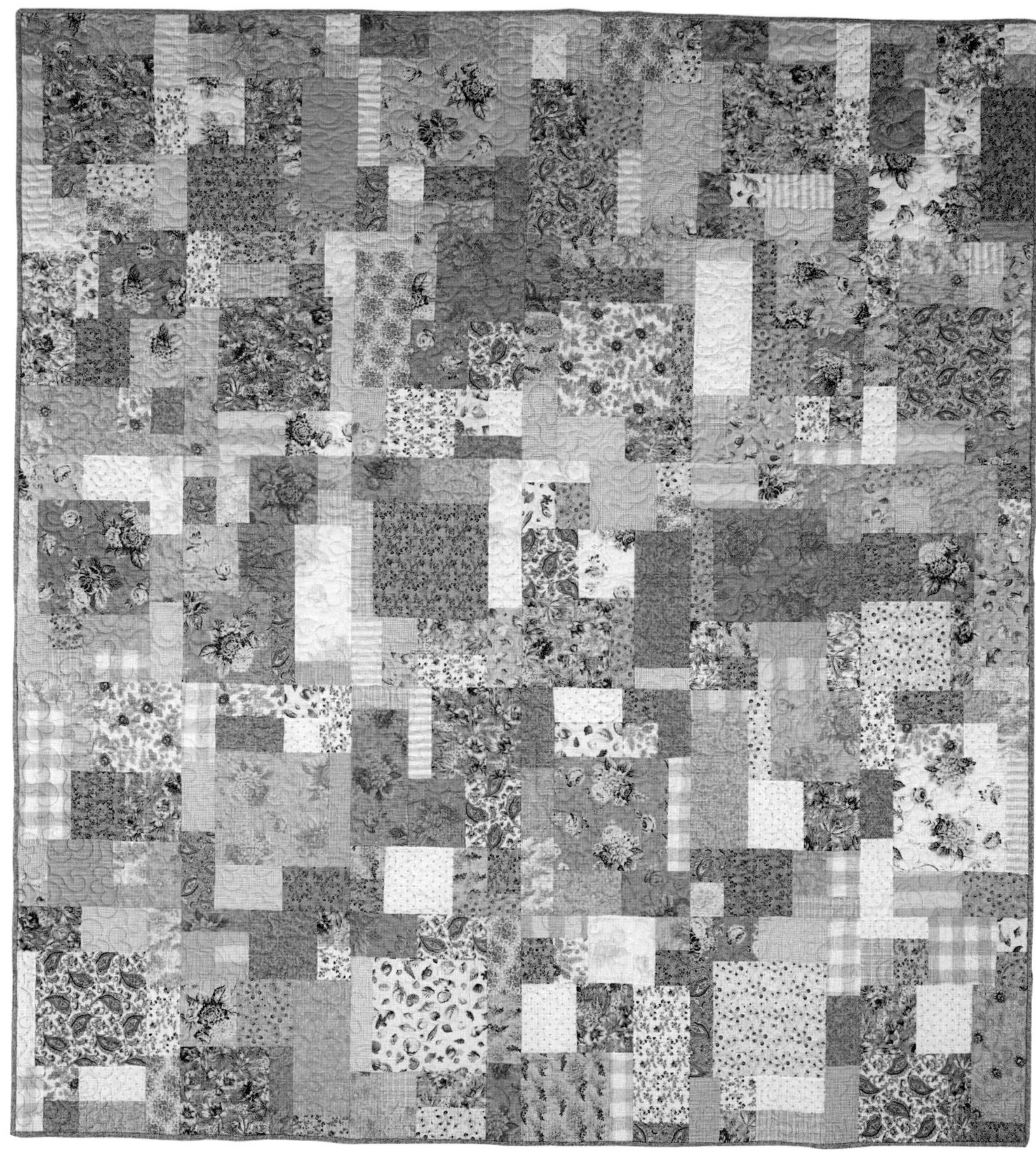

Materials

8¾ yards total of assorted pastel prints in yellow, pink, green, and white for blocks

⅞ yard of green print for binding

8 yards of backing fabric

96×106" of quilt batting

Finished quilt top: 90×100"

Cut the Fabrics

To make the best use of your fabrics, cut the pieces in the order that follows.

From assorted pastel prints, cut:

- 15—10½" squares
- 15—8½" squares
- 15—6½" squares
- 15—5½×12½" rectangles
- 30—5½×6½" rectangles
- 30—4½×6½" rectangles

- 30—3½x7½" rectangles
- 60—3½x6½" rectangles
- 30—3½x4½" rectangles
- 60—3½" squares
- 15—2½x10½" rectangles
- 15—2½x8½" rectangles
- 15—2½x6½" rectangles
- 15—2½x5½" rectangles

From green print, cut:

- 10—2½x42" binding strips

Assemble the Blocks

1. Referring to Assemble Block A on *page 66,* steps 1 and 2, use the appropriate assorted pastel print pieces to make an A block. Repeat to make a total of 15 A blocks.

2. Referring to Assemble Block B on *page 66,* steps 1 and 2, use the appropriate assorted pastel print pieces to make a B block. Repeat to make a total of 15 B blocks.

Assemble the Quilt Top

1. Referring to the photograph *opposite* and the Quilt Assembly Diagram, lay out the 30 blocks in six vertical rows, alternating blocks A and B. *Note:* In this quilt, the blocks are laid vertically. They were laid horizontally in "Daisy Mania."

2. Sew together the blocks in each row. Press the seam allowances toward the B blocks. Then join the rows to make the quilt top. Press the seam allowances in one direction.

Complete the Quilt

1. Layer the quilt top, batting, and backing according to the instructions in Quilter's Schoolhouse, which begins on *page 150.*

2. Quilt as desired. The quilt shown was machine-quilted with an allover flower design.

3. Use the green print 2½x42" strips to bind the quilt according to the instructions in Quilter's Schoolhouse.

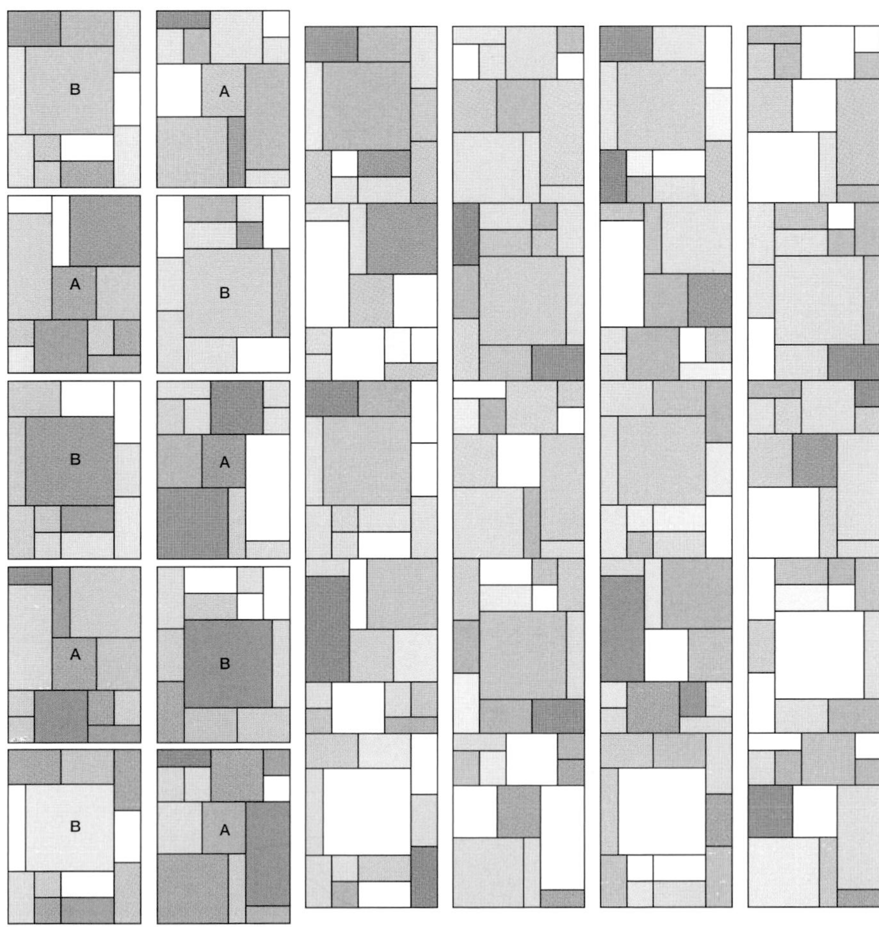

Quilt Assembly Diagram

SLICE AND *Dice*

Sit and sew now, and square up blocks later with designer Mabeth Oxenreider's fast and fun piecing method.

Materials

10—¼-yard pieces of dark batiks for blocks
10—¼-yard pieces of light batiks for blocks
¼ yard of solid orange for inner border
1½ yards of purple print for outer border and binding
2⅞ yards of backing fabric
52" square of quilt batting
6½"-square see-through acrylic ruler (optional)

Finished quilt top: 46" square
Finished block: 4" square

Quantities are for 44/45"-wide, 100% cotton fabrics. All measurements include a ¼" seam allowance. Sew with right sides together unless otherwise stated.

Designer Notes

It's often the fabric that inspires Mabeth Oxenreider to create her quilt designs.

"I was working on a quilt of Square-in-a-Square blocks with these fabrics," she says. "I loved the fabrics so much, I thought, *Why don't I try to make something that's just a little off?*

"Sometimes it takes time for me to live with and look at a fabric before I decide what kind of quilt it belongs in."

Cut the Fabrics

To make the best use of your fabrics, cut the pieces in the order that follows.

Cut the outer border strips and binding strips lengthwise (parallel to the selvage).

From assorted dark batiks, cut:
- 41 sets of 4 matching 2½×5" rectangles

From assorted light batiks, cut:
- 40 sets of 4 matching 2½×5" rectangles

From solid orange, cut:
- 2—1½×38½" inner border strips
- 2—1½×36½" inner border strips

From purple print, cut:
- 2—4½×46½" outer border strips
- 2—4½×38½" outer border strips
- 5—2½×42" binding strips

Assemble the Blocks

1. From a light batik scrap cut an asymmetrical, four-sided piece for a block center. (The edges of the center pieces in the featured quilt range from 1½" to 3½".) Repeat to cut from scraps a total of 41 light batik block centers and 40 dark batik block centers in varying sizes.

continued

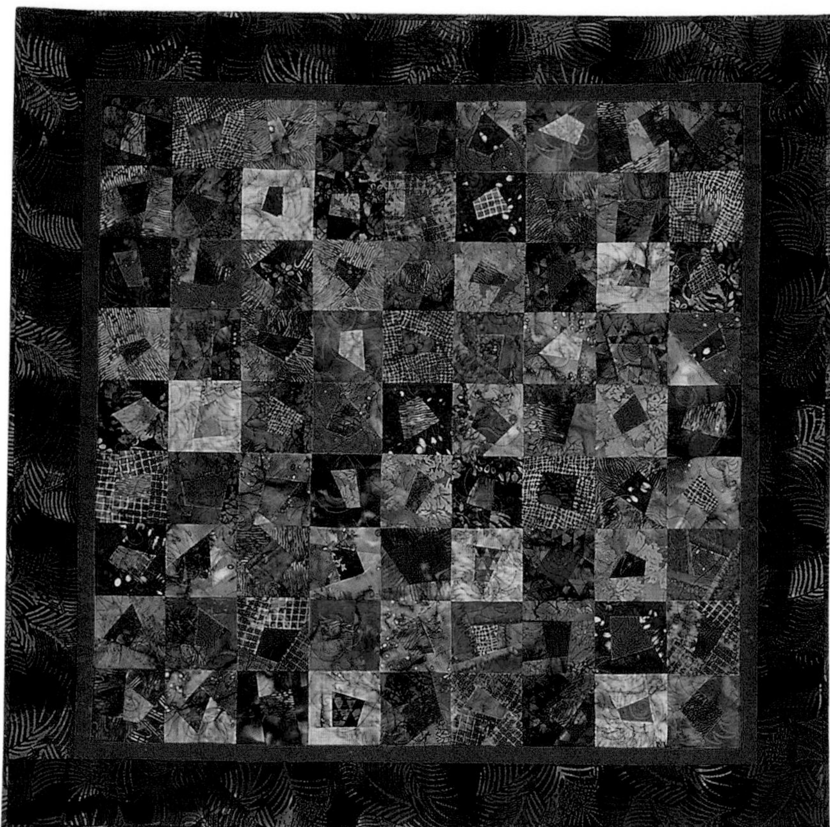

2. Center a light batik block center facedown on a long edge of a dark batik 2½×5" rectangle (see Diagram 1); join. Press the pieces open (see Diagram 2).

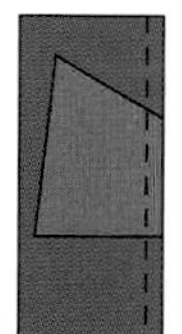

Diagram 1

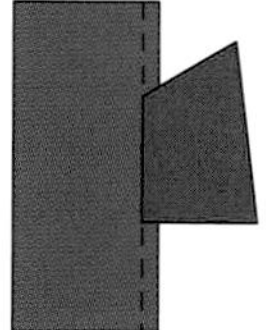

Diagram 2

3. Referring to Diagram 3, position a dark batik 2½×5" rectangle from the same set on the Step 2 pieced unit and sew together. Press open as before (see Diagram 4).

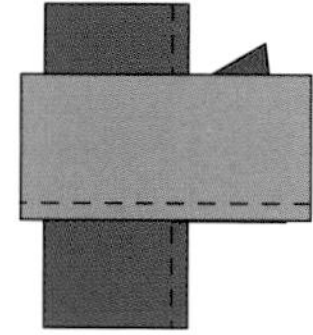

Diagram 3

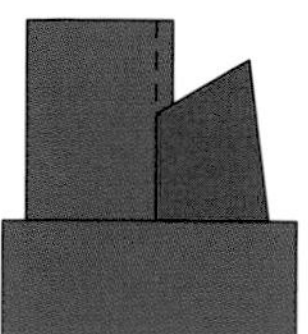

Diagram 4

4. In the same manner, join the remaining dark batik 2½×5" rectangles in the set to the remaining edges of the block center and press open (see Diagram 5).

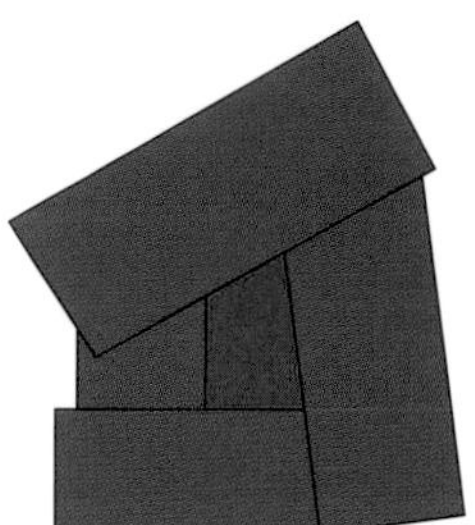

Diagram 5

5. Place the 6½" square acrylic ruler over the pieced unit at any angle (see Diagram 6); trim the pieced unit to 4½" square to make a dark batik block.

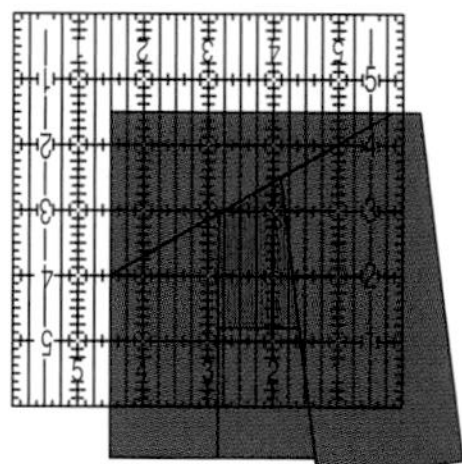

Diagram 6

6. Repeat steps 2 through 5 to make a total of 41 dark batik blocks.

7. Repeat steps 2 through 5 using the light batik 2½×5" rectangles and the dark batik block centers to make a total of 40 light batik blocks.

Assemble the Quilt Center

1. Referring to the photograph *above left* for placement, lay out the 41 dark batik blocks and the 40 light batik blocks in nine horizontal rows, alternating light and dark blocks.

2. Sew together the blocks in each row. Press the seam allowances in one direction, alternating the direction with each row. Then join the rows to make the quilt center. Press the seam allowances in one direction. The quilt center should measure 36½" square, including the seam allowances.

Add the Borders

1. Sew the solid orange 1½×36½" inner border strips to opposite edges of the pieced quilt center. Then join the solid orange 1½×38½" inner border strips

to the remaining edges of the pieced quilt center. Press the seam allowances toward the border.

2. Sew the purple print 4½x38½" outer border strips to opposite edges of the pieced quilt center. Then join the purple print 4½x46½" outer border strips to the remaining edges of the pieced quilt center to complete the quilt top. Press the seam allowances toward the outer border.

Complete the Quilt

1. Layer the quilt top, batting, and backing according to the instructions in Quilter's Schoolhouse, which begins on *page 150*. Quilt as desired.

2. Use the purple print 2½x42" strips to bind the quilt according to the instructions in Quilter's Schoolhouse.

optional colors

Quilt tester Laura Boehnke saw the potential for a baby quilt when she made her "Slice and Dice" color option with novelty prints.

"I chose these fabrics because I thought the pattern could showcase a large print," Laura says. "I fussy-cut about half of the block centers so I could center a motif in the blocks. Then I repeated that same large-motif fabric in the borders."

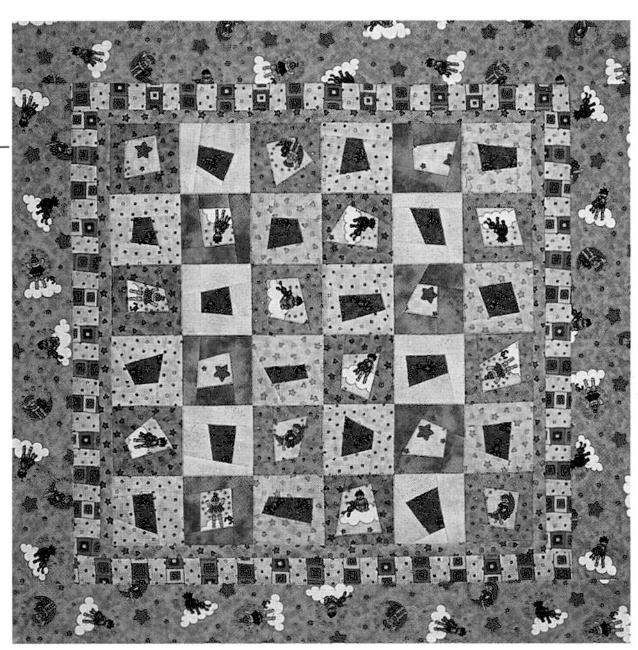

Slice and Dice

optional sizes

If you'd like to make this quilt in a size other than for a wall hanging, use the information *below*.

Alternate quilt sizes	Twin	Full/Queen	King
Number of dark batik blocks	124	200	265
Number of light batik blocks	123	199	264
Number of blocks wide by long	13x19	19x21	23x23
Finished size	62x86"	86x94"	102" square
Yardage requirements			
Assorted dark batiks	7 yards	8⅔ yards	11⅜ yards
Assorted light batiks	7 yards	8⅔ yards	11⅜ yards
Solid orange	⅜ yard	½ yard	⅝ yard
Purple print	2⅓ yards	2⅝ yards	3 yards
Backing	5⅛ yards	7⅔ yards	9 yards
Batting	68x92"	92x100"	108" square

Note: The method used for making this quilt results in an unusually large amount of wasted fabric. Save the scraps from this project for use on another scrap quilt.

RED-AND-WHITE LAP QUILT

This fresh two-color quilt is great for a summer picnic blanket or a game-day throw.

Materials

4 yards total of assorted red prints for blocks

4 yards total of assorted white prints for blocks

½ yard of mottled red for binding

3¼ yards of backing fabric

58" square of quilt batting

Finished quilt top: 52" square

Cut the Fabrics

To make the best use of your fabrics, cut the pieces in the order that follows.

From assorted red prints, cut:
- 85 sets of 4 matching 2½×5" rectangles

From assorted white prints, cut:
- 84 sets of 4 matching 2½×5" rectangles

From mottled red, cut:
- 6—2½×42" binding strips

Assemble the Blocks

1. From a white print scrap cut an asymmetrical, four-sided piece for a block center. (The edges of the center pieces in the quilt *opposite* range from 1" to 3".) Repeat to cut a total of 85 white print block centers and 84 red print block centers in varying sizes.

2. Referring to Assemble the Blocks on *page 74,* steps 2 through 5, use one white print block center and four matching red print 2½×5" rectangles to make a red print block.

3. Repeat Step 2 to make a total of 85 red print blocks.

4. Repeat Step 2 using one red print block center and four matching white print 2½×5" rectangles to make a white print block. Repeat to make a total of 84 white print blocks.

Assemble the Quilt Top

1. Referring to the photograph *above,* lay out the 85 red print blocks and the 84 white print blocks in 13 rows, alternating red and white blocks.

2. Sew together the blocks in each row. Press the seam allowances in one direction, alternating the direction with each row. Then join the rows to make the quilt top. Press the seam allowances in one direction.

Complete the Quilt

1. Layer the quilt top, batting, and backing according to the instructions in Quilter's Schoolhouse, which begins on *page 150.* Quilt as desired.

2. Use the mottled red 2½×42" strips to bind the quilt according to the instructions in Quilter's Schoolhouse.

EARTH-TONE TABLE MAT

Warm fall colors make these quilt blocks look like a swirl of falling leaves.

Lighter colors on the outside give way to darker colors toward the center of the mat.

Materials

1⅔ yards total of assorted dark prints in green, red, brown, and black for blocks

⅔ yard total of assorted light tan prints for blocks

½ yard total of assorted gold prints for blocks

⅝ yard of black stripe for inner border and binding

½ yard of burgundy floral for outer border

1¼ yards of backing fabric

41" square of quilt batting

Finished quilt top: 35" square

Cut the Fabrics

To make the best use of your fabrics, cut the pieces in the order that follows.

From assorted dark prints, cut:
- 29 sets of 4 matching 2½×5" rectangles

From assorted light tan prints, cut:
- 12 sets of 4 matching 2½×5" rectangles

From assorted gold prints, cut:
- 8 sets of 4 matching 2½×5" rectangles

From black stripe, cut:
- 4—2½×42" binding strips
- 2—1¼×30" inner border strips
- 2—1¼×28½" inner border strips

From burgundy floral, cut:

- 2—3¼×35½" outer border strips
- 2—3¼×30" outer border strips

Assemble the Blocks

1. From a dark print scrap cut an asymmetrical, four-sided piece for a block center. (The edges of the center pieces in the quilt *opposite* range from 1" to 3".) Repeat to cut a total of 29 assorted dark print block centers in varying sizes. Then repeat to cut a total of 20 block centers in varying sizes from scraps of assorted light tan prints and gold prints.

2. Referring to Assemble the Blocks on *page 74*, steps 2 through 5, use one dark print block center and four matching light tan print 2½×5" rectangles to make a light tan print block.

3. Repeat Step 2 to make a total of 12 light tan print blocks.

4. Repeat Step 2 using one dark print block center and four matching gold print 2½×5" rectangles to make a gold print block. Repeat to make a total of eight gold print blocks.

5. Repeat Step 2 using one assorted light tan, gold, or dark print block center and four matching dark print 2½×5" rectangles to make a dark print block. Repeat to make a total of 29 dark print blocks.

Assemble the Quilt Center

1. Lay out nine dark print blocks in three horizontal rows. Referring to the photograph *right* for placement, lay out the eight gold print blocks and eight dark print blocks around the nine center blocks, alternating gold print and dark print blocks. For the outer row, lay out the 12 light tan print blocks and the remaining 12 dark print blocks, alternating light tan print and dark print blocks.

2. Sew together the blocks in each horizontal row. Press the seam allowances in one direction, alternating the direction with each row. Then join the rows to make the quilt center. Press the seam allowances in one direction. The quilt center should measure 28½" square, including the seam allowances.

Add the Borders

1. Sew the black stripe 1¼×28½" inner border strips to opposite edges of the quilt center. Then join the black stripe 1¼×30" inner border strips to the remaining edges of the quilt center. Press all seam allowances toward the inner border. The pieced quilt center should now measure 30" square, including the seam allowances.

2. Sew the burgundy floral 3¼×30" outer border strips to opposite edges of the quilt center. Then join the burgundy floral 3¼×35½" outer border strips to the remaining edges of the quilt center to complete the quilt top. Press all seam allowances toward the outer border.

Complete the Quilt

1. Layer the quilt top, batting, and backing according to the instructions in Quilter's Schoolhouse, which begins on *page 150*. Quilt as desired.

2. Use the black stripe 2½×42" strips to bind the quilt according to the instructions in Quilter's Schoolhouse.

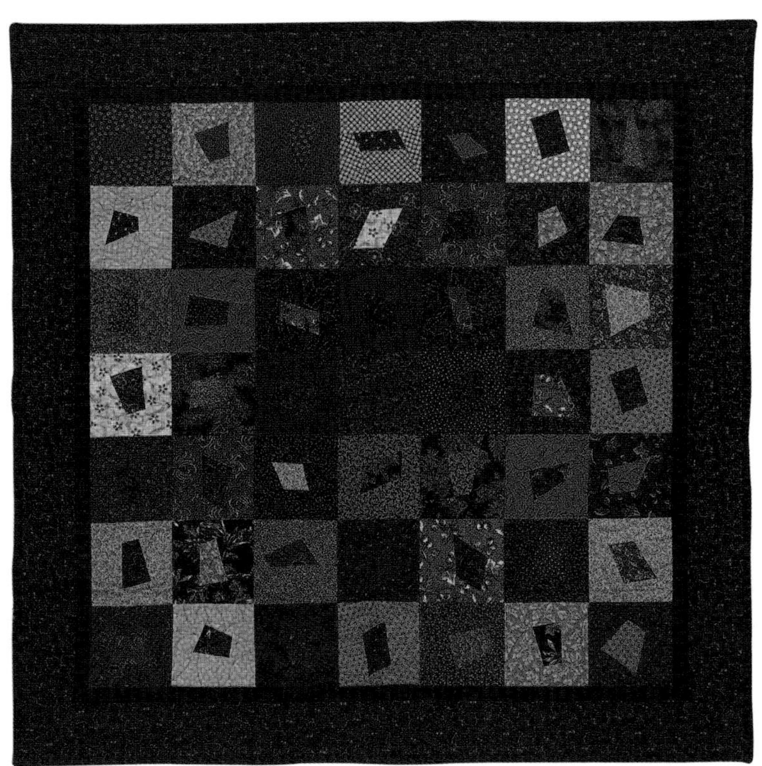

Completely *Dotty*

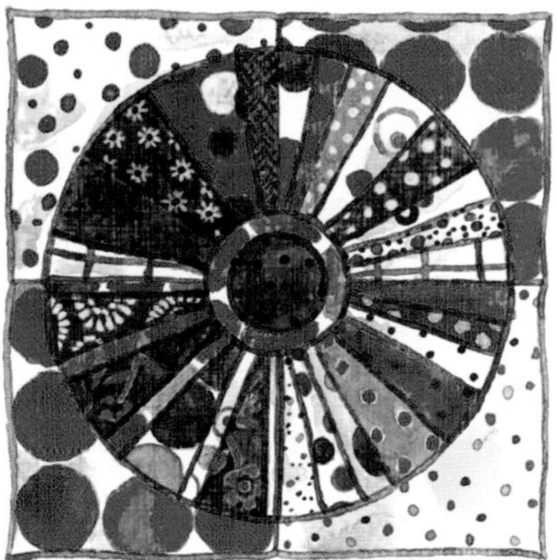

Foundation piecing ensures that your seams hit their spots and revolve into this beauty from Piece O' Cake designers Becky Goldsmith and Linda Jenkins.

Materials

3⅞ yards total of assorted light prints for blocks and sashing

2⅔ yards total of assorted dark prints for blocks and border

¾ yard of pink polka dot for binding

3½ yards of backing fabric

58×62" of quilt batting

Lightweight tracing paper or vellum

Finished quilt top: 52×56"
Finished block: 12" square

Quantities are for 44/45"-wide, 100% cotton fabrics. All measurements include a ¼" seam allowance. Sew with right sides together unless otherwise stated.

Designer Notes

After choosing the many polka-dot prints for this quilt, quiltmaker Becky Goldsmith sorted them into two piles—one a range of lights and one a range of darks. She concentrated the lightest lights in the block backgrounds and used the darkest lights in the blocks. She saved the darkest darks for the string-pieced border.

Cut the Fabrics

To make the best use of your fabrics, cut the pieces in the order that follows. Because units 1–5 are foundation-pieced, the fabric pieces used to make them are cut larger than necessary. You'll trim the pieces to the correct size after stitching them to the foundation papers. When cutting fabrics, don't worry about grain lines; the foundation papers will stabilize the fabric pieces. *Note:* When foundation-piecing, you'll sew from the wrong side of the units, so the finished unit will be the mirror-image of the foundation paper.

The patterns are on *Pattern Sheet 1*. To make templates of the patterns, follow the instructions in Quilter's Schoolhouse, which begins on *page 150*. If you're using traditional appliqué, as was done on this project, remember to add a 3⁄16" seam allowance when cutting out the appliqué pieces (B, C, D, and E).

From assorted light prints, cut:

- 48 of Pattern A
- 8 of Pattern B
- 2 of Pattern E
- 56—2⅝×5" rectangles
- 19—2¾×4½" rectangles
- 30—2½×4½" rectangles
- 38—2¼×4½" rectangles
- 30—2×4½" rectangles
- 70—1½×4½" rectangles

continued

From assorted dark prints, cut:

- 4 *each* of patterns B, C, and D
- 2 of Pattern E
- 118—2⅝×5" rectangles
- 38—2¾×4½" rectangles
- 15—2½×4½" rectangles
- 56—2⅜×4½" rectangles
- 45—2×4½" rectangles

From pink polka dot, cut:

- 1—26" square, cutting it into enough 2½"-wide bias strips to total 230" in length for binding (For specific instructions, see Cutting Bias Strips in Quilter's Schoolhouse.)

Make the Foundation Papers

The foundation patterns (units 1–5) are on *Pattern Sheet 1*. With a pencil, trace the foundation patterns onto lightweight tracing paper the number of times that follow, tracing all lines and numbers. Cut out the tracings on the outer dotted cutting lines to make the foundation papers.

- 14 of Unit 1
- 15 of Unit 2
- 19 of Unit 3
- 24 of Unit 4
- 2 of Unit 5

Assemble the Arcs

Unit 1 Arcs

1. To make a unit 1 arc, you'll need five light print 1½×4½" rectangles and four dark print 2⅜×4½" rectangles (see Diagram 1).

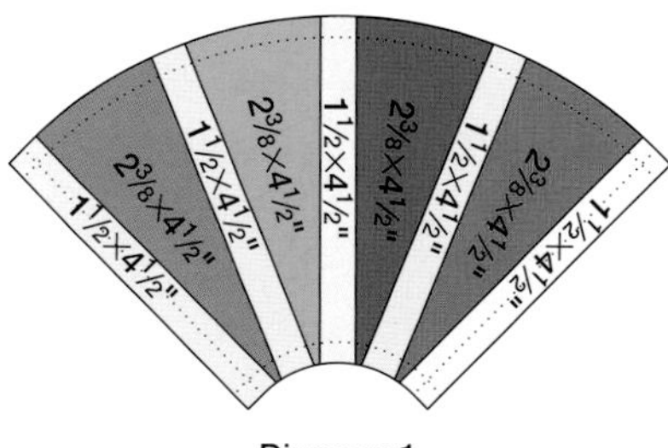

Diagram 1

2. With right sides together, place a light print 1½×4½" rectangle atop a dark print 2⅜×4½" rectangle, aligning a pair of long edges. Put a Unit 1 foundation paper on top of the light print strip so the light print strip is under area No. 1 (see Diagram 2). The aligned long edges of the strips should be a scant ¼" beyond the first stitching line and the top edges should extend about ⅛" above the foundation paper.

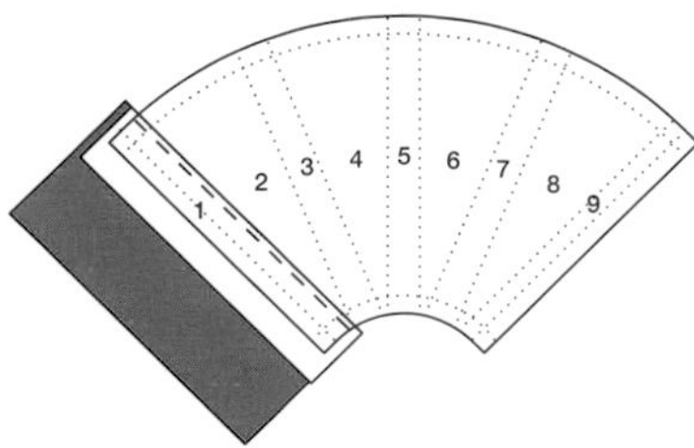

Diagram 2

3. With the foundation paper on top, sew on the first stitching line through all layers. Trim the fabric seam allowance to a scant ¼" if necessary. Press the rectangles open, pressing the seam allowance toward the dark print rectangle. Trim the dark print rectangle to a scant ¼" beyond the next stitching line (see Diagram 3). Trim both pieces even with the edges of the foundation paper (see Diagram 4).

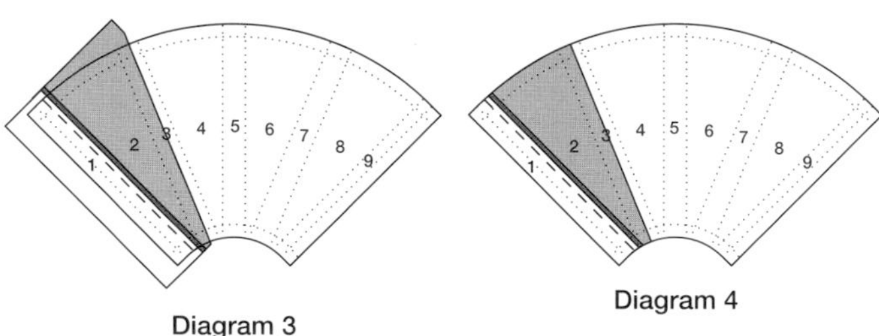
Diagram 3

Diagram 4

4. With right sides together, position a second light print 1½×4½" rectangle under the trimmed dark print piece with the right edge a scant ¼" beyond the second stitching line. Sew on the second stitching line as before (see Diagram 5).

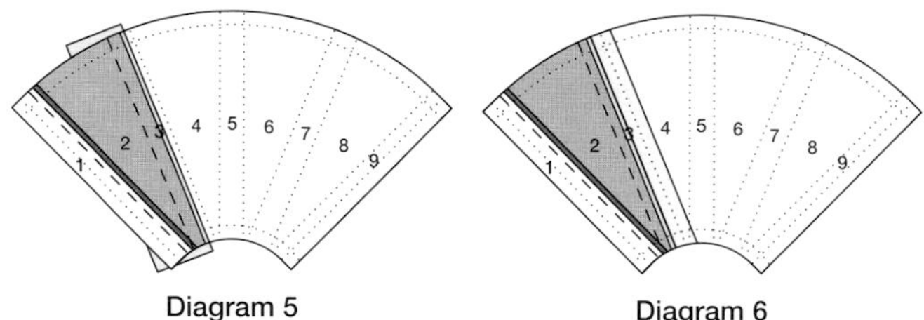
Diagram 5

Diagram 6

5. Trim the fabric seam allowance if needed. Press the pieces open, pressing the seam allowance toward the light print rectangle (see Diagram 6). Trim the second light print rectangle to a scant ¼" beyond the next sewing line and even with the edges of the foundation paper.

6. In the same manner, continue alternately adding dark and light print rectangles to the foundation paper in numerical order until you've pieced the entire foundation paper (see Diagram 7). With the blunt edge of a seam ripper, remove the foundation paper to complete a unit 1 arc.

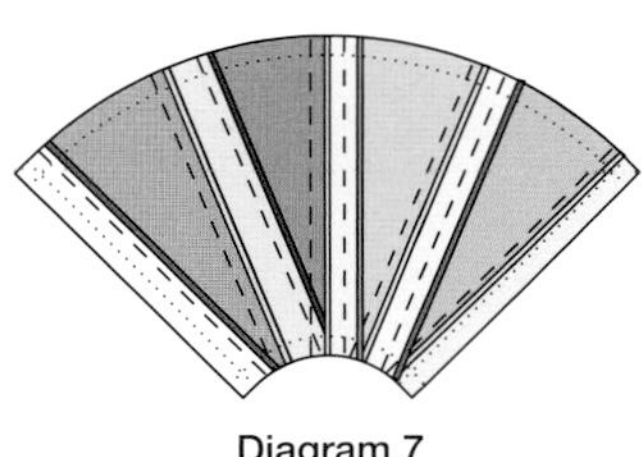
Diagram 7

7. Repeat steps 1 through 6 to make a total of 14 unit 1 arcs.

Unit 2 Arcs

1. To make a unit 2 arc, you will need two light print 2×4½" rectangles, two light print 2½×4½" rectangles, three dark print 2×4½" rectangles, and one dark print 2½×4½" rectangle.

2. Referring to Assemble the Arcs, Unit 1 Arcs, steps 2 through 6, and Diagram 8 on *page 86,* sew the

continued

rectangles to a Unit 2 foundation paper to make a Unit 2 arc. Repeat to make a total of 15 unit 2 arcs.

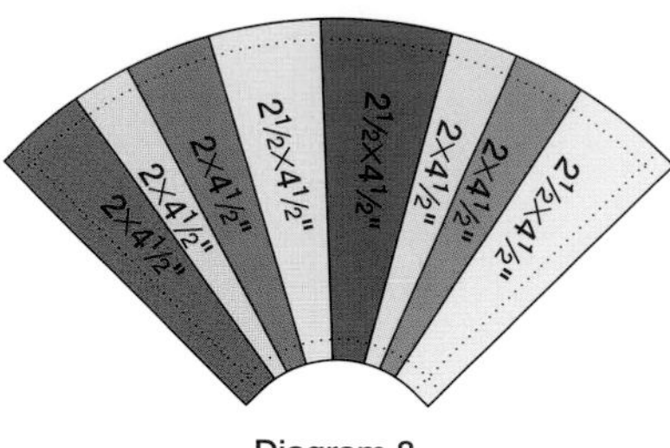

Diagram 8

Unit 3 Arcs

1. To make a unit 3 arc, you will need two light print 2¼×4½" rectangles, one light print 2¾×4½" rectangle, and two dark print 2¾×4½" rectangles.

2. Referring to Assemble the Arcs, Unit 1 Arcs, steps 2 through 6, and Diagram 9, sew the rectangles to a Unit 3 foundation paper to make a unit 3 arc. Repeat to make a total of 19 unit 3 arcs.

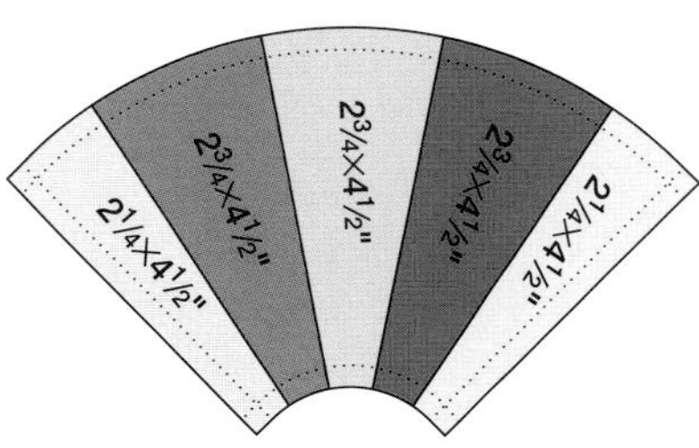

Diagram 9

Assemble the Blocks

1. Pin the center bottom of a light print A piece to the center top of a pieced unit 1 arc; the centers are marked with Xs on the patterns. Then pin each end. Pin generously between the ends and the center (see Diagram 10), using slender pins and picking up only a few threads at each position. Sew together, removing each pin just before your needle reaches it, to make a unit 1 square.

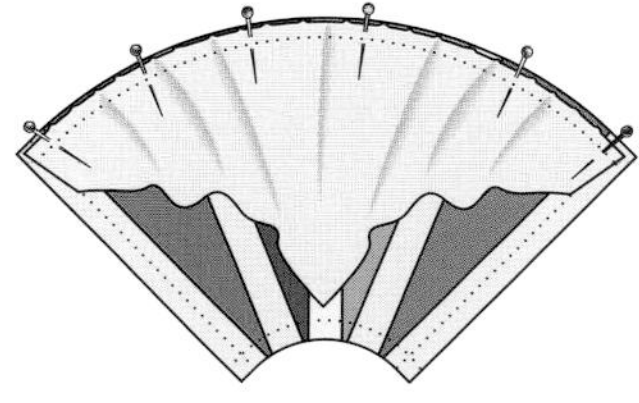

Diagram 10

2. Repeat Step 1 to join each unit 1 arc, unit 2 arc, and unit 3 arc to a light print A piece to make a total of 14 unit 1 squares, 15 unit 2 squares, and 19 unit 3 squares.

3. Referring to the Quilt Assembly Diagram, lay out the unit 1, 2, and 3 squares in sets of four. Sew together the squares in each set to make a total of 12 pieced blocks; the center of each block will be an open circle. Press the seam allowances in one direction. Each pieced block should measure 12½" square, including the seam allowances.

4. Referring to the photograph on *page 85* and the Quilt Assembly Diagram, use threads that match the fabrics to appliqué a C, D, or E piece to each B piece to make 12 block centers; press.

5. Pin a block center over the opening of each pieced block and appliqué in place.

Assemble the Sashing Rectangles and Border Units

1. Referring to Assemble the Arcs, Unit 1 Arcs, steps 2 through 6, sew seven light print 2⅝×5" rectangles to a Unit 4 foundation paper to make a light print unit 4 rectangle; do not remove the foundation paper. Repeat to make a total of eight light print unit 4 rectangles.

2. Repeat Step 1 using 112 dark print 2⅝×5" rectangles to make a total of 16 dark print unit 4 rectangles.

3. In the same manner, use the remaining six dark print 2⅝×5" rectangles and the unit 5 foundation papers to make a total of two unit 5 squares.

Assemble the Quilt Center

1. Referring to the Quilt Assembly Diagram, lay out the 12 pieced blocks and the eight light print unit 4 rectangles in five vertical rows.

2. Sew together the pieces in each row. Press the seam allowances in one direction, alternating the direction with each row. Then join the rows to make the quilt center. Press the seam allowances in one direction. The pieced quilt center should measure 44½×48½", including the seam allowances.

Add the Border

1. Join four dark print unit 4 rectangles together to make a border strip. The pieced border strip should measure 4½×48½", including the seam allowances. Repeat to make a total of four border strips.

Quilt Assembly Diagram

2. Sew a border strip to each long edge of the quilt center. Press the seam allowances toward the border.

3. Sew a pieced unit 5 square to one end of each remaining border strip. Then join the border strips to the remaining edges of the pieced quilt center to complete the quilt top. Press the seam allowances toward the border. Remove all of the remaining foundation papers.

Complete the Quilt

1. Layer the quilt top, batting, and backing according to the instructions in Quilter's Schoolhouse, which begins on *page 150*. Quilt as desired.

2. Use the pink polka-dot 2½"-wide bias strips to bind the quilt according to the instructions in Quilter's Schoolhouse.

Completely Dotty

optional sizes

If you'd like to make this quilt in a size other than for a throw, use the information *below*.

Alternate quilt sizes	Crib/Wall	Full/Queen	King
Number of blocks	6	35	48
Number of blocks wide by long	2×3	5×7	6×8
Finished size	36×44"	84×92"	100×104"
Number of unit 1	4	35	52
Number of unit 2	11	52	52
Number of unit 3	9	53	64
Number of unit 4	15 (3 sashing, 12 border)	56 (28 sashing, 28 border)	72 (40 sashing, 32 border)
Number of unit 5	0	0	2
Yardage requirements			
Assorted light prints	2¼ yards	10¼ yards	13⅛ yards
Assorted dark prints	1⅞ yards	6 yards	7⅛ yards
Pink polka dot	¾ yard	1 yard	1⅛ yards
Backing	1½ yards	7½ yards	8⅞ yards
Batting	42×50"	90×98"	106×110"

optional colors

Quilt tester Laura Boehnke selected a variety of country prints for her table runner *below*.

"I made four of each arc pattern, then moved them around on my design wall until I was pleased with their combination," Laura says. "I also was more random in my placement of lights and darks than the original quilt. It was easier for me to keep sewing along without having to stop and think about specific color placement."

BIG-BLOCK DUVET COVER

Showcase the foundation-pieced circles on the turn back of this duvet cover composed of hand-dyed fabrics.

continued

Materials

1¼ yards *each* of eight assorted hand-dyed blues and greens for blocks and duvet cover front

8 yards of blue batik for duvet cover back

Lightweight tracing paper or vellum

8 hook-and-loop tape tabs

Finished duvet cover: 90" square (fits a full/queen-size comforter)

Cut the Fabrics

To make the best use of your fabrics, cut the pieces in the order that follows. Cut the blue batik rectangle lengthwise (parallel to the selvage).

This project uses "Completely Dotty" patterns A and B and Foundation Pattern Unit 3, which are on *Pattern Sheet 1*. To make templates of patterns A and B, follow the instructions in Quilter's Schoolhouse, which begins on *page 150*. If you're using traditional appliqué, remember to add a 3⁄16" seam allowance when cutting out the B appliqué pieces.

From assorted hand-dyed blues and greens, cut:

- 15—18½x30½" rectangles
- 6—1½x12½" sashing rectangles
- 28 of Pattern A
- 84—2¾x4½" rectangles
- 56—2¼x4½" rectangles
- 7 of Pattern B

From blue batik, cut:

- 1—12½x90½" rectangle

From remaining blue batik, cut and piece:

- 1—90½" square

Assemble the Duvet Cover Front

1. Referring to the photograph *opposite top*, lay out the 15 assorted hand-dyed blue and green 18½x30½" rectangles in three horizontal rows.

2. Sew together the rectangles in each row. Press the seam allowances in one direction, alternating the direction with each row. Then join the rows to make the duvet cover front. Press the seam allowances in one direction. The pieced duvet cover front should measure 90½" square, including the seam allowances.

Assemble the Duvet Cover

1. Referring to Make the Foundation Papers on *page 84*, make a total of 28 Unit 3 foundation papers.

2. Referring to Assemble the Arcs, Unit 3 Arcs, on *page 86*, use the assorted hand-dyed blue and green 2¼x4½" and 2¾x4½" rectangles to make a total of 28 unit 3 arcs.

3. Referring to Assemble the Blocks on *page 86*, Step 1, use the assorted hand-dyed blue and green A pieces and the 28 unit 3 arcs to make a total of 28 unit 3 squares.

4. Referring to Assemble the Blocks, Step 3, join the 28 unit 3 squares to make a total of seven pieced blocks.

5. Referring to Assemble the Blocks, Step 5, appliqué a B circle to the center of each pieced block.

6. Referring to the photograph *opposite bottom* for placement, lay out the seven pieced blocks and the six assorted hand-dyed blue and green 1½x12½" sashing rectangles in a horizontal row. Sew together the pieces to make a patchwork row; press the seam allowances toward the sashing rectangles. The patchwork row should measure 90½x12½", including the seam allowances.

7. On the right side of one long edge of the blue batik 90½x12½" rectangle, sew the hook portion of the hook-and-loop tape tabs at even intervals ¾" from the edge.

8. With right sides together, join the edge of the blue batik 90½x12½" rectangle that has the hook-and-loop tape tabs to one long edge of the patchwork row. Press the seam allowance open. Then fold the patchwork row and batik rectangle with wrong sides together and press to make the back border (see Diagram 11).

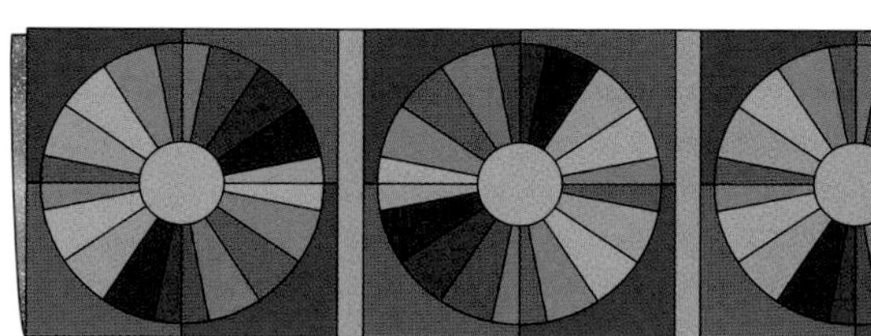

Diagram 11

9. Turn under ¼" along one edge of the blue batik 90½" square; press. Then fold the same edge under 4", creating a hem. Topstitch the hem in place to make the duvet cover back.

10. With right sides together, pin the raw edges of the back border to the top edge of the pieced duvet cover front. Then add the hemmed duvet cover back, aligning the bottom edge with the duvet cover front; the upper edge will overlap the back border (see Diagram 12). Sew together around all the outside edges to create the duvet cover (see Diagram 13). Turn the duvet cover right side out and press. The border will lap over the back to form an envelope.

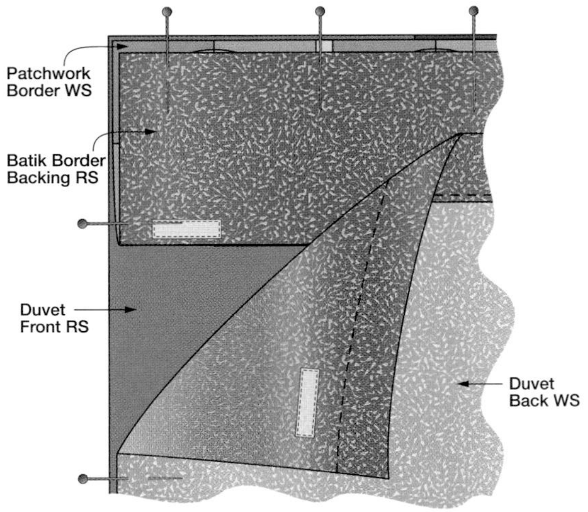

Diagram 12

Diagram 13

11. Sew the loop portion of the hook-and-loop tape tabs along the back hemmed edge to align with those on the back border. Insert a comforter through the envelope-style opening and latch the hook-and-loop tape tabs to secure.

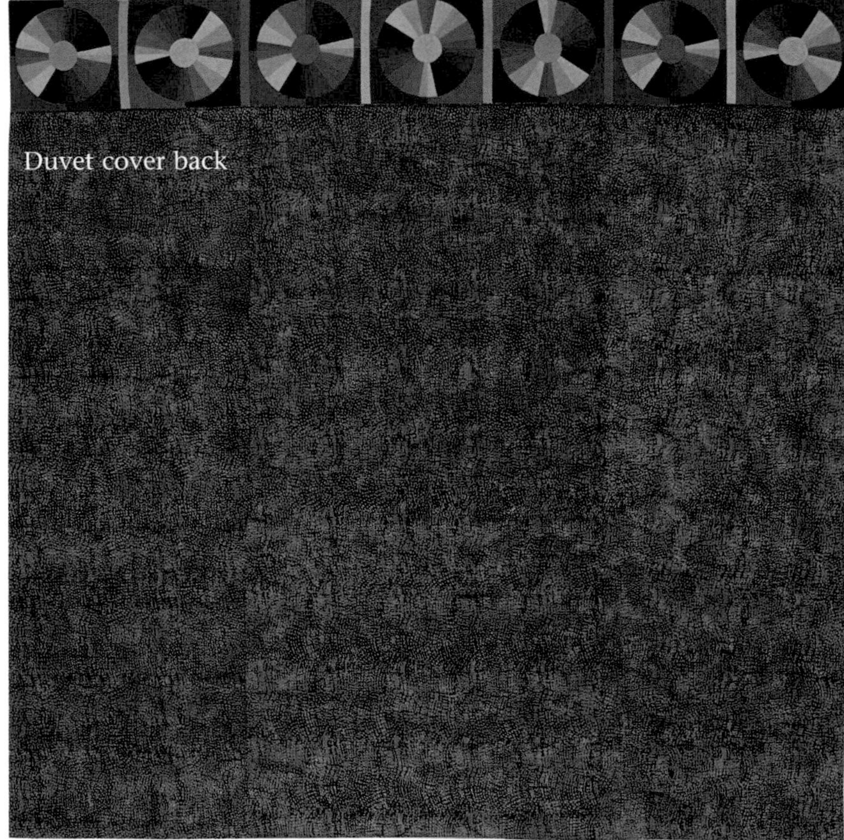

SOUTHWESTERN STRIPED THROW

Long fabric strips interspersed with just a few foundation-pieced rows make this a quick-to-finish project.

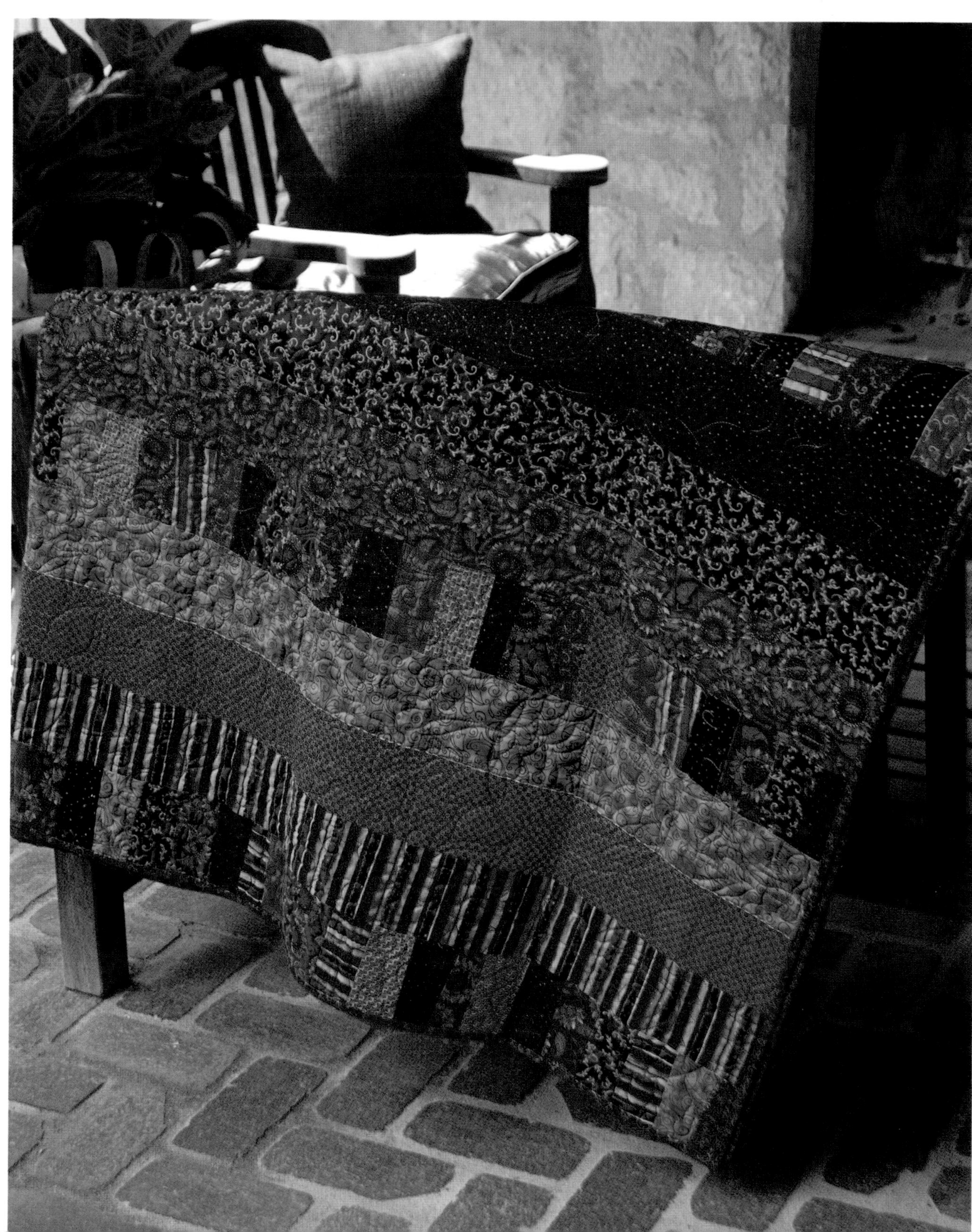

Materials

17—⅝-yard pieces of assorted prints in blue, red, green, brown, purple, and gold for quilt top

¾ yard of rust print for binding

7¼ yards of backing fabric

86×94" of quilt batting

Lightweight tracing paper or vellum

Finished quilt top: 80×88"

Cut the Fabrics

To make the best use of your fabrics, cut the pieces in the order that follows. This project uses "Completely Dotty" foundation pattern units 4 and 5, which are on *Pattern Sheet 1.*

From *each* assorted print, cut:

- 2—4½×42" strips
- 15—2⅝×5" rectangles for a total of 255 rectangles (you'll have 15 leftover rectangles)

From rust print, cut:

- 9—2½×42" binding strips

Make the Foundation Papers

Referring to Make the Foundation Papers on *page 84,* use foundation pattern units 4 and 5 to make a total of 30 unit 4 foundation papers and 10 unit 5 foundation papers.

Assemble the Pieced Rows

1. Referring to Assemble the Sashing Rectangles and Border Units, on *page 86,* Step 1, sew seven assorted print 2⅝×5" rectangles to a Unit 4 foundation paper to make a unit 4 rectangle; do not remove the foundation paper. Repeat to make a total of 30 unit 4 rectangles.

2. In the same manner, sew 30 assorted print 2⅝×5" rectangles to the Unit 5 foundation papers to make a total of 10 unit 5 squares.

3. Lay out six unit 4 rectangles and two unit 5 squares in a row, rotating the rectangles as desired; join to make a pieced row. The pieced row should measure 4½×80½", including the seam allowances. Repeat to make a total of five pieced rows.

Assemble the Quilt Top

1. Cut and piece two matching blue, red, green, brown, purple, or gold print 4½×42" strips to make one 4½×80½" strip. Repeat with the remaining sets of assorted print 4½×42" strips to make a total of 17 assorted print 4½×80½" strips.

2. Referring to the photograph *below,* lay out the 17 assorted print strips and the five pieced rows. Sew together the rows to complete the quilt top. Press the seam allowances in one direction. Remove the foundation papers.

Complete the Quilt

1. Layer the quilt top, batting, and backing according to the instructions in Quilter's Schoolhouse, which begins on *page 150.* Quilt as desired.

2. Use the rust print 2½×42" strips to bind the quilt according to the instructions in Quilter's Schoolhouse.

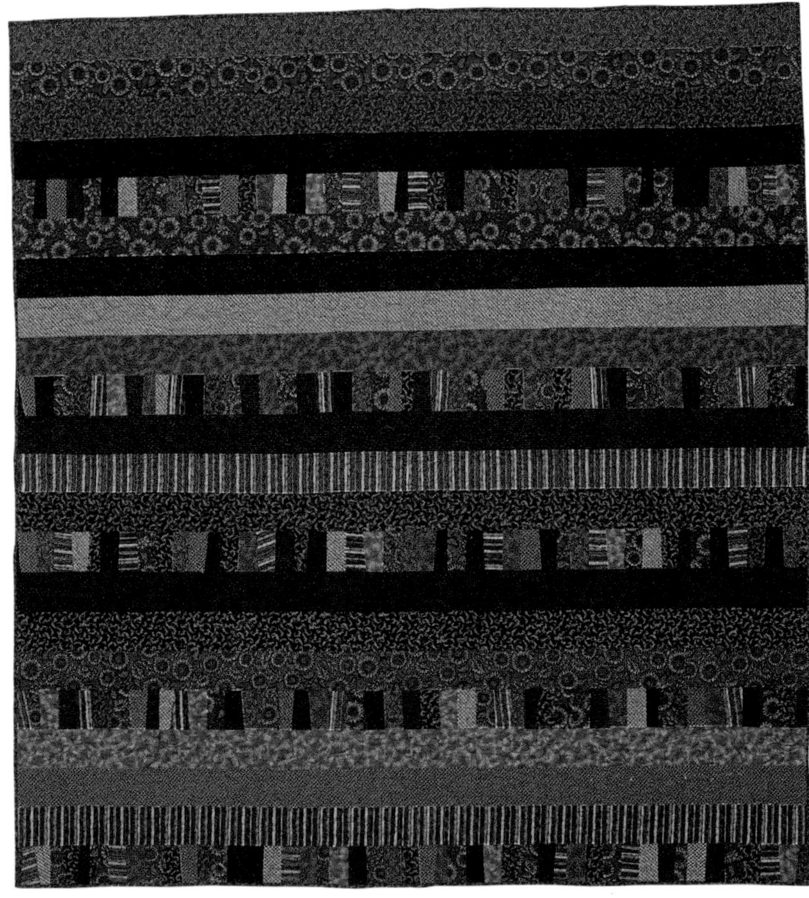

TALL TIMBERS

Trees symbolize life and growth and record the passing of each season. Walk down a new quilting path as you make the traditional "Tree of Life," the strippy "Winter Skies," and the graphic "Through the Woods." Then venture into more new territory by stitching a dramatic variation on each of these quilts.

TREE OF *Life*

In the late 1800s, quiltmakers frequently paired indigo and white fabrics in patterns that offered large open spaces to showcase their hand quilting. This antique quilt exemplifies the exquisite work done more than 100 years ago.

Materials

4¾ yards of muslin for blocks, setting squares and triangles, and corner triangles
2¼ yards of blue print for blocks
⅝ yard of solid blue for binding
3¼ yards of backing fabric
57×83" of quilt batting

Finished quilt top: 51×76½"
Finished block: 9" square

Quantities are for 44/45"-wide, 100% cotton fabrics. All measurements include a ¼" seam allowance. Sew with right sides together unless otherwise stated.

Cut the Fabrics

To make the best use of your fabrics, cut the pieces in the order that follows.

The patterns are on *Pattern Sheet 1*. To make templates for the patterns, follow the instructions in Quilter's Schoolhouse, which begins on *page 150*.

From muslin, cut:

- 4—14" squares, cutting each diagonally twice in an X for a total of 16 setting triangles
- 15—9½" setting squares
- 2—7¼" squares, cutting each in half diagonally for a total of four corner triangles
- 48—2×4" rectangles
- 24 *each* of patterns A and A reversed
- 24—3⅞" squares, cutting each in half diagonally for a total of 48 large triangles
- 12—3⅜" squares, cutting each in half diagonally for a total of 24 medium triangles
- 360—1⅞" squares
- 72—1½" squares

From blue print, cut:

- 12—4⅞" squares, cutting each in half diagonally for a total of 24 extra-large triangles
- 24—1⅞×3⅜" rectangles
- 24 of Pattern B
- 360—1⅞" squares
- 72—1⅞" squares, cutting each in half diagonally for a total of 144 small triangles

From solid blue, cut:

- 7—2½×42" binding strips

continued

Make the Triangle-Squares

1. Use a quilter's pencil to mark a diagonal line on the wrong side of the 360 muslin 1⅞" squares. (To prevent the fabric from stretching as you draw the lines, place 220-grit sandpaper under the squares.)

2. Layer each marked muslin square atop a blue print 1⅞" square. Sew each pair together with two seams, stitching ¼" on each side of the drawn line (see Diagram 1).

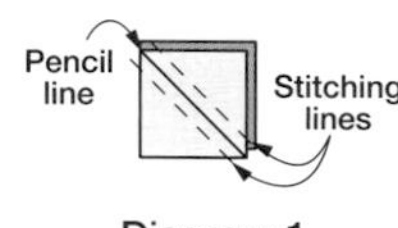

Diagram 1

To save time, chain-piece the layered squares. To chain-piece, machine-sew the pairs together one after the other without lifting the presser foot or clipping threads between units. First, sew along one side of the drawn lines, then turn the row of pairs around and sew along the other side of the lines (see Diagram 2). Clip the connecting threads between pairs.

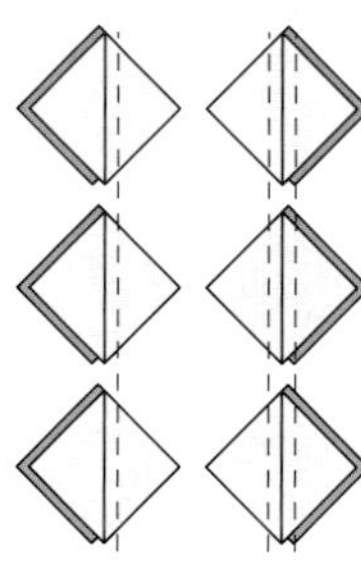

Diagram 2

3. Cut a pair apart on the drawn line to make two triangle units (see Diagram 3). Press the triangle units open to make two triangle-squares (see Diagram 4). Each triangle-square should measure 1½" square, including the seam allowances.

Diagram 3

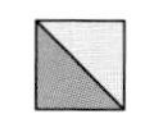

Diagram 4

4. Repeat Step 3 to make a total of 720 triangle-squares.

Assemble the Tree Blocks

The following instructions result in one tree block. Repeat the instructions to make a total of 24 blocks.

This block requires setting in seams. For specific instructions, see Setting in Seams in Quilter's Schoolhouse, which begins on *page 150.*

1. Join muslin A and A reversed pieces to the long edges of a blue print 1⅞×3⅜" rectangle (see Diagram 5); do not sew into the seam allowances in the angled corners. Press the seam allowances toward the blue print rectangle.

2. Sew a blue print extra-large triangle to the long edge of the Step 1 subunit.

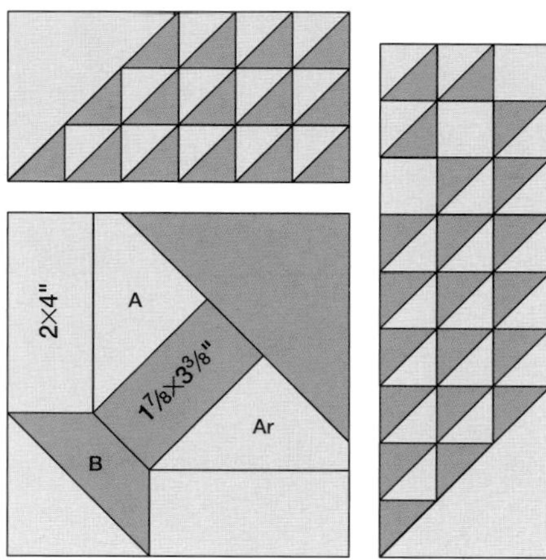

Diagram 5

3. Sew muslin 2×4" rectangles to the muslin edges of the Step 2 subunit; do not sew into the seam allowances in the angled corners. Press the seam allowances toward the muslin rectangles.

4. Sew together a muslin medium triangle and a blue print B piece. Set this unit into the Step 3 subunit to complete the tree trunk unit.

5. Referring to Diagram 5, lay out 30 triangle-squares, six blue print small triangles, and three muslin 1½" squares in two units of horizontal rows. Sew together the pieces in each row. Press the seam allowances in one direction, alternating the direction with each row. Then join the rows into two units; press the seam allowances in one direction. Join a muslin large triangle to the diagonal end of each unit to make the short and long tree branch units.

6. Join the short tree branch unit to the tree trunk unit; press the seam allowance toward the tree trunk unit. Then add the long tree branch unit to complete a tree block. The pieced tree block should measure 9½" square, including the seam allowances.

continued

Assemble the Quilt Top

1. Referring to the photograph on *page 99,* lay out the 24 tree blocks, the 15 muslin 9½" setting squares, and the 16 muslin setting triangles in diagonal rows. Sew together the pieces in each row. Press the seam allowances in one direction, alternating the direction with each row. Then join the rows to make the quilt center. Press the seam allowances in one direction.

2. Add the four muslin corner triangles to complete the quilt top. Press the seam allowances toward the corner triangles.

Complete the Quilt

1. Layer the quilt top, batting, and backing according to the instructions in Quilter's Schoolhouse, which begins on *page 150.*

2. Quilt as desired. The antique quilt is hand-quilted with a feathered wreath in each setting piece. Each tree block is outline-quilted ¼" from the seams.

3. Use the solid blue 2½×42" strips to bind the quilt according to the instructions in Quilter's Schoolhouse.

optional colors

Quilt tester Laura Boehnke chose to re-create "Tree of Life" as a four-block wall hanging. The metallic gold in the background print provides a shimmer that resembles the moon shining on a clear winter night.

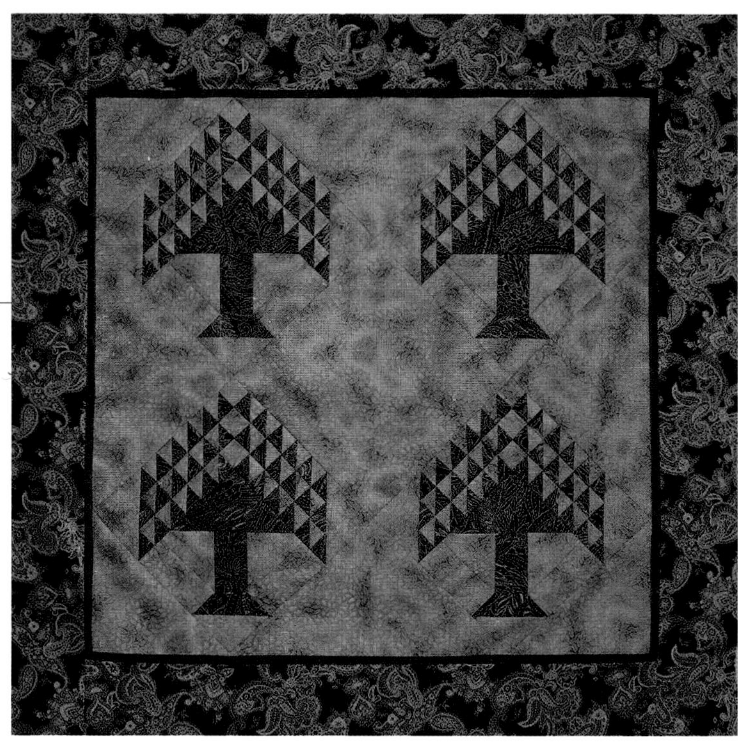

Tree of Life

optional sizes

If you'd like to make this quilt in a size other than for a throw, use the information *below.*

Alternate quilt sizes	Wall	Full/Queen	King
Number of blocks	9	56	64
Number of blocks wide by long	3×3	7×8	8×8
Finished size	38¼" square	89¼×102"	102" square
Yardage requirements			
Muslin	2⅛ yards	10 yards	11¼ yards
Blue print	1 yard	4⅜ yards	4¾ yards
Solid blue	½ yard	⅞ yard	⅞ yard
Backing	2½ yards	8 yards	9 yards
Batting	45" square	96×108"	108" square

BRIGHT WALL HANGING

A black background sets off bright fabrics, giving a contemporary look to a lone tree block.

Materials

⅓ yard of black polka dot for block and corner triangles

⅓ yard total of assorted bright prints for block and binding

⅝ yard of backing fabric

19" square of quilt batting

Finished quilt top: 12¾" square

Cut the Fabrics

To make the best use of your fabrics, cut the pieces in the order that follows.

This project uses "Tree of Life" patterns, which are on *Pattern Sheet 1.* To make templates for the patterns, follow the instructions in Quilter's Schoolhouse, which begins on *page 150.*

From black polka dot, cut:

- 2—7¼" squares, cutting each in half diagonally for a total of 4 corner triangles
- 2—2×4" rectangles
- 1 *each* of patterns A and A reversed
- 1—3⅞" square, cutting it in half diagonally for a total of 2 large triangles
- 1—3⅜" square, cutting it in half diagonally for a total of 2 medium triangles (you'll have 1 leftover triangle)
- 15—1⅞" squares
- 3—1½" squares

From assorted bright prints, cut:

- 1—4⅞" square, cutting it in half diagonally for a total of 2 extra-large triangles (you'll have 1 leftover triangle)
- 1—1⅞×3⅜" rectangle
- 1 of Pattern B
- 15—1⅞" squares
- 3—1⅞" squares, cutting each in half diagonally for a total of 6 small triangles
- Enough 2½"-wide strips in lengths varying from 5" to 12" to total 65" in length for binding

Make the Triangle-Squares

Referring to Make the Triangle-Squares on *page 98,* steps 1 through 3, use the black polka-dot 1⅞" squares and the assorted bright print 1⅞" squares to make a total of 30 triangle-squares.

Assemble the Block

Referring to Assemble the Tree Blocks on *page 98* and the photograph *above,* use the black polka-dot A and A reversed pieces, the bright print 1⅞×3⅜" rectangle, a bright print extra-large triangle, two black polka-dot 2×4" rectangles, a black polka-dot medium triangle, the bright print B piece, the 30 triangle-squares, six assorted bright print small triangles, three black polka-dot 1½" squares, and two black polka-dot large triangles to make a tree block.

Assemble the Quilt Top

Sew black polka-dot corner triangles to opposite edges of the tree block (see Diagram 6 on *page 102*); press the seam allowances toward the triangles. Then add black polka-dot corner triangles to the

continued

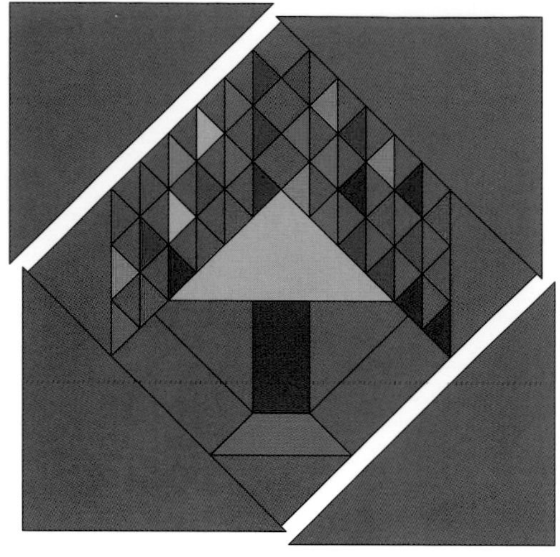
Diagram 6

remaining edges of the tree block to complete the quilt top; press as before.

Complete the Quilt

1. Layer the quilt top, batting, and backing according to the instructions in Quilter's Schoolhouse, which begins on *page 150.* Quilt as desired.

2. Using diagonal seams, sew together the assorted bright print 2½"-wide strips of varying lengths to make a pieced 2½"-wide strip. Use the pieced strip to bind the quilt according to the instructions in Quilter's Schoolhouse.

SCRAPPY LAP QUILT

This throw uses just one portion of the tree block, which creates a Double X block.

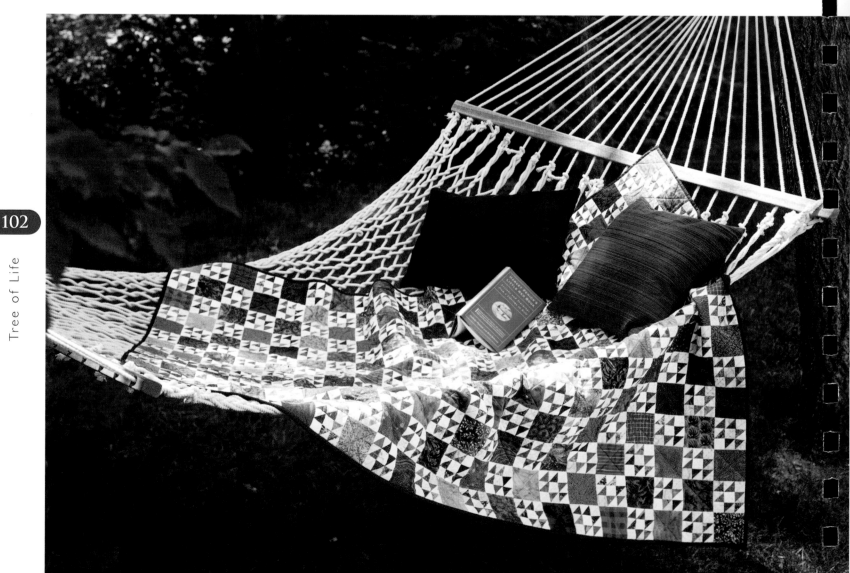

Materials

2⅔ yards total of assorted light prints for blocks

3⅜ yards total of assorted medium to dark prints for blocks and setting squares

½ yard of burgundy print for binding

3¼ yards of backing fabric

57×69" of quilt batting

Finished quilt top: 51×63"
Finished block: 3" square

Cut the Fabrics

To make the best use of your fabrics, cut the pieces in the order that follows.

From assorted light prints, cut:
- 534—1⅞" squares
- 534—1½" squares

From assorted medium and dark prints, cut:
- 179—3½" setting squares
- 534—1⅞" squares

From burgundy print, cut:
- 6—2½×42" binding strips

Make the Triangle-Squares

Referring to Make the Triangle-Squares on *page 98,* steps 1 through 3, use the assorted light print 1⅞" squares and the assorted medium and dark print 1⅞" squares to make a total of 1,068 triangle-squares.

Assemble the Blocks

Referring to Diagram 7 for placement, lay out six triangle-squares and three assorted light print 1½" squares in three rows. Sew together the pieces in each row. Press the seam allowances in one direction, alternating the direction with each row. Then join the rows to make a Double X block; press the seam allowances in one direction. The pieced block should measure 3½" square, including the seam allowances. Repeat to make a total of 178 Double X blocks.

Diagram 7

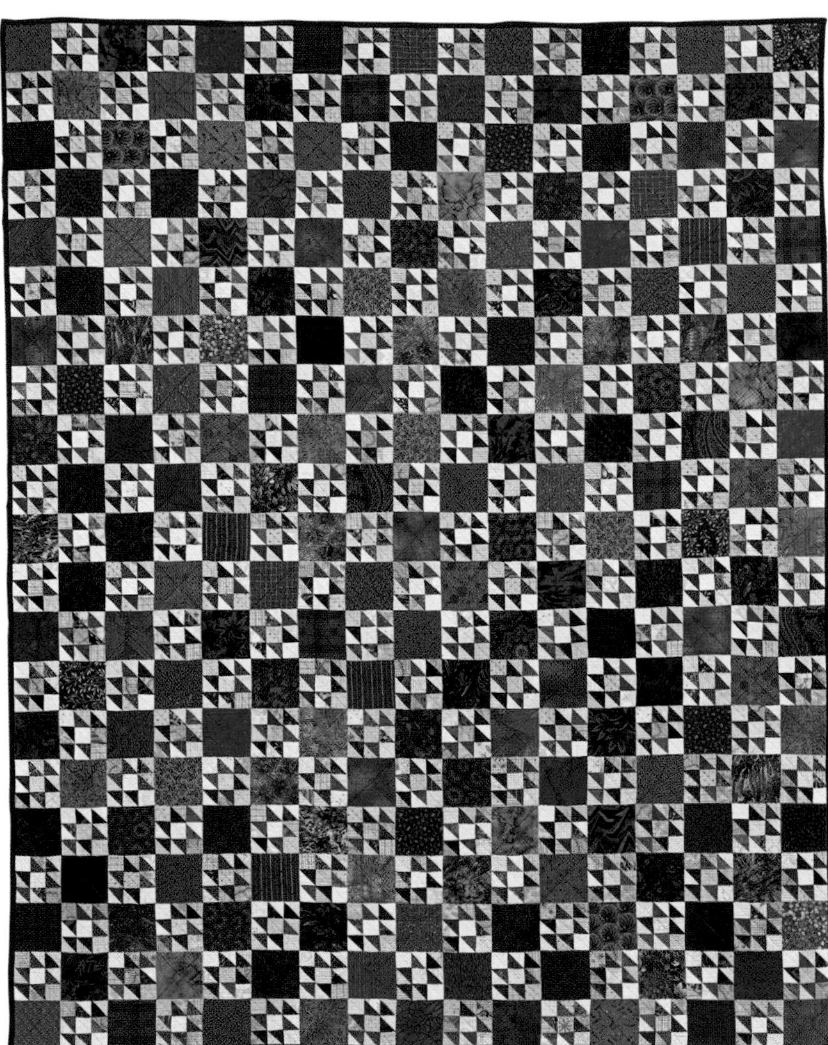

Assemble the Quilt Top

Referring to the photograph *above,* lay out the 178 Double X blocks and the 179 assorted medium and dark print 3½" setting squares in 21 horizontal rows. Sew together the pieces in each row. Press the seam allowances in one direction, alternating the direction with each row. Then join the rows to complete the quilt top. Press the seam allowances in one direction.

Complete the Quilt

1. Layer the quilt top, batting, and backing according to the instructions in Quilter's Schoolhouse, which begins on *page 150.* Quilt as desired.

2. Use the burgundy print 2½×42" strips to bind the quilt according to the instructions in Quilter's Schoolhouse.

WINTER *Skies*

The background and trees on this intricate-looking quilt from designer Kim Diehl are composed entirely of strips.

Materials

⅝ yard total of assorted gold prints for center star block and star border

⅜ yard total of assorted red prints for center star block and star border

1⅓ yards total of assorted blue prints for center star block and tree border

⅛ yard of brown print for center star block and trunk appliqués

½ yard total of assorted green prints for tree border

⅞ yard total of assorted dark blue prints for star border

½ yard of dark green print for binding

2⅝ yards of backing fabric

46" square of quilt batting

Freezer paper

Fabric glue stick

300 assorted white buttons

Finished quilt top: 40" square
Finished center star block: 20" square

Quantities are for 44/45"-wide, 100% cotton fabrics. All measurements include a ¼" seam allowance. Sew with right sides together unless otherwise stated.

Designer Notes

A blizzard of buttons embellishes this quilt from designer Kim Diehl. She says she "threw a handful of buttons up in the air over the quilt and took notice of how they fell" to decide their placement.

"Sprinkle just a handful of buttons randomly to look like twinkling stars instead of snowflakes," Kim says. "Or use sequins if you want sparkle."

Cut the Fabrics

To make the best use of your fabrics, cut the pieces in the order that follows.

From assorted gold prints, cut:
- 8—5½" squares
- 8—3" squares
- 108—1½" squares

From assorted red prints, cut:
- 8—3" squares
- 108—1½" squares

From assorted blue prints, cut:
- 10—1½×24" strips
- 4—1½×12½" strips
- 4—1½×11½" strips
- 4—1½×10½" strips
- 8—1½×9½" strips
- 8—1½×7½" strips

continued

- 16—1½x6½" strips
- 16—1½x5½" strips
- 8—1½x4½" strips
- 8—1½x3½" strips
- 8—1½x2½" strips
- 8—1½" squares

From brown print, cut:

- 4 of Tree Trunk Pattern (See Appliqué the Center Star Block on *page 108* for cutting instructions.)
- 20—1½" squares

From assorted green prints, cut:

- 20—1½x6½" strips
- 16—1½x5½" strips
- 16—1½x4½" strips
- 4—1½x3½" strips
- 4—1½x2½" strips

From assorted dark blue prints, cut:

- 62—1½x6½" strips
- 4—1½x5½" strips
- 4—1½x4½" strips
- 4—1½x3½" strips
- 40—1½x2½" strips
- 4—1½" squares

From dark green print, cut:

- 5—2½x42" binding strips

Piece the Center Star Block Units

16-Patch Unit

1. Referring to Diagram 1 for placement, lay out the eight gold print 3" squares and the eight red print 3" squares in four rows, alternating colors.

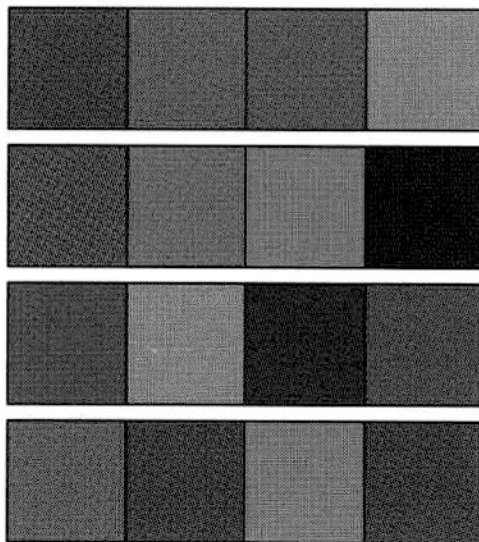

Diagram 1

2. Sew together the squares in each row. Press the seam allowances toward the red print squares. Join the rows to make a 16-Patch unit. Press the seam allowances in one direction. The pieced unit should measure 10½" square, including the seam allowances.

Star Point Units

1. Aligning long edges, sew together five blue print 1½x24" strips to make a strip set (see Diagram 2). Press the seam allowances in one direction. Repeat to make a second strip set.

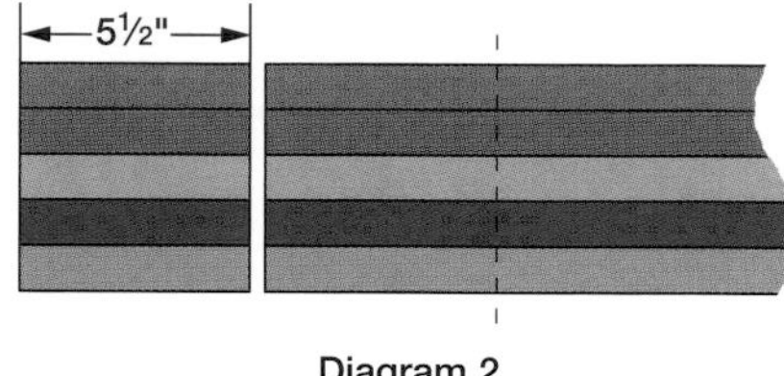

Diagram 2

2. Cut the two strip sets into a total of eight 5½"-wide segments.

3. Use a quilter's pencil to mark a diagonal line on the wrong side of the gold print 5½" squares. (To prevent the fabric from stretching as you draw the lines, place 220-grit sandpaper under the squares.)

4. Layer a marked gold print 5½" square atop a 5½"-wide blue strip segment. Sew on the drawn line. Trim the seam allowance on one side of the stitched line to ¼" (see Diagram 3). Press the triangles open, pressing the seam allowance toward the gold print triangle, to make a star point unit (see Diagram 4). Repeat to make a total of four star point units.

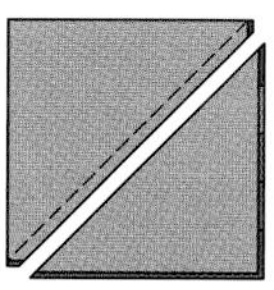

Diagram 3

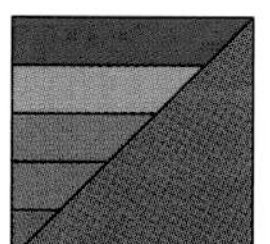

Diagram 4

5. Repeat Step 4, changing the direction of the drawn line as shown in Diagram 5, to make a mirror-image star point unit (see Diagram 6). Repeat to make four mirror-image star point units.

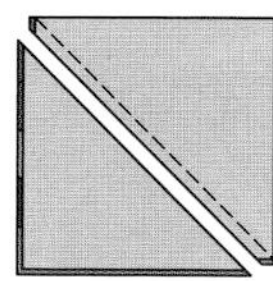

Diagram 5

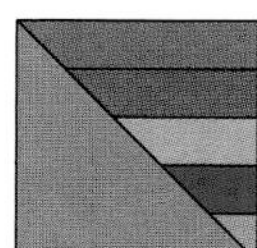

Diagram 6

Log Cabin Corner Units

1. To make one Log Cabin corner unit, you'll need two blue print 1½" squares, two blue print 1½x2½" strips, two blue print 1½x3½" strips, two blue print 1½x4½" strips, and five brown print 1½" squares.

2. Pair each blue print 1½" square with a brown print 1½" square; sew together. Press the seam allowances toward the brown print squares. Referring to Diagram 7, join the pairs to make a Four-Patch subunit. Press the seam allowance in one direction.

Diagram 7

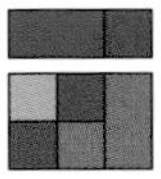

Diagram 8

3. Join a blue print 1½×2½" strip to the right-hand edge of the Four-Patch subunit (see Diagram 8); press the seam allowance toward the blue print strip. Then add a brown print 1½" square to the second blue print 1½×2½" strip; press the seam allowance toward the blue print strip. Join this pieced segment to the top edge of the Four-Patch subunit so that the brown print squares align diagonally; press the seam allowance toward the outside.

continued

4. Referring to diagrams 9 and 10, add the remaining blue print 1½"-wide strips and brown print 1½" squares in the same manner to make a Log Cabin corner unit. The pieced Log Cabin corner unit should measure 5½" square, including the seam allowances.

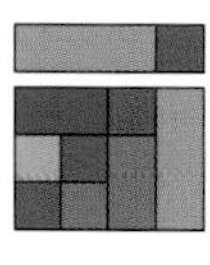

Diagram 9

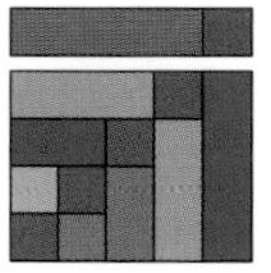

Diagram 10

5. Repeat steps 1 through 4 to make a total of four Log Cabin corner units.

Assemble the Center Star Block

1. Referring to Diagram 11, lay out the 16-Patch unit, the eight star point units, and the four Log Cabin corner units in three horizontal rows.

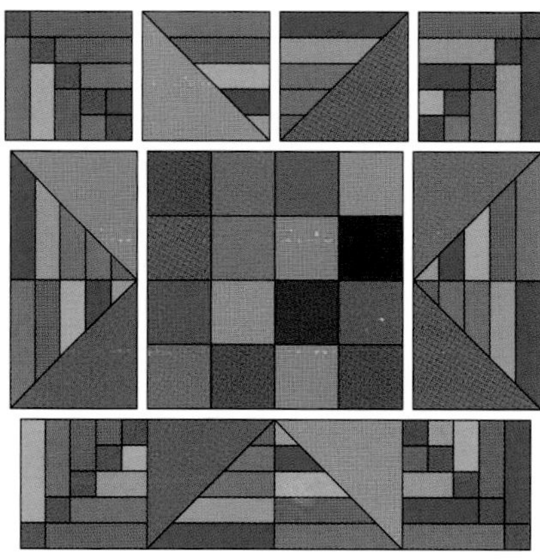

Diagram 11

2. Join each pair of star point units; press the seam allowances in one direction. Then sew together the pieces in each row. Press the seam allowances toward the star point units. Join the rows to make the center star block. Press the seam allowances toward the block center. The pieced center star block should measure 20½" square, including the seam allowances.

Appliqué the Center Star Block

1. Position the freezer paper, shiny side down, over the Tree Trunk Pattern on *Pattern Sheet 1*. With a pencil, trace the pattern four times. Cut out the freezer-paper templates on the traced lines.

2. Place a small amount of fabric glue on the matte side of the freezer-paper templates and anchor them to the back of the brown print, leaving about ½" between templates. Cut out the fabric shapes about ¼" beyond the freezer-paper edges.

3. Use the point of a hot, dry iron to press under the seam allowances of the trunk pieces.

4. Referring to the photograph on *page 107*, position the trunk pieces on the center star block; use the seam lines as placement guides. Baste the trunk pieces in place.

5. Using brown thread, appliqué the trunk pieces in place with a slip stitch. Trim away the foundation behind the appliqués, leaving ¼" seam allowances, and gently peel away the paper templates.

Piece and Add the Borders

The tree and star borders are pieced in rows, then added to the center star block one at a time in Courthouse Steps style. This means once the rows are pieced, one row is added to the top edge of the center star block, then one to the bottom edge, then one to a side edge, and finally one to the remaining side edge, always pressing the seam allowances away from the center. This process continues until the quilt top is complete.

To streamline the assembly process, designate one edge of the center star block as the top; attach a safety pin a few inches below that raw edge so you can tell at a glance which one it is.

Note: The measurements shown in the Tree Border Assembly and Star Border Assembly diagrams indicate the length of each 1½"-wide strip.

Tree Rows

1. Referring to the Tree Border Assembly Diagram, sew together the strips in each row, starting in the center and stitching diagonal 45-degree seams (see diagrams 12 and 13 as examples). Note that the diagonal seams run in opposite directions on either side of the center and colors are repeated to create mirror-image halves. Trim away the excess fabric at each seam, leaving a ¼" seam allowance; press the seam allowances to one side.

2. Join the rows to the center star block in Courthouse Steps style as described above.

Star Rows

1. For accurate sewing lines, use a quilter's pencil to mark a diagonal line on the wrong side of 72 gold print 1½" squares and 72 red print 1½" squares.

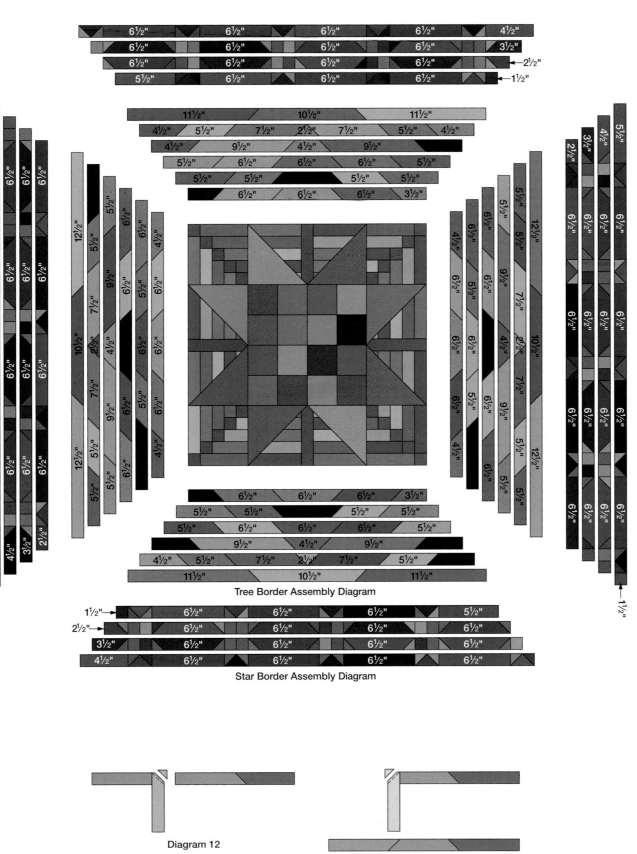

Tree Border Assembly Diagram

Star Border Assembly Diagram

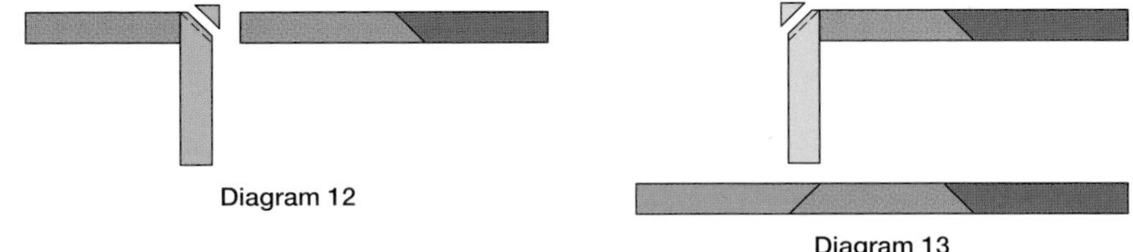

Diagram 12

Diagram 13

continued

2. Align a marked gold print square with one end of a dark blue print 1½×2½" strip (see Diagram 14, noting the direction of the drawn line). Stitch on the marked line; trim away the excess fabric, leaving a ¼" seam allowance. Press the attached triangle open.

Diagram 14

3. Align a second marked gold print square with the opposite end of the dark blue print rectangle (see Diagram 14, again noting the direction of the drawn line). Stitch, trim, and press as before to make a gold Flying Geese unit. The pieced Flying Geese unit should still measure 1½×2½", including the seam allowances.

4. Repeat steps 2 and 3 to make a total of 18 gold Flying Geese units.

5. Repeat steps 2 and 3 using marked red print 1½" squares and dark blue print 1½×2½" strips to make a total of 18 red Flying Geese units (see Diagram 15).

Diagram 15

6. Align a marked red print square and a marked gold print square with the ends of a dark blue print 1½×6½" strip (see Diagram 16, noting the direction of the drawn lines). Stitch, trim, and press to make a rectangle unit. The pieced rectangle unit should still measure 1½×6½", including the seam allowances. Repeat to make a total of 16 rectangle units.

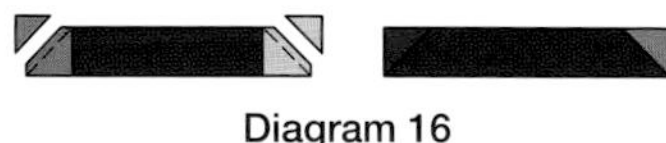

Diagram 16

7. Repeat Step 6, reversing the placement of the marked gold and red print squares (see Diagram 17), to make a total of 16 additional rectangle units.

Diagram 17

8. Referring to Diagram 18, align marked gold print squares with one end of one dark blue print 1½×4½" strip, two dark blue print 1½×3½" strips, and one dark blue print 1½×2½" strip (note the direction of the drawn line for each strip length). Stitch, trim, and press to make four more rectangle units.

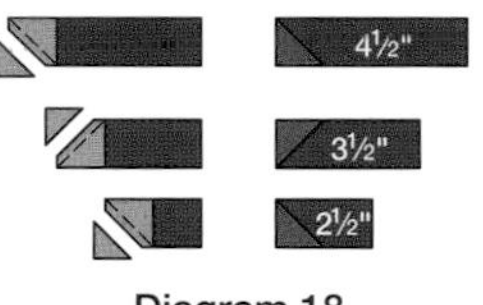

Diagram 18

9. Repeat Step 8 using marked red print squares to make four more rectangle units.

10. Lay out the Flying Geese units, the rectangle units, and the remaining gold print 1½" squares and red print 1½" squares in rows, referring to the Star Border Assembly Diagram on *page 109.* Sew together the units in each row.

11. Join the rows to the center star block in Courthouse Steps style, as described on *page 108,* to complete the quilt top.

Complete the Quilt

1. Layer the quilt top, batting, and backing according to the instructions in Quilter's Schoolhouse, which begins on *page 150.* Quilt as desired.

2. Hand-sew 300 assorted white buttons onto the blue background areas of the quilt with heavy thread. Slide the needle between the fabric layers to hide the thread behind each button.

3. Use the dark green print 2½×42" strips to bind the quilt according to the instructions in Quilter's Schoolhouse.

1930S BED QUILT

This cheerful quilt couples crisp white fabric with whimsical 1930s prints.

Materials

3⅞ yards of white print for blocks and setting squares

3½ yards total of assorted prints in pink, blue, green, peach, red, purple, and yellow for blocks and outer border

1¼ yards of blue print for inner border and binding

8 yards of backing fabric

96×106" of quilt batting

Finished quilt top: 90×100"
Finished block: 10" square

Cut the Fabrics

To make the best use of your fabrics, cut the pieces in the order that follows.

From white print, cut:
- 28—10½" setting squares
- 224—3" squares

From assorted prints, cut:
- Enough 9½"-wide strips in lengths varying from 6" to 15" to total 365" for outer border
- 28 sets of eight matching 3" squares

From blue print, cut:
- 10—2½x42" binding strips
- 8—1½x42" strips for inner border

Assemble the 16-Patch Blocks

Referring to Piece the Center Star Block Units, 16-Patch Unit, on *page 106*, and Diagram 19, use eight white print 3" squares and a set of eight matching assorted print 3" squares to make a 16-Patch block. Repeat to make a total of twenty-eight 16-Patch blocks.

Diagram 19

Assemble the Quilt Center

1. Referring to the photograph *opposite*, lay out the twenty-eight 16-Patch blocks and the 28 white print 10½" setting squares in eight horizontal rows.

2. Sew together the blocks in each row. Press the seam allowances toward the 16-Patch blocks. Join the rows to make the quilt center. Press the seam allowances in one direction. The pieced quilt center should measure 70½x80½", including the seam allowances.

Assemble and Add the Borders

1. Cut and piece the blue print 1½x42" strips to make the following:
- 2—1½x80½" inner border strips
- 2—1½x72½" inner border strips

2. Sew the long blue print inner border strips to the side edges of the pieced quilt center. Then join the short blue print inner border strips to the remaining edges of the quilt center. Press all seam allowances toward the inner border. The quilt center should now measure 72½x82½", including the seam allowances.

3. Sew together the assorted print 9½"-wide strips of varying lengths to make the following:
- 2—9½x90½" outer border strips
- 2—9½x82½" outer border strips

4. Sew the short pieced outer border strips to the side edges of the quilt center. Then join the long pieced outer border strips to the remaining edges of the quilt center to complete the quilt top. Press all seam allowances toward the inner border.

Complete the Quilt

1. Layer the quilt top, batting, and backing according to the instructions in Quilter's Schoolhouse, which begins on *page 150*. Quilt as desired.

2. Use the blue print 2½x42" strips to bind the quilt according to the instructions in Quilter's Schoolhouse.

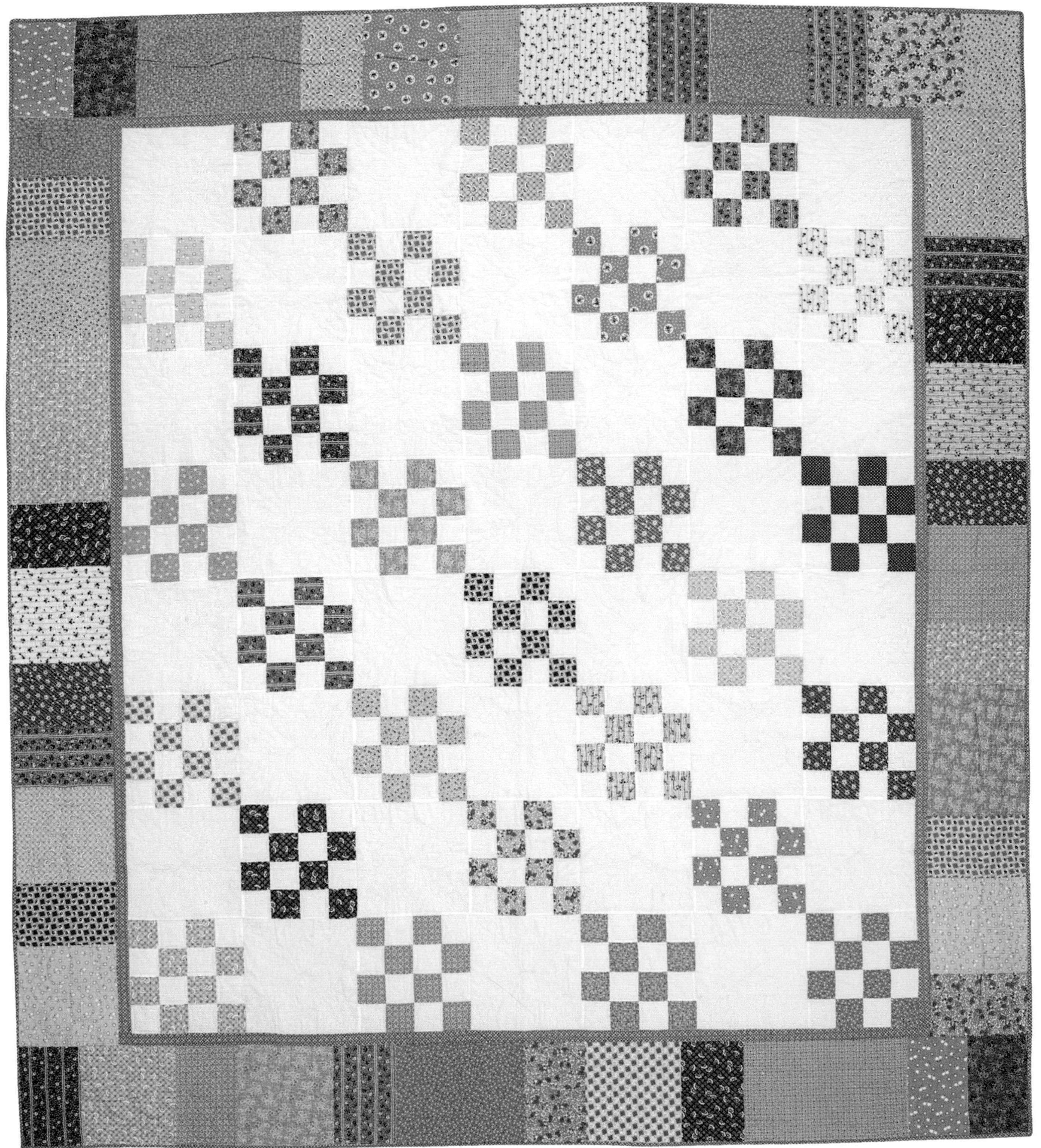

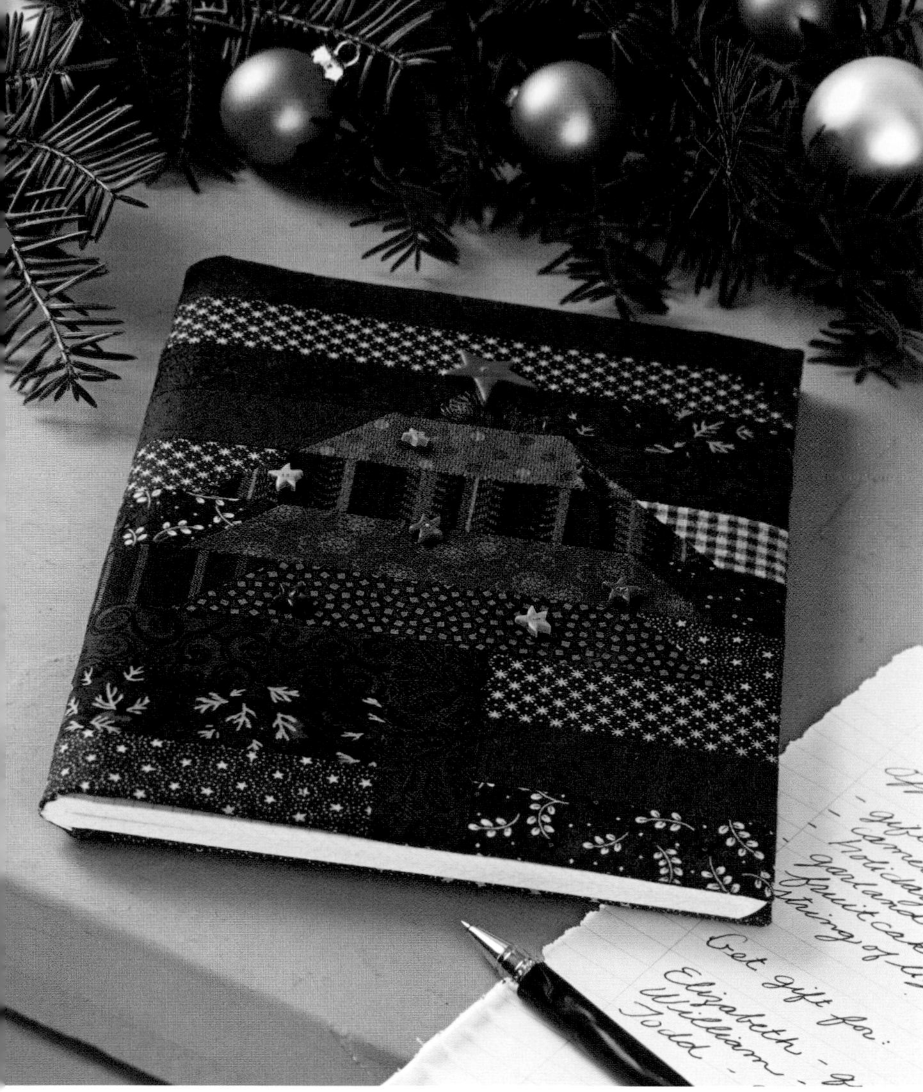

PIECED JOURNAL COVER

Stitch a cozy Christmas-theme book cover to create a journal for recording holiday memories.

Materials

Scrap of brown print for tree trunk appliqué

½ yard total of assorted red prints for background

⅛ yard total of assorted green prints for tree and binding

Lightweight fusible web

Assorted star-shape buttons: 1 large, 7 small

Finished journal cover: 7½×10"
(fits a standard composition book)

Cut the Fabrics

To make the best use of your fabrics, cut the pieces in the order that follows.

To use fusible web for appliquéing the tree trunk, complete the following steps.

1. Use a pencil to draw a 1×3½" rectangle on the paper side of the fusible web. Cut out the fusible-web rectangle roughly ¼" outside the drawn lines.

2. Following the manufacturer's instructions, press the fusible-web rectangle onto the wrong side of the brown print scrap; let cool. Cut out the fabric rectangle on the drawn lines and peel off the paper backing to make the tree trunk appliqué.

From assorted red prints, cut:

- 1—1½×18½" strip
- 1—1½×15" strip
- 2—1½×14½" strips
- 1—1½×12½" strip
- 2—1½×11½" strips
- 4—1½×11" strips
- 3—1½×9½" strips
- 2—1½×9¼" strips
- 2—1½×8¼" strips
- 1—1½×7½" strip
- 2—1½×7¼" strips
- 5—1½×6½" strips
- 1—1½×6" strip
- 2—1½×5½" strips
- 4—1½×5" strips
- 2—1½×4" strips
- 1—1½×2" strip

From assorted green prints, cut:

- 2—1½×10½" binding strips
- 3—1½×6½" strips
- 1—1½×4½" strip
- 1—1½×2½" strip

Piece the Journal Cover

1. Lay out the strips for the journal cover top in rows, referring to Diagram 20. The measurements shown indicate the length of each 1½"-wide strip.

2. Referring to Piece and Add the Borders, Tree Rows, on *page 108,* sew together the strips in each row, stitching diagonal 45-degree seams (see diagrams 12 and 13 on *page 109* as examples).

First sew together the rows with the green print strips; start with the green print strips and add red print strips to either side. Trim away the excess fabric at each seam, leaving a ¼" seam allowance; press the seam allowances to one side.

Repeat this process with the rows of red print strips. *Note:* The three seams that will be hidden under the tree trunk appliqué are sewn straight, not diagonally.

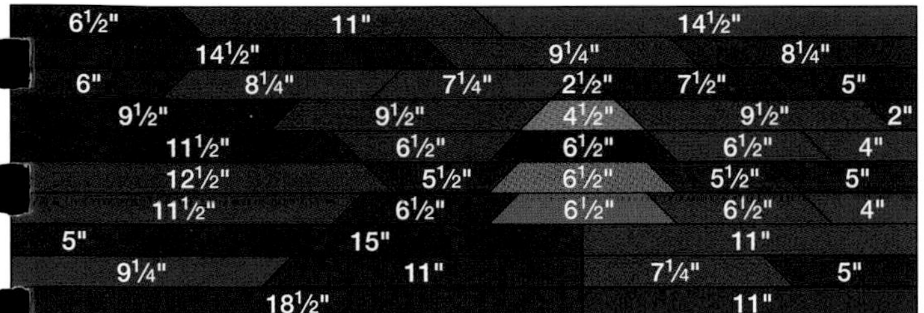

Diagram 20

3. Sew together the bottom three pieced rows, aligning the straight seams. Press the seam allowances open for the least bulk. Center the tree trunk appliqué over the straight seams; fuse in place. Zigzag-stitch along the long edges of the tree trunk appliqué.

4. Sew the seven remaining pieced rows to the Step 3 unit, aligning the centers of the green print strips with the appliquéd tree trunk, to make a pieced rectangle; press as before. The pieced rectangle should measure 10½×29", including the seam allowances.

Complete the Journal Cover

1. Sew a green print 1½×10½" binding strip to one short end of the pieced rectangle, aligning the raw edges. Turn the binding strip over the edge of the pieced rectangle to the back. Turn under the raw edge of the binding strip ¼", and hand-stitch the folded edge to the pieced rectangle. Repeat to bind the remaining short end of the pieced rectangle with the remaining green print 1½×10½" binding strip. *Note:* Refer to the photograph *above right* to see the binding on the finished journal cover.

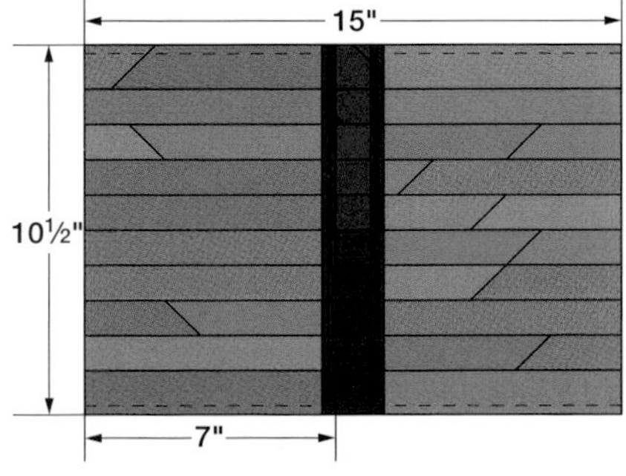

Diagram 21

2. With right sides together, fold each bound end of the pieced rectangle 7" toward the center to create a 10½×15" rectangle. Sew along the long edges of the folded rectangle, catching all layers, to complete the journal cover (see Diagram 21). Turn the journal cover right side out and press.

3. Referring to the photograph *above*, hand-sew the seven small star-shape buttons onto the tree, being careful to catch only the front layer of the journal cover. Sew the large star-shape button to the top of the tree.

THROUGH THE *Woods*

Quiltmaker Joy Hoffman's love of the traditional tree block results in an eye-catching wall hanging.

Materials

1 yard of off-white print for blocks

1 yard total of assorted green, gold, and rust prints for blocks

⅓ yard of mottled green for blocks

¾ yard of dark brown print for blocks and binding

1¾ yards of dark green print for blocks, setting pieces, and outer border

⅝ yard of green print for setting pieces

1¾ yards of tan-and-green print for inner border

3⅝ yards of backing fabric

65" square of quilt batting

Finished quilt top: 58½" square
Finished blocks: large tree, 18" square; small tree, 10" square

Quantities are for 44/45"-wide, 100% cotton fabrics. All measurements include a ¼" seam allowance. Sew with right sides together unless otherwise stated.

Cut the Fabrics

To make the best use of your fabrics, cut the pieces in the order that follows. The patterns are on *Pattern Sheet 2*. To make templates of the patterns, follow the instructions in Quilter's Schoolhouse, which begins on *page 150*.

Cut the outer border strips lengthwise (parallel to the selvage). The border strip measurements are mathematically correct. You may wish to cut your strips longer than specified to allow for possible sewing differences.

From off-white print, cut:

- 2 of Pattern A
- 2—6⅞" squares, cutting each in half diagonally for a total of 4 medium triangles (you'll have 1 leftover triangle)
- 8 *each* of patterns C and C reversed
- 51—2⅞" squares, cutting each in half diagonally for a total of 102 small triangles
- 9—2½" squares

From assorted green, gold, and rust prints, cut:

- 98—2⅞" squares, cutting each in half diagonally for a total of 196 small triangles
- 10—2½" squares

From mottled green, cut:

- 1—8⅞" square, cutting it in half diagonally for a total of 2 large triangles (you'll have 1 leftover triangle)

continued

- 4—6⅞" squares, cutting each in half diagonally for a total of 8 medium triangles

From dark brown print, cut:
- 6—2½×42" binding strips
- 1 of Pattern B
- 8 of Pattern D

From dark green print, cut:
- 4—2¾×60" outer border strips
- 4 *each* of patterns E and E reversed
- 2—8" squares, cutting each in half diagonally for a total of 4 corner triangles

From green print, cut:
- 4 of Pattern F

From tan-and-green print, cut:
- 8 of Pattern G

Make the Triangle-Squares

1. Sew together an off-white print small triangle and an assorted green, gold, or rust print small triangle to make a light triangle-square (see Diagram 1). Press the seam allowance toward the green, gold, or rust print triangle. The pieced light triangle-square should measure 2½" square, including the seam allowances.

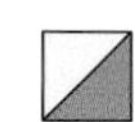
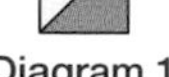
Diagram 1

2. Repeat Step 1 to make a total of 94 light triangle-squares.

3. Repeat Step 1 using 96 assorted green, gold, or rust print small triangles to make a total of 48 dark triangle-squares. Press the seam allowance toward the darker fabric in each triangle-square.

Assemble the Tree Blocks

The tree blocks require setting in seams. For specific instructions, see Setting in Seams in Quilter's Schoolhouse, which begins on *page 150.*

1. Referring to Diagram 2, set the two off-white print A pieces into the dark brown print B piece to make an ABA unit, clipping into the seam allowance of the B piece at the inside corners as needed. Sew an off-white print medium triangle and a mottled green large triangle to opposite edges of the ABA unit to make the large tree trunk unit.

2. Lay out 14 light triangle-squares; 16 dark triangle-squares; six green, gold, or rust print small triangles; two green, gold, or rust print 2½" squares; and one off-white print 2½" square in two units of horizontal rows as shown in Diagram 2. Sew

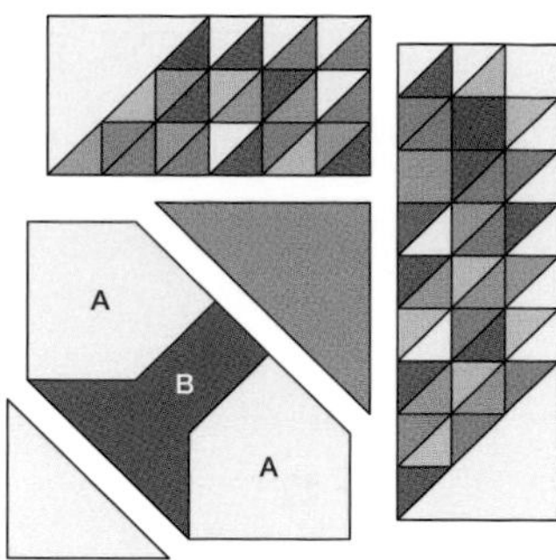

Diagram 2

together the pieces in each row. Press the seam allowances in one direction, alternating the direction with each row. Join the rows into units; press seam allowances in one direction. Join an off-white print medium triangle to the diagonal end of each unit to make short and long tree branch units.

3. Join the short tree branch unit to the tree trunk unit; press the seam allowance toward the tree trunk unit. Then add the long tree branch unit to complete the large tree block. The pieced block should measure 18½" square, including the seam allowances.

4. Referring to Diagram 3, set the off-white print C and C reversed pieces into the dark brown print D piece to make a CDCr unit, clipping the seam allowance of the D piece at the inside corners as needed. Sew an off-white print small triangle and a mottled green medium triangle to opposite edges of the CDCr unit to complete a small tree trunk unit.

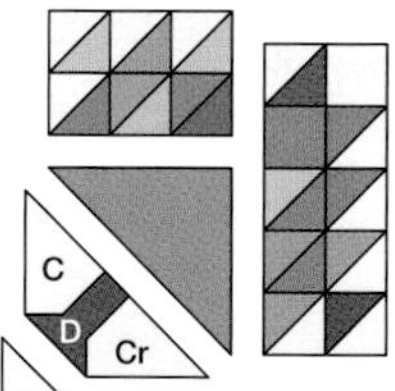

Diagram 3

5. Lay out 10 light triangle-squares; four dark triangle-squares; one green, gold, or rust print 2½" square; and one off-white print 2½" square in two units of horizontal rows as shown in Diagram 3. Sew together the pieces in each row, then join the rows to make the short and long tree branch units; press as for the large tree block.

6. Repeat Step 3 to join the tree branch units to the small tree trunk unit to make a small tree block. The pieced small tree block should measure 10½" square, including the seam allowances.

7. Repeat steps 4 through 6 to make a total of eight small tree blocks.

Assemble the Quilt Top

1. Referring to Diagram 4 for placement, join one dark green print E piece, one dark green print E reversed piece, and one green print F piece to a small tree block, setting in seams as necessary; in order to set in the pieces, do not sew into the seam allowances in the angled corners. Add a dark green print corner triangle to make a side setting unit. Noting the placement of each small tree block, repeat to make a total of four side setting units.

2. Sew a side setting unit to opposite edges of the large tree block, again noting the placement of the small tree blocks; do not sew into the seam allowances. In the same manner, add the remaining side setting units to the remaining edges of the large tree block to make the center unit.

3. Referring to Diagram 5, set the four remaining small tree blocks into the center unit.

4. Sew together two tan-and-green print G pieces to make an inner border unit; in order to set in the seams, do not sew into the seam allowances in the angled corners. Repeat to make a total of four inner border units.

5. Sew an inner border unit to opposite corners of the center unit, setting in seams as necessary. Then join the remaining inner border units to the center unit to make the quilt center.

6. Center and sew a dark green print 2¾×60" outer border strip to each edge of the quilt center, beginning and ending ¼" from each corner. Follow the instructions in Quilter's Schoolhouse, which begins on *page 150,* to miter the border corners, completing the quilt top.

Complete the Quilt

1. Layer the quilt top, batting, and backing according to the instructions in Quilter's Schoolhouse. Quilt as desired.

2. Use the dark brown print 2½×42" strips to bind the quilt according to the instructions in Quilter's Schoolhouse.

Diagram 4

Diagram 5

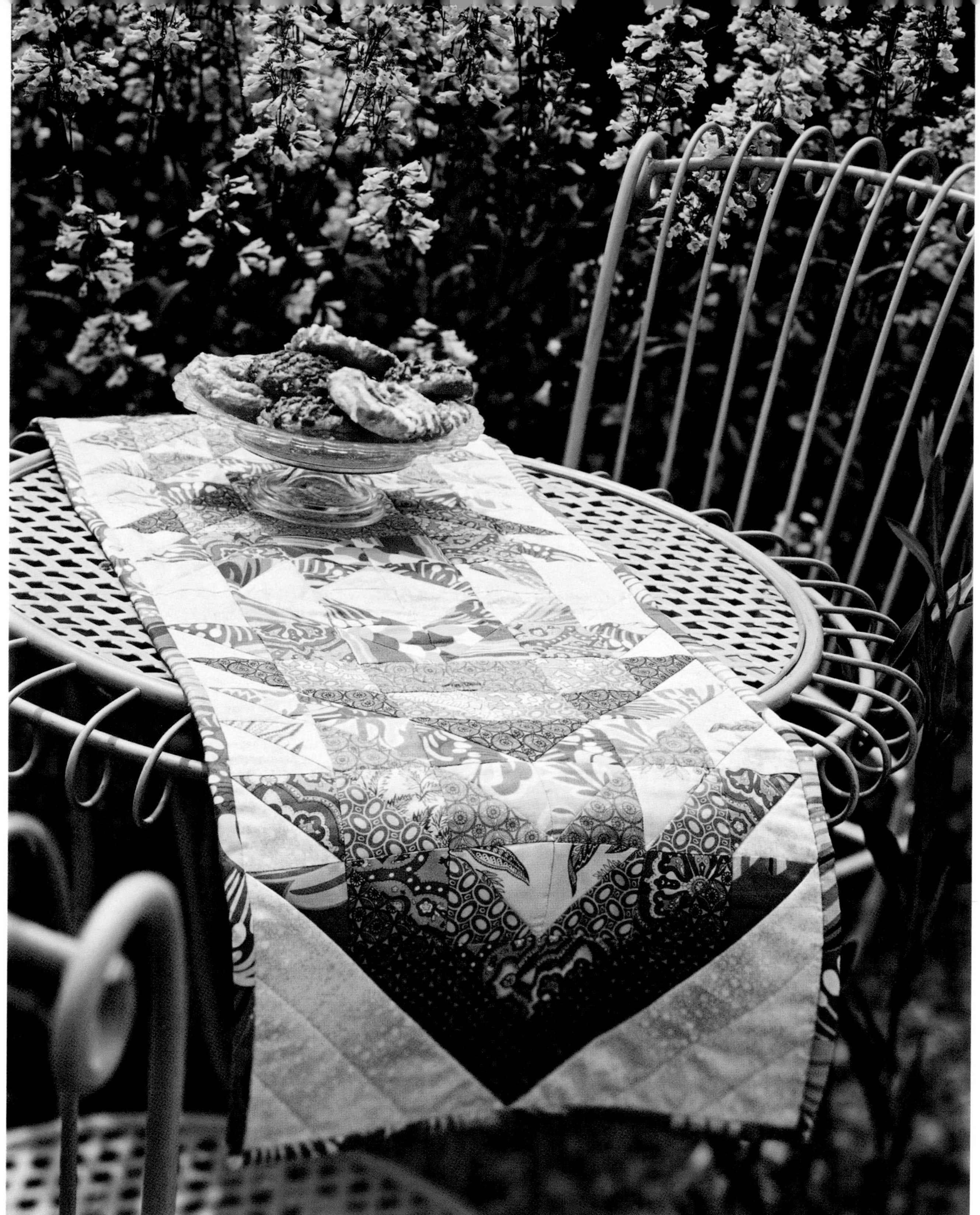

PASTEL TABLE RUNNER

Transform a branch section of the tree block into a table runner

using a mix of large and small prints.

Materials

⅜ yard of cream print

½ yard total of assorted orange and pink prints

⅛ yard total of assorted green prints

⅓ yard of multicolor print for binding

½ yard of backing fabric

16×40" of quilt batting

Finished quilt top: 12×36"

Plan the Quilt

If you'd like to duplicate the mirror-imaged halves on the featured table runner, use a design wall to plan the number and color placement of each triangle-square combination. Refer to the Quilt Assembly Diagram and the photograph *opposite* for guidance and lay out your triangle-squares as you stitch them.

Cut the Fabrics

To make the best use of your fabrics, cut the pieces in the order that follows.

From cream print, cut:

- 2—6⅞" squares, cutting each in half diagonally for a total of 4 medium triangles
- 14—2⅞" squares, cutting each in half diagonally for a total of 28 small triangles
- 4—2½" squares

From assorted orange and pink prints, cut:

- 58—2⅞" squares, cutting each in half diagonally for a total of 116 small triangles
- 4—2½" squares

From assorted green prints, cut:

- 6—2⅞" squares, cutting each in half diagonally for a total of 12 small triangles
- 4—2½" squares

From multicolor print, cut:

- 3—2½×42" binding strips

Make the Triangle-Squares

1. Referring to Make the Triangle-Squares on *page 118,* Step 1, use one cream print small triangle and one assorted orange, pink, or green print small triangle to make a light triangle-square. Repeat to make a total of 28 light triangle-squares.

2. In the same manner, use 88 assorted orange, pink, and green print small triangles to make a total of 44 dark triangle-squares.

Assemble the Branch Units

1. Referring to Assemble the Tree Blocks on *page 118,* Step 2, and Diagram 6, use seven light triangle-squares; 11 dark triangle-squares; one cream print medium triangle; one cream print 2½" square; one green print 2½" square; one orange or pink print 2½" square; and three assorted orange, pink, or green print small triangles to make a long tree branch unit. Repeat to make a second long tree branch unit.

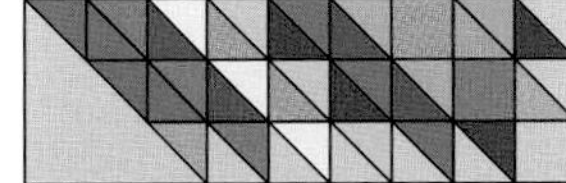

Diagram 6

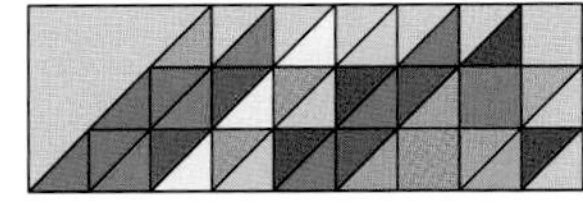

Diagram 7

2. Referring to Diagram 7, repeat Step 1 to make two reversed long tree branch units.

Assemble the Quilt Top

1. Referring to the Quilt Assembly Diagram, lay out the long tree branch units and the reversed long tree branch units, noting the direction of the triangle-squares' seams in each unit.

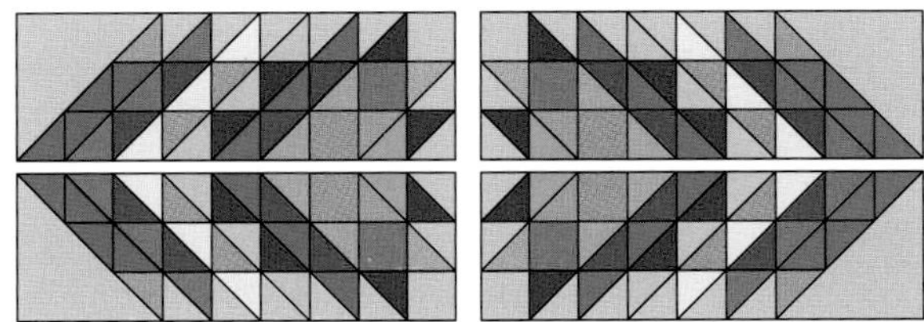

Quilt Assembly Diagram

2. Sew together the units in pairs. Press the seam allowances in opposite directions. Then join the pairs to complete the quilt top. Press the seam allowance in one direction.

Complete the Quilt

1. Layer the quilt top, batting, and backing according to the instructions in Quilter's Schoolhouse, which begins on *page 150.* Quilt as desired.

2. Use the multicolor print 2½×42" strips to bind the quilt according to the instructions in Quilter's Schoolhouse.

FOUR-SEASONS WALL ART

Display all four blocks throughout the year, or hang up one block at a time for seasonal decorating.

Materials to Make Four Blocks

9×22" piece (fat eighth) *each* of light blue, light green, tan, and dark tan batiks for backgrounds

⅛ yard of dark brown batik for tree trunks

9×22" piece (fat eighth) *each* of dark gray, bright pink, dark green, and brown batiks for blocks

Scraps of assorted blue, green, pink, orange, red, purple, and brown batiks for blocks

9×22" piece (fat eighth) *each* of dark blue, lime green, dark orange, and light brown batiks for bindings

4—16" squares of backing fabric

4—16" squares of quilt batting

Finished quilt blocks: 10" square

Cut the Fabrics

To make the best use of your fabrics, cut the pieces in the order that follows in each section.

This project uses "Through the Woods" patterns C and D, which are on *Pattern Sheet 2*. To make templates for the patterns, follow the instructions in Quilter's Schoolhouse, which begins on *page 150*.

Cut and Assemble the Winter Tree Block

From light blue batik, cut:

- 1 *each* of patterns C and C reversed
- 6—2⅞" squares, cutting each in half diagonally for a total of 12 small triangles (you'll have 1 leftover triangle)
- 1—2½" square

From dark brown batik, cut:

- 1 of Pattern D

From dark gray batik, cut:

- 1—6⅞" square, cutting it in half diagonally for a total of 2 medium triangles (you'll have 1 leftover triangle)
- 2—2⅞" squares, cutting each in half diagonally for a total of 4 small triangles
- 1—2½" square

From scraps of assorted blue and green batiks, cut:

- 7—2⅞" squares, cutting each in half diagonally for a total of 14 small triangles

From dark blue batik, cut:

- 2—2½×22" binding strips

1. Referring to Make the Triangle-Squares on *page 118,* Step 1, use one light blue batik small triangle and an assorted blue or green batik small triangle to make a light triangle-square. Repeat to make a total of 10 light triangle-squares.

2. Repeat Step 1 using four dark gray batik small triangles and four assorted blue or green batik small triangles to make a total of four dark triangle-squares.

3. Referring to Assemble the Tree Blocks on *page 118,* steps 4 through 6, and the photograph *below right,* use the light blue batik C and C reversed pieces, one dark brown batik D piece, one light blue batik small triangle, one dark gray batik medium triangle, the 10 light triangle-squares, the four dark triangle-squares, the light blue batik 2½" square, and the dark gray batik 2½" square to make the winter tree block.

Cut and Assemble the Spring Tree Block

To make the spring block, follow the instructions in Cut and Assemble the Winter Tree Block, substituting light green batik for the light blue batik; bright pink batik for the dark gray batik; assorted blue, green, and pink batiks for the assorted blue and green batiks; and lime green batik for the dark blue batik.

Cut and Assemble the Summer Tree Block

To make the summer block, follow the instructions in Cut and Assemble the Winter Tree Block, substituting tan batik for the light blue batik; dark green batik for the dark gray batik; assorted green, orange, red, and purple batiks for the assorted blue and green batiks; and dark orange batik for the dark blue batik.

Cut and Assemble the Autumn Tree Block

To make the autumn block, follow the instructions in Cut and Assemble the Winter Tree Block, substituting dark tan batik for the light blue batik; brown batik for the dark gray batik; assorted green, orange, red, and brown batiks for the assorted blue and green batiks; and light brown batik for the dark blue batik.

Complete the Quilts

1. Layer each quilt block, batting, and backing according to the instructions in Quilter's Schoolhouse, which begins on *page 150.* Quilt as desired.

2. Use the dark blue, lime green, dark orange, and light brown batik 2½×42" strips to bind the corresponding tree blocks according to the instructions in Quilter's Schoolhouse.

3. The tree blocks shown *opposite* were each mounted on cream mat board in frames with a 15½"-square opening.

Winter Tree Block

Spring Tree Block

Summer Tree Block

Autumn Tree Block

ALWAYS APPLIQUÉ

Create a bouquet of projects with these appliquéd quilts. "Prairie Flowers" features needle-turn appliqué flowers reinterpreted in fusible-web appliqué and embroidery. Designs from "Trumpet Blooms" spring up in wool and Asian prints. And "Tulip Fancy" has dainty blooms perfect for a pillow with yarn couching or a lovely bed-size quilt. Let these appliquéd projects blossom into ideas for your next quilt.

PRAIRIE *Flowers*

Designer Jo Morton's needle-turn appliqué wall hanging suggests lush, abundant fields.

Materials

5—18×22" pieces (fat quarters) of cream plaids and stripes for appliquéd blocks and pieced blocks

Scraps of assorted red, green, and brown prints for flower, leaf, stem, and bird appliqués

1⅓ yards of red floral for pieced blocks and outer border

¼ yard of green print for inner border

Scraps of yellow print for inner border corners

18×22" piece (fat quarter) of green plaid for outer border corners

½ yard of red-and-green print for binding

2⅞ yards of backing fabric

50" square of quilt batting

Finished quilt top: 43¼" square
Finished block: 6¼" square

Quantities are for 44/45"-wide, 100% cotton fabrics. All measurements include a ¼" seam allowance. Sew with right sides together unless otherwise stated.

Cut the Fabrics

To make the best use of your fabrics, cut the pieces in the order that follows. The appliqué foundations are cut larger than necessary to allow for ease in appliquéing; you'll trim them to correct size later.

The patterns are on *Pattern Sheet 2*. To make templates of the patterns, follow the instructions in Quilter's Schoolhouse, which begins on *page 150*. Remember to add a 3⁄16" seam allowance when cutting out the appliqués.

From assorted cream plaids and stripes, cut:
- 17—1¾×22" strips
- 12—7" squares

From red print scraps, cut:
- 1 *each* of patterns E, F, G, AAA, BBB, FFF, and KKK
- 2 *each* of patterns I, N, U, V, JJ, EEE, and LLL
- 3 of Pattern CC
- 9 *each* of patterns QQ and QQ reversed
- 18 of Pattern WW
- 4 of Pattern RRR

From green print scraps, cut:
- 1 *each* of patterns A, B, C, C reversed, D, H, J, K, L, P, Q, R, S, T, T reversed, AA, DD, DD reversed, EE, FF, GG, HH, HH reversed, KK, NN, OO, RR, SS, TT, TT reversed, UU, XX, YY, ZZ, CCC, DDD reversed, GGG, HHH, III, NNN, OOO, PPP, and QQQ
- 2 *each* of patterns II, LL, LL reversed, and MMM
- 3 *each* of patterns O and VV
- 10 of Pattern BB
- 4 *each* of patterns MM and DDD

continued

- 7 of Pattern PP
- 5 of Pattern JJJ

From brown print scraps, cut:
- 1 *each* of patterns W, X, Y, and Z

From red floral, cut:
- 4—5½x33¾" outer border strips
- 18—1¾x22" strips

From green print, cut:
- 4—1½x31¾" inner border strips

From yellow print scraps, cut:
- 4—1½" squares for inner border
- 3 of Pattern M

From green plaid, cut:
- 4—5½" squares for outer border

From red-and-green print, cut:
- 5—2½x42" binding strips

Appliqué the Blocks

1. Referring to the Quilt Assembly Diagram, arrange the designated appliqué pieces for one appliqué block atop a cream plaid or stripe 7" square appliqué foundation. Be sure to allow for a seam allowance along each edge of the square. When pleased with the arrangement, baste in place.

2. Using threads in colors that match the fabrics, appliqué each piece to the foundation, turning the edges under with your needle as you work. Begin with the pieces on the bottom and work up.

3. Press the appliquéd block from the back; with the design centered, trim the block to measure 6¾" square, including the seam allowances.

4. Repeat steps 1 through 3 to appliqué a total of 12 blocks, one of each design shown in the Quilt Assembly Diagram.

Assemble the 25-Patch Blocks

1. Referring to Diagram 1 for placement, sew together three red floral 1¾x22" strips and two cream plaid or stripe 1¾x22" strips to make a strip set A. Press the seam allowances toward the red floral strips. Repeat to make a total of four of strip set A. Cut the strip sets into a total of thirty-nine 1¾"-wide A segments.

2. Referring to Diagram 2, sew together three cream plaid or stripe 1¾x22" strips and two red floral 1¾x22" strips to make a strip set B. Press the seam allowances toward the red floral strips. Repeat to make a total of three of strip set B. Cut the strip sets into a total of twenty-six 1¾"-wide B segments.

3. Referring to Diagram 3, sew together three A segments and two B segments to make a 25-Patch block. Press the seam allowances toward the A segments. The pieced 25-Patch block should measure 6¾" square, including the seam allowances. Repeat to make a total of thirteen 25-Patch blocks.

Assemble the Quilt Center

1. Referring to the Quilt Assembly Diagram, lay out the 12 appliquéd blocks and the thirteen 25-Patch blocks in five rows.

2. Sew together the blocks in each row. Press the seam allowances toward the appliquéd blocks. Then join the rows to make the quilt center. Press the seam allowances in one direction. The pieced quilt center should measure 31¾" square, including the seam allowances.

Add the Borders

1. Sew green print 1½x31¾" inner border strips to opposite edges of the pieced quilt center. Press the seam allowances toward the inner border.

2. Sew a yellow print 1½" square to each end of the remaining green print 1½x31¾" inner border strips to make inner border units. Press the seam

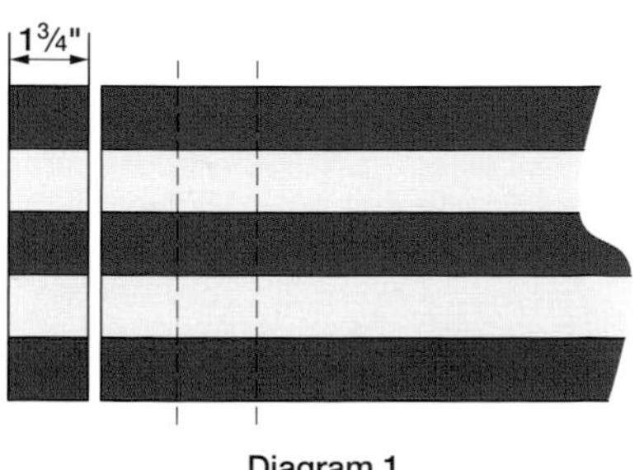

Diagram 1

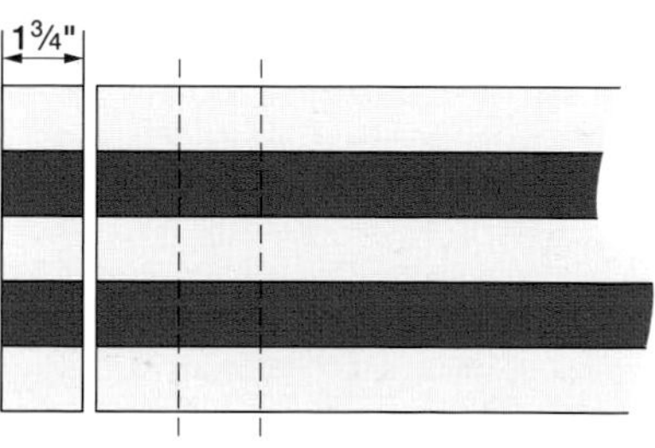

Diagram 2

Diagram 3

allowances toward the green print strips. Sew the inner border units to the remaining edges of the pieced quilt center. Press the seam allowances toward the inner border.

3. Sew red floral 5½×33¾" outer border strips to opposite edges of the pieced quilt center. Press the seam allowances toward the outer border.

4. Sew a green plaid 5½" square to each end of the remaining red floral 5½×33¾" outer border strips to make outer border units. Press the seam allowances toward the red floral strips. Sew the outer border units to the remaining edges of the pieced quilt center to complete the quilt top. Press the seam allowances toward the outer border.

Complete the Quilt

1. Layer the quilt top, batting, and backing according to the instructions in Quilter's Schoolhouse, which begins on *page 150*. Quilt as desired.

2. Use the red-and-green print 2½×42" strips to bind the quilt according to the instructions in Quilter's Schoolhouse.

Quilt Assembly Diagram

FRIENDSHIP QUILTS

Reproduce your favorite flower block in cheerful batiks for a special pal as a token of your friendship.

Materials for Two Quilts

18×22" piece (fat quarter) of blue-green batik for appliqué foundation and binding

9×22" piece (fat eighth) of green batik for appliqué foundation

Scraps of bright pink, yellow, and olive green batiks for flower, leaf, and stem appliqués

⅛ yard of teal batik for flower appliqués, border, and covered cording

⅛ yard of pink batik for border and covered cording

⅛ yard of light green batik for border

9×22" piece (fat eighth) of orange batik for binding

⅜ yard of backing fabric

2—13" squares of quilt batting

2⅓ yards of $\frac{1}{16}$"-diameter cording

Machine embroidery thread: bright pink, yellow, olive green, teal, orange, and gold (optional)

Lightweight fusible web

Finished quilt tops: 8¾" square

Cut the Fabrics

To make the best use of your fabrics, cut the pieces in the order that follows. This project uses "Prairie Flowers" patterns, which are on *Pattern Sheet 2*. To use fusible web for appliquéing, follow these steps.

1. Lay the fusible web, paper side up, over the patterns. With a pencil, trace each pattern the number of times indicated, leaving ½" between tracings. Cut out each fusible-web shape roughly ¼" outside the traced lines.

2. Following the manufacturer's instructions, press the fusible-web shapes onto the backs of the designated fabrics; let cool. Cut out the fabric shapes on the lines. Peel off the paper backings.

From blue-green batik, cut:
- 2—2½×22" binding strips
- 1—7" square

From green batik, cut:
- 1—7" square

From bright pink batik scraps, cut:

- 1 *each* of patterns F reversed, H reversed, and J reversed

From yellow batik scraps, cut:

- 1 *each* of patterns E reversed, G reversed, and I reversed

From olive green batik scraps, cut:

- 1 *each* of patterns A reversed, B reversed, C reversed, D reversed, K reversed, L reversed, NN reversed, and OO reversed
- 3 of Pattern PP reversed

From teal batik, cut:

- 1—¾×42" strip for covered cording
- 12—1¾" squares
- 9 *each* of patterns QQ and QQ reversed

From pink batik, cut:

- 1—¾×42" strip for covered cording
- 12—1¾" squares

From light green batik, cut:

- 24—1¾" squares

From orange batik, cut:

- 2—2½×22" binding strips

From cording, cut:

- 2—42" pieces

Appliqué the Blocks

1. Referring to the Quilt Assembly Diagram on *page 129* and the photographs *above right,* arrange the designated appliqué pieces for each block atop the blue-green batik and green batik 7" squares. (Because this project uses fusible appliqué, the pieces for each block will be the reverse of those specified in the diagram.) When you're pleased with the arrangement, fuse the pieces in place to make a bright pink appliquéd block and a teal blue appliquéd block.

2. Using machine-embroidery threads in colors that match the appliqués and working from the bottom layer to the top, straight-stitch around each appliqué piece, $^1/_{16}$" from the edges. Using contrasting machine-embroidery threads and a free-motion zigzag, stitch around the flower appliqués and add flower centers.

3. With the design centered, trim each block to measure 6¾" square, including seam allowances.

Add the Borders

1. Lay out three pink batik 1¾" squares and two light green batik 1¾" squares in a row, alternating

colors. Join the pieces to make a short border unit. Repeat to make a second short border unit.

2. Lay out four light green batik 1¾" squares and three pink batik 1¾" squares in a row, alternating colors. Sew together to make a long border unit. Repeat to make a second long border unit.

3. Sew the short border units to opposite edges of the bright pink appliquéd block. Join the long border units to the remaining edges of the bright pink appliquéd block to complete the pink quilt top. Press the seam allowances toward the border.

4. Repeat steps 1 through 3 with the teal batik 1¾" squares, the remaining light green batik 1¾" squares, and the teal appliquéd block to complete the teal blue quilt top.

Complete the Quilts

1. Layer each quilt top, batting and backing according to the instructions in Quilter's Schoolhouse, which begins on *page 150.* Quilt as desired. Trim the batting and backing even with each quilt top.

2. Cover one cording piece with the teal batik ¾×42" strip (see Covered Cording in Quilter's Schoolhouse for instructions). Cut the covered cording into four 9¼" lengths. Aligning raw edges and using a machine cording foot, stitch a length of covered cording to each edge of the pink quilt.

3. Repeat Step 2 with the remaining cording piece and the pink batik ¾×42" strip to make covered cording and attach it to the teal quilt.

4. Use the orange batik 2½×22" strips to bind the pink quilt and use the blue-green batik 2½×22" strips to bind the teal quilt according to the instructions in Quilter's Schoolhouse.

EMBROIDERED WALL HANGING

Replace the appliqués with "greenwork" embroidery in this botanical wall hanging.

Materials

1¼ yards total of assorted cream and light tan prints for pieced blocks and embroidery foundations

⅞ yard total of assorted green and tan prints for pieced blocks and inner border corners

¼ yard of cream vine print for inner border

⅞ yard of green polka dot for outer border

18×22" piece (fat quarter) of green vine print for outer border corners

½ yard of dark green print for binding

2⅞ yards of backing fabric

50" square of quilt batting

Embroidery floss: assorted greens

Finished quilt top: 43¼" square

Cut the Fabrics

To make the best use of your fabrics, cut the pieces in the order that follows.

This project uses the "Prairie Flowers" patterns, which are on *Pattern Sheet 2*. To make templates of the patterns, follow the instructions in Quilter's Schoolhouse, which begins on *page 150*.

From assorted cream and light tan prints, cut:
- 17—1¾×22" strips
- 12—7" squares

From assorted green and tan prints, cut:
- 18—1¾×22" strips
- 4—1½" squares

From one green or tan print, cut:
- 4—1½" squares for inner border

From cream vine print, cut:
- 4—1½×31¾" inner border strips

From green polka dot, cut:
- 4—5½×33¾" outer border strips

From green vine print, cut:

- 4—5½" squares for outer border

From dark green print, cut:

- 5—2½×42" binding strips

Embroider the Blocks

1. Referring to the Quilt Assembly Diagram on *page 129,* arrange the designated appliqué templates for one block atop a cream or light tan print 7" square. Be sure to allow for a ¼" seam allowance along each edge of the square. When you're pleased with the arrangement, pin in place. With a quilter's pencil, trace around each appliqué template. Remove the templates and add detail lines (flower centers, leaf veins, and bird feathers) as desired. Repeat with the remaining appliqué templates and assorted cream and light tan print 7" squares.

2. Using a stem-stitch and two strands of embroidery floss, embroider the designs. If desired, use an embroidery hoop when stitching to keep the fabric taut.

To stem-stitch, pull your needle up at A (see diagram *below*). Insert your needle back into the fabric at B, about ¼" away from A. Holding the floss out of the way, bring your needle back up at C and pull the floss through so it lies flat against the fabric. The distances between points A, B, and C should be equal. Pull with equal tautness after each stitch.

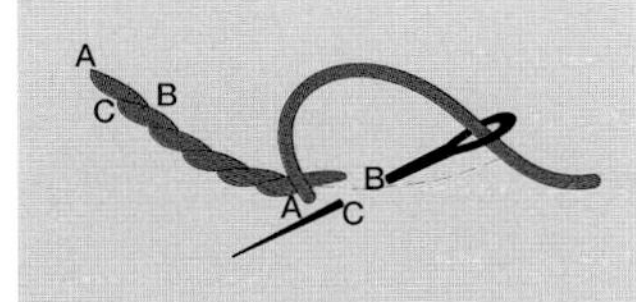

Stem Stitch Diagram

3. Press the embroidered block from the back; center the design and trim the block to measure 6¾" square, including the seam allowances.

Assemble the 25-Patch Blocks

Referring to Assemble the 25-Patch Blocks on *page 128,* use the assorted cream and light tan print 1¾×22" strips and the assorted green and tan print 1¾×22" strips to make a total of thirteen 25-Patch blocks.

Assemble the Quilt Top

1. Referring to Assemble the Quilt Center on *page 128,* use the 12 embroidered blocks and the thirteen 25-Patch blocks to make the quilt center.

2. Referring to Add the Borders on *page 128,* use the green or tan print 1½" squares, the cream vine print 1½×31¾" inner border strips, the green polka dot 5½×33¾" outer border strips, and the green vine print 5½" squares to assemble and add the inner and outer borders to complete the quilt top.

Complete the Quilt

1. Layer the quilt top, batting, and backing according to the instructions in Quilter's Schoolhouse, which begins on *page 150.* Quilt as desired.

2. Use the dark green print 2½×42" strips to bind the quilt according to the instructions in Quilter's Schoolhouse.

Trumpet *Blooms*

Fusible-web appliqué makes designer Pat Sloan's lap-size quilt quick to make.

Variegated thread was used to machine-appliqué for added interest.

Materials

2½ yards of tan floral for blocks and border

1⅛ yards of tan plaid for blocks

⅛ yard of yellow print for circle appliqués

⅛ yard of orange print for circle appliqués

¼ yard of dark purple print for circle appliqués

1¾ yards of olive green plaid for stem appliqués, sashing, and binding

½ yard of red-orange print for flower appliqués and sashing

½ yard of olive green print for leaf appliqués

3⅞ yards of backing fabric

68" square of quilt batting

Olive green variegated thread

2⅝ yards of lightweight fusible web

Finished quilt top: 62" square
Finished block: 14" square

Quantities are for 44/45"-wide, 100% cotton fabrics. All measurements include a ¼" seam allowance. Sew with right sides together unless otherwise stated.

Cut the Fabrics

To make the best use of your fabrics, cut the pieces in the order that follows.

Cut the border strips the length of the fabric (parallel to the selvage). The border strips are mathematically correct. You may wish to cut your strips longer than specified to allow for possible sewing differences.

The patterns are on *Pattern Sheet 2*. To use fusible web for appliquéing, as was done in this project, complete the following steps.

1. Lay the fusible web, paper side up, over the appliqué patterns. Use a pencil to trace each pattern the number of times indicated, leaving ½" between tracings. Cut out each piece roughly ¼" outside the traced lines.

2. Following the manufacturer's instructions, press the fusible web shapes onto the wrong side of the designated fabrics; let cool. Cut out the fabric shapes on the drawn lines. Peel off the paper backings.

From tan floral, cut:
- 2—7½×62½" border strips
- 2—7½×48½" border strips
- 18—7½" squares

From tan plaid, cut:
- 18—7½" squares

continued

From yellow print, cut:
- 9 of Pattern A

From orange print, cut:
- 9 of Pattern B

From dark purple print, cut:
- 9 of Pattern C

From olive green plaid, cut:
- 7—2½×42" binding strips
- 24—2×14½" sashing strips
- 36 of Pattern D

From red-orange print, cut:
- 16—2" sashing squares
- 36 of Pattern E

From olive green print, cut:
- 36 *each* of patterns F and F reversed

Piece and Appliqué the Blocks

1. Sew together two tan plaid 7½" squares and two tan floral 7½" squares in pairs (see Diagram 1). Press the seam allowances in opposite directions. Then join the pairs to make a Four-Patch block. Press the seam allowance in one direction. The pieced Four-Patch block should measure 14½" square, including the seam allowances.

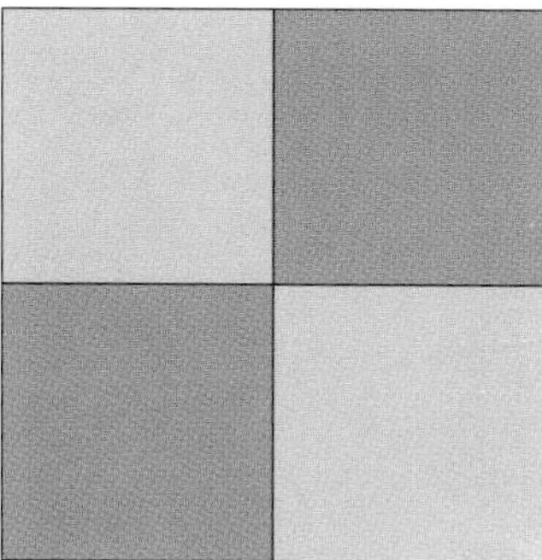

Diagram 1

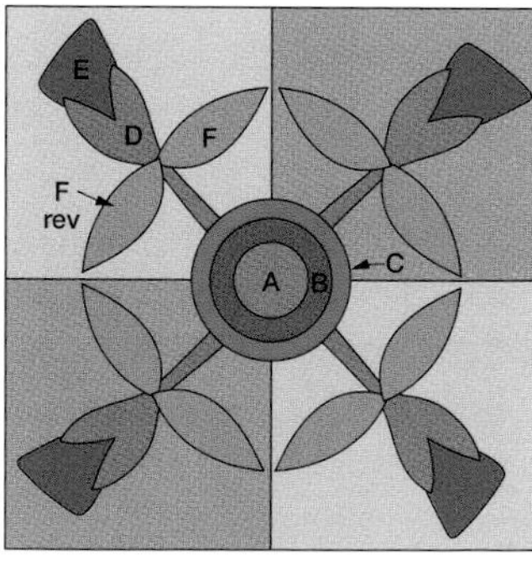

Diagram 2

2. Referring to Diagram 2, lay out one yellow print A circle, one orange print B circle, one dark purple print C circle, four olive green plaid D stems, four red-orange print E flowers, four olive green print F leaves, and four olive green print F reversed leaves on the Four-Patch block. When you are pleased with the arrangement, fuse the pieces in place.

3. Using olive green variegated thread and working from the bottom layer to the top, machine-blanket-stitch the pieces in place to make an appliquéd Four-Patch block.

4. Repeat steps 1 through 3 to make a total of nine appliquéd Four-Patch blocks.

Assemble the Quilt Center

1. Referring to the photograph *opposite* for placement, lay out the nine appliquéd Four-Patch blocks, the 24 olive green plaid 2×14½" sashing strips, and the 16 red-orange print 2" sashing squares in seven horizontal rows.

2. Sew together the pieces in each row. Press the seam allowances toward the sashing strips. Then join the rows to make the quilt center. Press the seam allowances in one direction. The pieced quilt center should measure 48½" square, including the seam allowances.

Add the Border

1. Add the tan floral 7½×48½" border strips to opposite edges of the pieced quilt center. Press the seam allowances toward the border.

2. Join the tan floral 7½×62½" border strips to the remaining edges of the pieced quilt center to complete the quilt top. Press the seam allowances toward the border.

Complete the Quilt

1. Layer the quilt top, batting, and backing according to the instructions in Quilter's Schoolhouse, which begins on *page 150*. Quilt as desired.

2. Use the olive green plaid 2½×42" strips to bind the quilt according to the instructions in Quilter's Schoolhouse.

Trumpet Blooms

optional sizes

If you'd like to make this quilt in a size other than for a throw, use the information *below.*

Alternate quilt sizes	**Twin**	**Full/Queen**	**King**
Number of blocks	15	25	36
Number of blocks wide by long	3×5	5×5	6×6
Finished size	62×93"	93" square	108" square
Yardage requirements			
Tan floral	3⅜ yards	4⅝ yards	5⅞ yards
Tan plaid	1½ yards	2⅓ yards	3⅜ yards
Yellow print	⅛ yard	⅛ yard	⅛ yard
Orange print	¼ yard	⅓ yard	½ yard
Dark purple print	⅓ yard	½ yard	⅝ yard
Olive green plaid	2⅛ yards	3¼ yards	4 yards
Red-orange print	⅝ yard	⅞ yard	1¼ yards
Olive green print	⅝ yard	⅞ yard	1¼ yards
Backing	5½ yards	8¼ yards	9½ yards
Batting	68×99"	99" square	114" square
Fusible web	4½ yards	7¼ yards	9⅞ yards

WOOL THROW AND PILLOWS

Fashion one purchased blanket into two dotty wool pillows and a matching throw for a playful accent to your home decor.

Materials

Purchased twin-size (66×90") blue wool blanket

11—6×13" pieces of assorted yellow, red, pink, orange, purple, green, and blue felted wool for circle appliqués

1—5½×12" piece of green plaid felted wool for pillow rectangle appliqué

20"-square pillow form

16×12" pillow form

Embroidery floss: yellow, red, pink, orange, purple, green, and blue

Finished throw: 60×66"
Finished pillows: 20" square and 16×12"

Quantities are for wool fabrics. All measurements include a ½" seam allowance.

Prepare the Throw

1. Trim one edge of the blue wool blanket to make a 60½×66" rectangle. Set aside the trimmed piece to make the pillows.

2. Finish the cut blanket edge in the same manner as the original blanket was finished to complete the throw. On the featured throw, the cut blanket edge was turned ½" to the back and blanket-stitched with blue yarn (see Appliqué the Throw for instructions on blanket stitching).

Cut the Fabrics

To make the best use of your fabrics, cut the pieces in the order that follows.

This project uses "Trumpet Blooms" patterns A, B, and C, which are on *Pattern Sheet 2*. To make templates of the patterns, follow the instructions in Quilter's Schoolhouse, which begins on *page 150*. It is not necessary to add seam allowances to these appliqué shapes because felted wool won't fray.

To felt wool, machine-wash it in a hot-water-wash, cool-rinse cycle with a small amount of detergent; machine-dry it on high heat and steam-press.

From leftover blue wool blanket piece, cut:

- 2—21" squares
- 2—17×13" rectangles

From assorted yellow, red, pink, orange, purple, green, and blue wool, cut:

- 13 of Pattern A
- 12 of Pattern B
- 17 of Pattern C

Appliqué the Throw

1. Referring to Diagram 3, lay out nine assorted wool C circles across one short edge of the throw, evenly spacing them across the width. Start and end the circles 2" from the long edges of the throw.

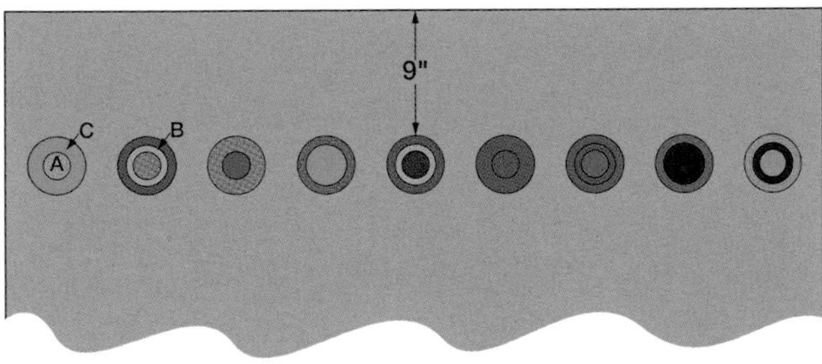

Diagram 3

2. Lay out six assorted wool B circles and seven assorted wool A circles atop the C circles. When you are pleased with the arrangement, pin the circles together.

3. Pick up one stack of pinned circle appliqués. Using two strands of contrasting floss, blanket-stitch around each A and B circle in the stack. Place the blanket-stitched circle stack back on the throw and blanket-stitch the C circle in place.

To blanket-stitch, first pull your needle up at A (see diagram *below*), form a reverse L shape with the floss, and hold the angle of the L shape in place with your thumb. Then push the needle down at B and come up at C to secure the stitch.

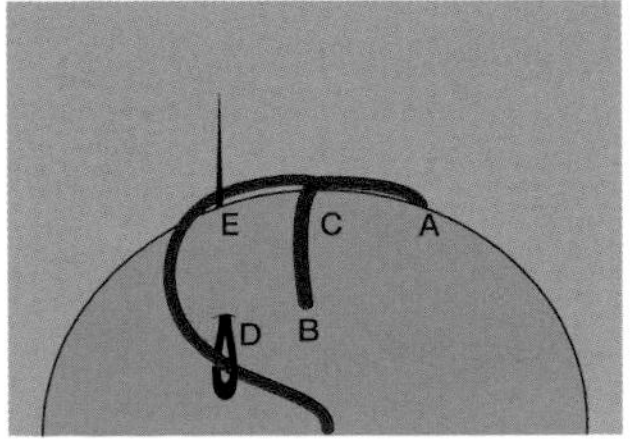

Blanket Stitch Diagram

4. Repeat Step 3 to appliqué each stack of pinned circle appliqués together and then to the throw.

Appliqué the Pillow Tops

1. Referring to the photograph *opposite*, lay out six assorted wool C circles evenly spaced in two vertical rows on a blue wool 21" square. Start and end the circles 3" from the top and bottom edges of the wool square. The side edges of the circles should be 5" from the side edges of the wool square.

2. Lay out four assorted wool B circles and five assorted wool A circles atop the C circles. When you are pleased with the arrangement, pin the circles together.

3. Referring to Appliqué the Throw, Step 3, appliqué each stack of circle appliqués together, then to the blue wool square to make the square pillow top.

4. Referring to the photograph *opposite*, lay out two assorted wool C circles evenly spaced on the green plaid wool 5½×12" rectangle.

5. Lay out two assorted wool B circles and one assorted wool A circle atop the C circles. When you are pleased with the arrangement, pin the circles together.

6. Referring to Appliqué the Throw, Step 3, appliqué each stack of circle appliqués together, then to the green plaid wool rectangle. Place the green plaid wool 5½×12" rectangle on the blue wool 17×13" rectangle, 4½" from one short end. Be sure to allow for a ½" seam allowance along each long edge of the blue wool rectangle. Blanket-stitch in place to make the rectangular pillow top.

Complete the Pillows

1. Layer the square pillow top, right side down, with the remaining blue wool 21" square. Sew around all edges with a ½" seam, leaving an opening along one side. Turn right side out through the opening and insert the 20"-square pillow form. Slipstitch the opening closed to complete the square pillow.

2. Repeat Step 1 with the rectangular pillow top, remaining blue wool 17×13" rectangle, and 16×12" pillow form to complete the rectangular pillow.

ASIAN BED QUILT

Put an international twist on this quilt by incorporating Asian fabrics.

The appliqué colors were inspired by the floral print used in the border.

Materials

2⅓ yards of white print for blocks

2⅓ yards of ivory print for blocks

⅛ yard of multicolor print for circle appliqués

⅓ yard of dark pink print for circle appliqués

½ yard of light pink print for circle appliqués

1 yard of green print for stem appliqués

⅞ yard of pink print for flower appliqués

1 yard of olive green print for leaf appliqués

1¾ yards of blue print for sashing

¼ yard of dark blue print for sashing squares

3⅜ yards of black floral for border and binding

8¼ yards of backing fabric

99" square of quilt batting

Black thread

7¼ yards of lightweight fusible web

Finished quilt top: 93" square

Cut the Fabrics

To make the best use of your fabrics, cut the pieces in the order that follows. Cut the border strips lengthwise (parallel to the selvage). The border strip measurements are mathematically correct. You may wish to cut your strips longer than specified to allow for possible sewing differences.

This project uses the "Trumpet Blooms" patterns, which are on *Pattern Sheet 2*. To use fusible web for appliquéing, as was done in this project, refer to Cut the Fabrics on *page 135,* steps 1 and 2.

From white print, cut:
• 50—7½" squares
From ivory print, cut:
• 50—7½" squares
From multicolor print, cut:
• 25 of Pattern A
From dark pink print, cut:
• 25 of Pattern B
From light pink print, cut:
• 25 of Pattern C
From green print, cut:
• 100 of Pattern D
From pink print, cut:
• 100 of Pattern E
From olive green print, cut:
• 100 *each* of patterns F and F reversed
From blue print, cut:
• 60—2×14½" sashing strips
From dark blue print, cut:
• 36—2" sashing squares
From black floral, cut:
• 10—2½×42" binding strips
• 2—7½×93½" border strips
• 2—7½×79½" border strips

Piece and Appliqué the Blocks

Referring to the photograph *above right* and Piece and Appliqué the Blocks on *page 136*, use the white print 7½" squares, the ivory print 7½" squares, the multicolor print A circles, the dark pink print B circles, the light pink print C circles, the green print D stems, the pink print E flowers, the olive green print F and F reversed leaves, and black thread to make a total of 25 appliquéd Four-Patch blocks.

Assemble the Quilt Center

1. Referring to the photograph *above right*, lay out the 25 appliquéd blocks, the 60 blue print 2×14½" sashing strips, and the 36 dark blue print 2" sashing squares in 11 horizontal rows.

2. Sew together the pieces in each row. Press the seam allowances toward the sashing strips. Then join the rows to make the quilt center. Press the seam allowances in one direction. The pieced quilt center should measure 79½" square, including the seam allowances.

Add the Border

1. Add the black floral 7½×79½" border strips to opposite edges of the pieced quilt center. Press the seam allowances toward the border.

2. Join the black floral 7½×93½" border strips to the remaining edges of the pieced quilt center to complete the quilt top. Press the seam allowances toward the border.

Complete the Quilt

1. Layer the quilt top, batting, and backing according to the instructions in Quilter's Schoolhouse, which begins on *page 150*. Quilt as desired.

2. Use the black floral 2½×42" strips to bind the quilt according to the instructions in Quilter's Schoolhouse.

TULIP *Fancy*

Celebrate spring with designer Linda Hohag's timeless throw. Using starch, Linda creates smooth, sharp edges for machine appliqué.

Materials

2⅞ yards of solid off-white for appliqué foundations and border No. 2

¾ yard of red check for circle and swag appliqués

1⅝ yards of dark green print for stem appliqués, border Nos. 1 and 4, and binding

1⅜ yards of green print for leaf appliqués and border No. 3

1⅞ yards of red print for circle, tulip, and swag appliqués

3¼ yards of backing fabric

57" square of quilt batting

Heat-resistant template plastic

Liquid starch

Cotton swabs

Finished quilt top: 50½" square
Finished block: 10" square

Quantities are for 44/45"-wide, 100% cotton fabrics. All measurements include a ¼" seam allowance. Sew with right sides together unless otherwise stated.

Cut the Fabrics

To make the best use of your fabrics, cut the pieces in the order that follows. Cut the border and binding strips the length of the fabric (parallel to the selvage). The border measurements are mathematically correct. You may wish to cut your strips longer than specified to allow for possible sewing differences.

The patterns are on *Pattern Sheet 1*. To make a template of Pattern A, follow the instructions in Quilter's Schoolhouse, which begins on *page 150*. Refer to Appliqué the Tulip Blocks on *page 144* for making templates for the remaining patterns.

From solid off-white, cut:
- 2—6½×44" border No. 2 strips
- 2—6½×32" border No. 2 strips
- 9—11½" squares

From red check, cut:
- 9 of Pattern A

From dark green print, cut:
- 2—3½×51" border No. 4 strips
- 2—3½×45" border No. 4 strips
- 6—2½×42" binding strips
- 2—1¼×32" border No. 1 strips
- 2—1¼×30½" border No. 1 strips

From green print, cut:
- 2—1×45" border No. 3 strips
- 2—1×44" border No. 3 strips

continued

Appliqué the Tulip Blocks

1. Place heat-resistant template plastic over Pattern B. Trace the pattern onto the plastic using a permanent fine-line marker (see Diagram 1). Cut out on the drawn lines to make a B template.

Diagram 1

2. Place the B template on the wrong side of the red print fabric. Cut out a B appliqué piece, adding a 3/16" seam allowance to the edges (see Diagram 2).

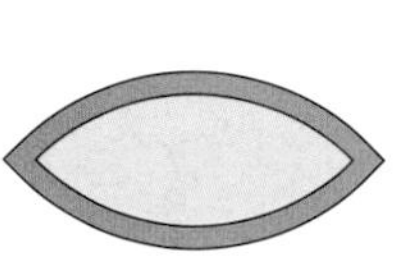
Diagram 2

Diagram 3

3. Pour a small amount of starch into a dish. Linda uses liquid starch, but spray starch sprayed into a small bowl works well, too. Place the template-topped fabric on a pressing surface covered with a tea towel or muslin. Dip a cotton swab in the starch and moisten the appliqué piece's seam allowance (see Diagram 3).

4. Use the tip of a hot, dry iron to turn the seam allowance over the edge of the template and press it in place until the fabric is dry (see Diagram 4). Press

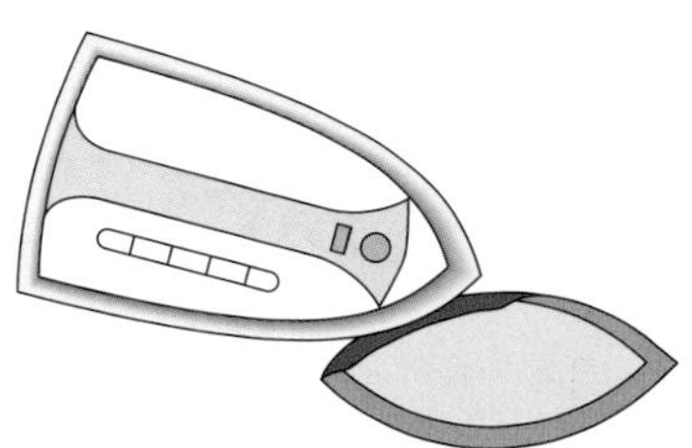
Diagram 4

the entire seam allowance in the same manner, adding starch as necessary.

5. Turn the template and appliqué piece over. Press the appliqué from the right side, then remove the template.

6. Repeat steps 2 through 5 to prepare a total of four red print B appliqués. Referring to the Tulip Block Appliqué Placement Diagram, arrange the pieces on top of a red check A piece; baste and appliqué in place to make a circle appliqué.

Tulip Block
Appliqué Placement Diagram

7. Referring to steps 1 through 5, use appropriate templates and fabrics to prepare a total of eight red print C tulips, 16 green print D leaves, and eight dark green print E stems.

8. Fold a solid off-white 11½" square in half vertically and horizontally. Lightly finger-press after each fold to create positioning guides for the appliqué pieces; unfold.

9. Referring to the Tulip Block Appliqué Placement Diagram, arrange the prepared appliqué pieces on the prepared foundation; baste. Stitch the pieces to the foundation, working from the bottom layer to the top, to make an appliquéd tulip block. *Note:* Linda machine-stitched her appliqués in place close to the crisp, folded edges using monofilament thread for nearly invisible stitches.

Rinse the appliquéd block in warm water to remove the starch. Lay flat and press on the wrong side while slightly damp. Trim the block to measure 10½" square, including the seam allowances.

10. Repeat steps 1 through 9 to make a total of nine appliquéd tulip blocks.

Assemble the Quilt Center and Add the First Border

1. Referring to the photograph *opposite,* lay out the nine tulip blocks in three rows. Sew together the blocks in each row. Press the seam allowances in one direction, alternating the direction with each row. Then join the rows to make the quilt center. Press the seam allowances in one direction. The pieced quilt center should measure 30½" square, including the seam allowances.

2. Sew the dark green print 1¼×30½" border No. 1 strips to opposite edges of the quilt center. Sew the dark green print 1¼×32" border No. 1 strips to the remaining edges of the quilt center. Press all seam allowances toward the border. The quilt center should now measure 32" square, including the seam allowances.

Add and Appliqué the Second Border

1. Referring to steps 1 through 5 of Appliqué the Tulip Blocks, use the appropriate templates and fabrics to prepare a total of 12 red print C tulips, 24 green print F leaves, eight red check G swags, eight red print H swags, four red check I swags, and four red print J swags.

2. With right sides up, place a red print H swag below a red check G swag, matching the center points marked on the patterns; pin. Stitch along the adjoining edges to make a side swag unit. Repeat to make a total of eight side swag units.

In the same manner, use a red print J swag and a red check I swag to make a corner swag unit. Repeat to make a total of four corner swag units.

3. Fold the solid off-white 6½×32" border No. 2 strips and 6½×44" border No. 2 strips in half crosswise. Lightly finger-press to mark the center; unfold.

Sew the solid off-white 6½×32" border No. 2 strips to opposite edges of the quilt center. Then sew the solid off-white 6½×44" border No. 2 strips to the remaining edges of the quilt center. Press all seam allowances toward border No. 1.

4. Referring to the photograph *opposite,* arrange the eight side swag units and the four corner swag units on border No. 2; the side swag units should meet at the center of the border No. 2 strips, and the bottom edge of the side swag units should be about ⅞" from the border strip edge. Position a red print

continued

C tulip and two green print F leaves where the swag units meet. When you are pleased with the arrangement, baste all of the appliqués, then stitch in place.

Rinse the appliquéd quilt center in warm water to remove the starch. Lay flat and press on the wrong side while slightly damp.

Add the Remaining Borders

1. Sew the green print 1×44" border No. 3 strips to opposite edges of the pieced quilt center. Then sew the green print 1×45" border No. 3 strips to the remaining edges of the pieced quilt center. Press all seam allowances toward border No. 3.

2. Sew the dark green print 3½×45" border No. 4 strips to opposite edges of the pieced quilt center. Sew the dark green print 3½×51" border No. 4 strips to the remaining edges of the pieced quilt center to complete the quilt top. Press all seam allowances toward border No. 4.

Complete the Quilt

1. Layer the quilt top, batting, and backing according to the directions in Quilter's Schoolhouse, which begins on *page 150*. Quilt as desired.

2. Use the dark green print 2½×42" strips to bind the quilt according to the directions in Quilter's Schoolhouse.

BATIK BED QUILT

Set the tulip blocks on point in a sea of beautiful, colorwashed batiks.

Materials

3⅝ yards of pale blue print for appliqué foundations

⅝ yard of multicolor batik for circle appliqués

⅝ yard total of assorted purple batiks for tulips

⅔ yard total of assorted green batiks for leaves

⅓ yard of dark periwinkle print for stems

⅓ yard total of assorted blue batiks for tulips

1⅝ yards of mottled dark purple for stem appliqués, inner border, and binding

3 yards of blue batik for setting pieces

1 yard of light blue batik for setting squares

2⅞ yards of dark blue batik for outer border

8¼ yards of backing fabric

98×112" of quilt batting

Lightweight fusible web

Finished quilt top: 91¼×105½"
Finished block: 10" square

Cut the Fabrics

To make the best use of your fabrics, cut the pieces in the order that follows. This project uses the "Tulip Fancy" patterns, which are on *Pattern Sheet 1*. To use fusible web for appliquéing, as was done in this project, follow these steps.

1. Lay the fusible web, paper side up, over the patterns. With a pencil, trace each pattern the number of times indicated, leaving ½" between tracings. Cut out each fusible-web shape roughly ¼" outside the traced lines.

2. Following the manufacturer's instructions, press the fusible-web shapes onto the backs of the designated fabrics; let cool. Cut out the fabric shapes on the drawn lines. Peel off the paper backings.

From pale blue print, cut:
- 28—11½" squares

From multicolor batik, cut:
- 112 of Pattern B

From assorted purple batiks, cut:
- 144 of Pattern C (18 sets of 8 each)

From assorted green batiks, cut:
- 188 of Pattern F
- 168 of Pattern D

From dark periwinkle print, cut:
- 144 of Pattern E

From assorted blue batiks, cut:
- 60 of Pattern C (10 sets of 6 each)

From mottled dark purple, cut:
- 19—2½×42" strips for inner border and binding
- 80 of Pattern E

From blue batik, cut:
- 5—15½" squares, cutting each diagonally twice in an X for a total of 20 setting triangles (you will have 2 left over)
- 14—10½" squares
- 2—8" squares, cutting each in half diagonally for a total of 4 corner triangles

From light blue batik, cut:
- 8—10½" squares

From dark blue batik, cut:
- 11—8½×42" strips for outer border

Appliqué the Tulip Blocks

1. Fold a pale blue print 11½" square in half vertically and horizontally. Lightly finger-press after each fold to create positioning guides for the appliqué pieces; unfold.

2. Referring to the Tulip Block Appliqué Placement Diagram on *page 145*, arrange four multicolor batik B pieces, eight matching purple batik C tulips, and eight dark periwinkle print E stems on the prepared foundation. Then randomly add six assorted green batik D leaves and six assorted green batik F leaves to the block as desired; fuse all of the appliqué pieces to the foundation.

3. Using threads that match the appliqués, zigzag-stitch the pieces to the foundation, working from the bottom layer to the top, to make a purple appliquéd tulip block. Trim to measure 10½" square, including the seam allowances.

4. Repeat steps 1 through 3 to make a total of 18 purple appliquéd tulip blocks.

5. Repeat steps 1 through 3 using the remaining appliqué pieces to make a total of 10 blue appliquéd tulip blocks. In the featured quilt, only six tulip appliqués were used in each blue appliquéd tulip block; the missing tulips were replaced with assorted green batik F leaves.

Assemble the Quilt Center

1. Referring to the photograph on *page 148*, lay out the purple appliquéd tulip blocks; the blue appliquéd tulip blocks; the blue batik 10½" setting squares, setting triangles, and corner triangles; and the light blue batik 10½" setting squares in diagonal rows. The purple appliquéd tulip blocks should form the outer row of the quilt, and the blue appliquéd tulip blocks should form the inner row.

2. Sew together the pieces in each row. Press the seam allowances in one direction, alternating the direction with each row. Join the rows to make the quilt center. Press the seam allowances in one direction. The quilt center should measure 71¾×86", including the seam allowances.

Add the Borders

1. Cut and piece mottled dark purple 2½×42" strips to make the following:
- 2—2½×86" inner border strips
- 2—2½×75¾" inner border strips

continued

2. Sew the long mottled dark purple inner border strips to the side edges of the pieced quilt center. Then join the short mottled dark purple inner border strips to the short edges of the quilt center. Press all seam allowances toward the border.

3. Cut and piece the dark blue batik 8½×42" strips to make the following:

- 2—8½×91¾" outer border strips
- 2—8½×90" outer border strips

4. Sew the short dark blue batik outer border strips to the side edges of the quilt center. Join the long dark blue batik outer border strips to the remaining edges of the quilt center to complete the quilt top. Press all seam allowances toward the outer border.

Complete the Quilt

1. Layer the quilt top, batting, and backing according to the directions in Quilter's Schoolhouse, which begins on *page 150*. Quilt as desired.

2. Use the remaining mottled dark purple 2½×42" strips to bind the quilt according to the directions in Quilter's Schoolhouse.

SPRINGTIME PILLOW

The tulip appliqué pattern becomes a guide for yarn couching on this pillow.

Materials

½ yard of solid off-white for pillow front and back

Scraps of assorted yarns in pink, orange, and yellow

3½ yards of green chenille yarn

2 yards of green beaded cording

14"-square pillow form

Finished pillow: 14" square

Cut the Fabrics

This project uses the "Tulip Fancy" Full-Size Appliqué Placement Diagram, which is on *Pattern Sheet 1*.

From solid off-white, cut:

- 1—16" square for pillow top
- 1—14½" square for pillow back

Couch the Pillow Top

1. Center and trace the Full-Size Appliqué Placement Diagram onto the solid off-white 16" square using a pencil and a light box. On the featured pillow, the B shapes were eliminated when tracing; instead, the arcs of the E stems were continued.

2. Set up your sewing machine with a couching foot (or any foot with an open center); a long, narrow zigzag or blind hem stitch; monofilament thread in the needle; and off-white cotton thread in the bobbin. Lay one strand of assorted yellow, orange, or pink yarn atop a drawn tulip shape on the solid off-white 16" square. Machine-couch the yarn to the fabric by stitching over the yarn on the drawn lines.

Referring to the photograph *above right* for color placement, couch the remaining drawn tulip shapes with the assorted yellow, orange, and pink yarn. Couch the remaining drawn shapes with green chenille yarn.

3. Trim the couched solid off-white square to 14½" square, including the seam allowances, to complete the pillow top.

Complete the Pillow

1. Aligning raw edges and using a machine cording foot, stitch the beaded cording to the pillow top in the same manner as for covered cording (see Covered Cording in Quilter's Schoolhouse, which begins on *page 150,* for instructions).

2. Sew together the pillow top and the solid off-white 14½"-square pillow back, leaving an opening to insert the pillow form. Turn right side out and insert the pillow form through the opening. Whipstitch the opening closed.

QUILTER'S SCHOOLHOUSE

GETTING STARTED

Before you begin any project, collect the tools and materials you'll need in one place.

Tools

CUTTING

Acrylic ruler: To aid in making perfectly straight cuts with a rotary cutter, choose a ruler of thick, clear plastic. Many sizes are available. A 6×24" ruler marked in ¼" increments with 30°, 45°, and 60° angles is a good first purchase.

Rotary-cutting mat: A rotary cutter should always be used with a mat designed specifically for it. The mat protects the table and helps keep the fabric from shifting while you cut. Often these mats are described as self-healing, meaning the blade does not leave slash marks or grooves in the surface, even after repeated usage. While many sizes and shapes are available, a 16×23" mat marked with a 1" grid, with hash marks at ⅛" increments and 45° and 60° angles, is a good choice.

Rotary cutter: The round blade of a rotary cutter will cut up to six fabric layers at once. Because the blade is so sharp, be sure to purchase one with a safety guard and keep the guard over the blade when you're not cutting. The blade can be removed from the handle and replaced when it gets dull. Commonly available in three sizes, a good first blade is a 45 mm.

Scissors: You'll need one pair for cutting fabric and another for cutting paper and plastic.

Pencils and other marking tools: Marks made with special quilt markers are easy to remove after sewing.

Template plastic: This slightly frosted plastic comes in sheets about 1⁄16" thick.

PIECING

Iron and ironing board

Sewing thread: Use 100-percent-cotton thread.

Sewing machine: Any machine in good working order with well-adjusted tension will produce pucker-free patchwork seams.

APPLIQUÉ

Fusible web: Instead of the traditional method, secure cutout shapes to the background of an appliqué block with this iron-on adhesive.

Hand-sewing needles: For hand appliqué, most quilters like fine quilting needles.

HAND QUILTING

Frame or hoop: You'll get smaller, more even stitches if you stretch your quilt as you stitch. A frame supports the quilt's weight, ensures even tension, and frees both your hands for stitching. However, once set up, it cannot be disassembled until the quilting is complete. Quilting hoops are more portable and less expensive.

Quilting needles: A "between" or quilting needle is short with a small eye. Common sizes are 8, 9, and 10; size 8 is best for beginners.

Quilting thread: Quilting thread is stronger than sewing thread.

Thimble: This finger cover relieves the pressure required to push a needle through several layers of fabric and batting.

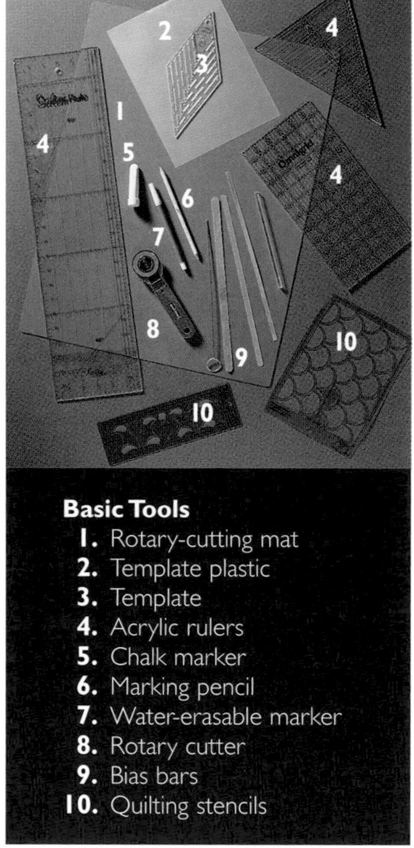

Basic Tools
1. Rotary-cutting mat
2. Template plastic
3. Template
4. Acrylic rulers
5. Chalk marker
6. Marking pencil
7. Water-erasable marker
8. Rotary cutter
9. Bias bars
10. Quilting stencils

Darning foot: You may find this tool, also called a hopper foot, in your sewing machine's accessory kit. If not, have your machine model and brand available when you go to purchase one. It is used for free-motion stitching.
Safety pins: They hold the layers together during quilting.
Table: Use a large work surface that's level with your machine bed.
Thread: Use 100-percent-cotton quilting thread, cotton-wrapped polyester quilting thread, or fine nylon monofilament thread.
Walking foot: This sewing-machine accessory helps you keep long, straight quilting lines smooth and pucker-free.

Choose Your Fabrics

It is no surprise that most quilters prefer 100-percent-cotton fabrics for quiltmaking. Cotton fabric minimizes seam distortion, presses crisply, and is easy to quilt.
Most patterns, including those in this book, specify quantities for 44/45"-wide fabrics unless otherwise noted. Our projects call for a little extra yardage in length to allow for minor errors and slight shrinkage.

Prepare Your Fabrics

There are conflicting opinions about the need to prewash fabric. The debate is a modern one because most antique quilts were made with unwashed fabric. However, the dyes and sizing used today are unlike those used a century ago.

Prewashing fabric offers quilters certainty as its main advantage. Today's fabrics resist bleeding and shrinkage, but some of both can occur in some fabrics. Some quilters find prewashed fabric easier to quilt. If you choose to prewash your fabric, press it well before cutting.

Other quilters prefer the crispness of unwashed fabric, especially for machine piecing. And, if you use fabrics with the same fiber content throughout a quilt, then any shrinkage that occurs in its first washing should be uniform. Some quilters find this small amount of shrinkage desirable, since it gives a quilt a slightly puckered, antique look.

We recommend prewashing a scrap of each fabric to test it for shrinkage and bleeding. If you choose to prewash an entire fabric piece, unfold it to a single layer. Wash it in warm water, which will allow the fabric to shrink and/or bleed. If the fabric bleeds, rinse it until the water runs clear. Do not use it in a quilt if it hasn't stopped bleeding. Hang the fabric to dry, or tumble it in the dryer until slightly damp; press well.

Select the Batting

For a small beginner project, a thin cotton batting is a good choice. It has a tendency to "stick" to fabric, so it requires less basting. Also, it's easy to stitch. It's wise to follow the stitch density (maximum distance between rows of stitching required to keep the batting from shifting and wadding up inside the quilt) recommendation printed on the packaging.

Polyester batting is lightweight and readily available. In general, it springs back to its original height when compressed, adding a puffiness to quilts. It tends to "beard" (work out between the weave of the fabric) more than natural fibers. Polyester fleece is denser and works well for pillow tops and place mats.

Wool batting has good loft retention and absorbs moisture, making it ideal for cool, damp climates. Read the label carefully before purchasing a wool batting; it may require special handling.

ROTARY CUTTING

We've taken the guesswork out of rotary cutting with this primer.

Plan for Cutting

Quilt-Lovers' Favorites™ instructions list pieces in the order in which they should be cut to make the best use of your fabrics. Always consider the fabric grain before cutting. The arrow on a pattern piece or template indicates which direction the fabric grain should run. One or more straight sides of the pattern piece or template should follow the fabric's lengthwise or crosswise grain.

The lengthwise grain, parallel to the selvage (the tightly finished edge), has the least amount of stretch. (Do not use the selvage of a woven fabric in a quilt. When washed, it may shrink more than the rest of the fabric.) Crosswise grain, perpendicular to the selvage, has a little more give. The edge of any pattern piece that will be on the outside of a block or quilt should always be cut on the lengthwise grain. Be sure to press the fabric before cutting to remove any wrinkles or folds.

Using a Rotary Cutter

When cutting, keep an even pressure on the rotary cutter and make sure the blade is touching the edge of the ruler. The less you

continued

move your fabric when cutting, the more accurate you'll be.

SQUARING UP THE FABRIC EDGE

Before rotary-cutting fabric into strips, it is imperative that one fabric edge be made straight, or squared up. Since all subsequent cuts will be measured from this straight edge, squaring up the fabric edge is an important step. There are several techniques for squaring up an edge, some of which involve the use of a pair of rulers. For clarity and simplicity, we have chosen to describe a single-ruler technique here. *Note:* The instructions are for right-handers.

1. Lay your fabric on the rotary mat with the right side down and one selvage edge away from you. Fold the fabric with the wrong side inside and the selvages together. Fold the fabric in half again, lining up the fold with the selvage edges. Lightly hand-crease all of the folds.

2. Position the folded fabric on the cutting mat with the selvage edges away from you and the bulk of the fabric length to your left. With the ruler on top of the fabric, align a horizontal grid line on the ruler with the lower folded fabric edge, leaving about 1" of fabric exposed along the ruler's right-hand edge (see Photo 1). Do not worry about or try to align the uneven raw edges along the right-hand side of the fabric. *Note:* If the grid lines on the cutting mat interfere with your ability to focus on the ruler grid lines, turn your cutting mat over and work on the unmarked side.

3. Hold the ruler firmly in place with your left hand, keeping your fingers away from the right-hand edge and spreading your fingers apart slightly. Apply pressure to the ruler with your fingertips to prevent it from slipping as you cut. With the ruler firmly in place, hold the rotary cutter so the blade is touching the right-hand edge of the ruler. Roll the blade along the ruler edge, beginning just off the folded edge and pushing the cutter away from you, toward the selvage edge.

4. The fabric strip to the right of the ruler's edge should be cut cleanly away, leaving you with a straight edge from which you can measure all subsequent cuts. Do not pick up the fabric once the edge is squared; instead, turn the cutting mat to rotate the fabric and begin cutting strips.

CUTTING AND SUBCUTTING STRIPS

To use a rotary cutter to its greatest advantage, first cut a strip of fabric, then subcut the strip into specific sizes. For example, if your instructions say to cut forty 2" squares, follow these steps.

1. First cut a 2"-wide strip crosswise on the fabric. Assuming you have squared up the fabric edge as described earlier, you can turn your cutting mat clockwise 180° with the newly squared-up edge on your left and the excess fabric on the right. Place the ruler on top of the fabric.

2. Align the 2" grid mark on the ruler with the squared-up edge of the fabric (see Photo 2). *Note:* Align only the vertical grid mark and the fabric raw edge; ignore the selvages at the lower edge that may not line up perfectly with the horizontal ruler grid. A good rule of thumb to remember when rotary-cutting fabric is "the piece you want to keep should be under the ruler." That way, if you accidentally swerve away from the ruler when cutting, the piece under the ruler will be "safe."

3. Placing your rotary cutter along the ruler's right-hand edge and holding the ruler firmly with your left hand, run the blade along the ruler, as in Step 3 of Squaring Up the Fabric Edge, *left,* to cut the strip. Remove the ruler.

4. Sliding the excess fabric out of the way, carefully turn the mat so the 2" strip is horizontal in relation to you. Refer to Squaring Up the Fabric Edge to trim off the selvage edges and square up the strip's short edges.

1

2

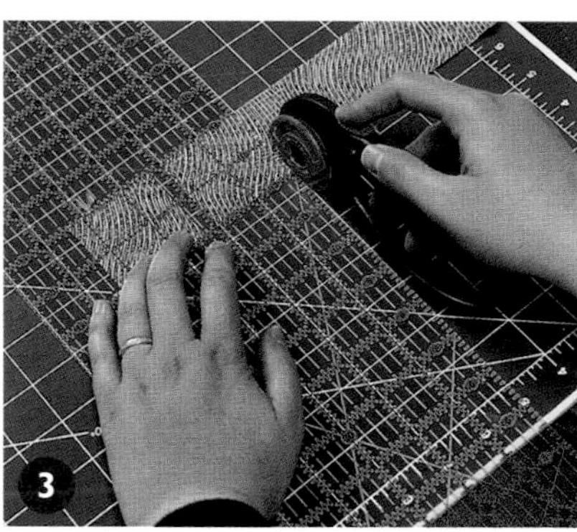

3

5. Align the ruler's 2" grid mark with a squared-up short edge of the strip (the 2" square you want to keep should be under the ruler). Hold the ruler with your left hand and run the rotary cutter along the right-hand ruler edge to cut a 2" square. To cut multiple 2" squares from one strip, slide the ruler over 2" from the previous cutting line and cut again (see Photo 3). From a 44/45"-wide strip, you'll likely be able to cut twenty-one 2" squares. Since in this example you need a total of 40, cut a second 2"-wide strip and subcut it into 2" squares.

CUTTING TRIANGLES

Right triangles also can be quickly and accurately cut with a rotary cutter. There are two common ways to cut triangles. An example of each method follows.

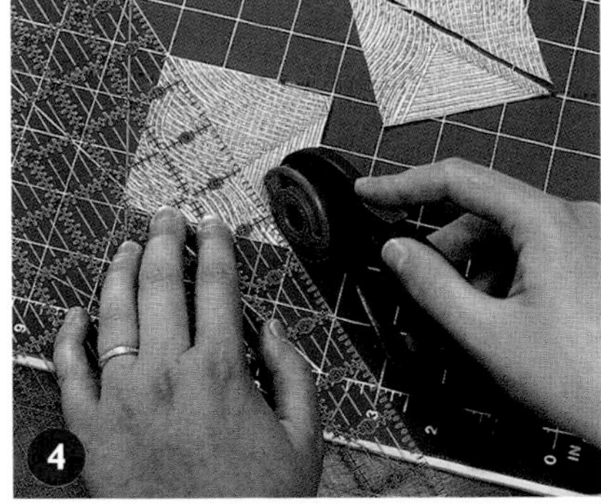

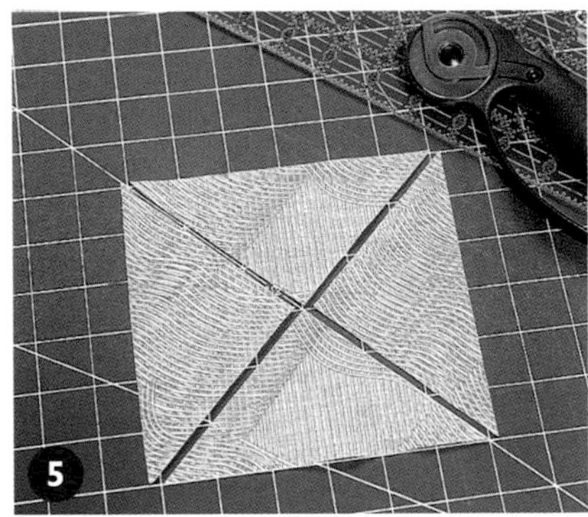

To cut two triangles from one square, the instructions may read:

From green print, cut:

- 20—3" squares, cutting each in half diagonally for a total of 40 triangles

1. Referring to Cutting and Subcutting Strips *opposite,* cut a 3"-wide fabric strip and subcut the strip into 3" squares.

2. Line up the ruler's edge with opposite corners of a square to cut it in half diagonally (see Photo 4). Cut along the ruler's edge. *Note:* The triangles' resultant long edges are on the bias. Avoid stretching or overhandling these edges when piecing so that seams don't become wavy and distorted.

To cut four triangles from one square, the instructions may read:

From green print, cut:

- 20—6" squares, cutting each diagonally twice in an X for a total of 80 triangles

3. Referring to Cutting and Subcutting Strips *opposite,* cut a 6"-wide fabric strip and subcut it into 6" squares.

4. Line up the ruler's edge with opposite corners of a square to cut it in half diagonally. Cut along the ruler's edge; do not separate the two triangles created. Line up the ruler's edge with the remaining corners and cut along the ruler's edge to make a total of four triangles (see Photo 5). *Note:* The triangles' resultant short edges are on the bias. Avoid stretching or overhandling these edges when piecing so that seams don't become wavy and distorted.

Cutting with Templates

A successful quilt requires precise cutting of pieces.

About Scissors

Sharp scissor blades are vital to accurate cutting, but keeping them sharp is difficult because each use dulls the edges slightly. Cutting paper and plastic speeds the dulling process, so invest in a second pair for those materials and reserve your best scissors for fabric.

Make the Templates

For some quilts, you'll need to cut out the same shape multiple times. For accurate piecing later, the individual pieces should be identical to one another.

A template is a pattern made from extra-sturdy material so you can trace around it many times without wearing away the edges. You can make your own templates by duplicating printed patterns (like those on the Pattern Sheets) on plastic.

To make permanent templates, we recommend using easy-to-cut template plastic. This material lasts indefinitely, and its transparency allows you to trace the pattern directly onto its surface.

To make a template, lay the plastic over a printed pattern. Trace the pattern onto the plastic using a ruler and a permanent marker. This will ensure straight lines, accurate corners, and permanency. *Note:* If the pattern you are tracing is a half-pattern to begin with, you must first make a full-size pattern. To do so, fold a piece of tracing paper in half and crease; unfold. Lay the tracing paper over the half-pattern, aligning the crease with the fold line indicated on the pattern. Trace the half-pattern. Then rotate the tracing paper, aligning the half-pattern on the opposite side of the crease to trace the other half of the pattern. Use this full-size pattern to create your template.

For hand piecing and appliqué, make templates the exact size of the finished pieces, without seam allowances, by tracing the patterns' dashed lines. For machine piecing, make templates with the seam allowances included.

For easy reference, mark each template with its letter designation, grain line if noted, and block name. Verify the template's size by placing it over the printed pattern. Templates must be accurate or the error, however small, will compound many times as you assemble the quilt. To check the accuracy of your templates, make a test block before cutting the fabric pieces for an entire quilt.

continued

Trace the Templates

To mark on fabric, use a special quilt marker that makes a thin, accurate line. Do not use a ballpoint or ink pen that may bleed if washed. Test all marking tools on a fabric scrap before using them.

To trace pieces that will be used for hand piecing or appliqué, place templates facedown on the wrong side of the fabric; position the tracings at least ½" apart (see Diagram 1, template A). The lines drawn on the fabric are the sewing lines. Mark cutting lines, or estimate a seam allowance around each piece as you cut out the pieces. For hand piecing, add a ¼" seam allowance; for hand appliqué, add a $\frac{3}{16}$" seam allowance.

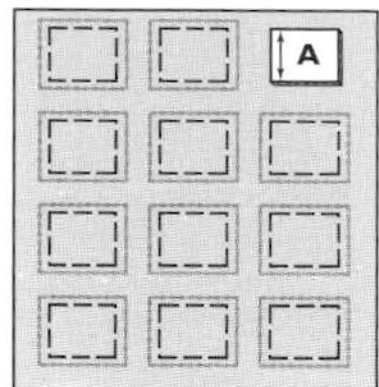

Diagram 1

Templates used to make pieces for machine piecing have seam allowances included so you can use common lines for efficient cutting. To trace, place templates facedown on the wrong side of the fabric; position them without space in between (see Diagram 2, template B). Using sharp scissors or a rotary cutter and ruler, cut precisely on the drawn (cutting) lines.

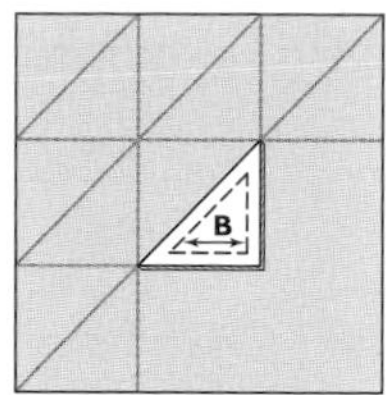

Diagram 2

Templates for Angled Pieces

When two patchwork pieces come together and form an angled opening, a third piece must be set into this angle. This happens frequently when using diamond shapes.

For a design that requires setting in, a pinhole or window template makes it easy to mark the fabric with each shape's exact sewing and cutting lines and the exact point of each corner on the sewing line. By matching the corners of adjacent pieces, you'll be able to sew them together easily and accurately.

To make a pinhole template, lay template plastic over a pattern piece. Trace both the cutting and sewing lines onto the plastic. Carefully cut out the template on the cutting line. Using a sewing-machine needle or any large needle, make a hole in the template at each corner on the sewing line (matching points). The holes must be large enough for a pencil point or other fabric marker to poke through.

Trace Angled Pieces

To mark fabric using a pinhole template, lay it facedown on the wrong side of the fabric and trace. Using a pencil, mark dots on the fabric through the holes in the template to create matching points, then cut out the fabric piece on the drawn line.

To mark fabric using a window template, lay it facedown on the wrong side of the fabric (see Diagram 3). With a marking tool, mark the cutting line, sewing line, and each corner on the sewing line (matching points). Cut out the fabric piece on the cutting lines, making sure all pieces have sewing lines and matching points marked.

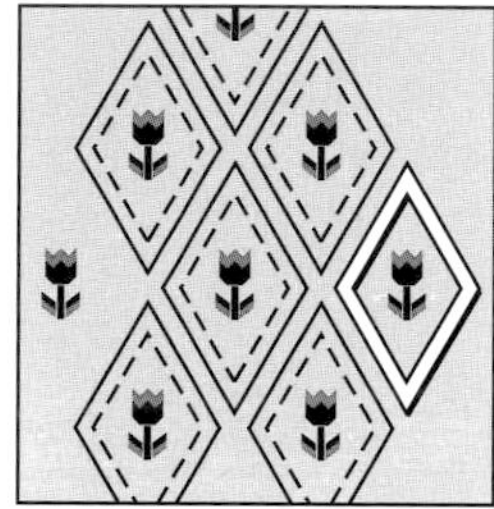

Diagram 3

PIECING

Patchwork piecing consists of sewing fabric pieces together in a specific pattern.

Hand Piecing

In hand piecing, seams are sewn only on the marked sewing lines; the seam allowances remain unstitched. Begin by matching the edges of two pieces with the fabrics' right sides together. Sewing lines should be marked on the wrong side of both pieces. Push a pin through both fabric layers at each corner (see Diagram 1). Secure the pins perpendicular to the sewing line. Insert more pins between the corners.

Insert a needle through both fabrics at the seam-line corner. Make one or two backstitches atop the first stitch to secure the thread. Weave the needle in and out of the fabric along the seam line, taking four to six tiny stitches at a time before you pull the thread taut (see Diagram 2). Remove the pins as you sew. Turn the work over occasionally to see that the stitching follows the marked sewing line on the other side.

Sew eight to 10 stitches per inch along the seam line. At the end of the seam, remove the last pin and make the ending stitch through the hole left by the corner pin.

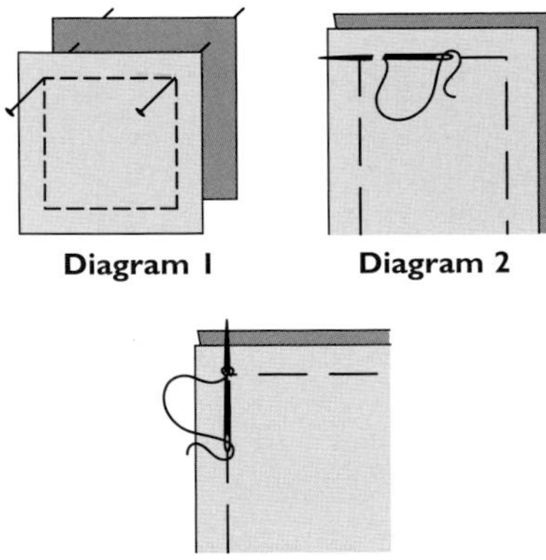

Diagram 1 Diagram 2

Diagram 3

Backstitch over the last stitch and end the seam with a loop knot (see Diagram 3).

To join rows of patchwork by hand, hold the sewn pieces with right sides together and seams matched. Insert pins at the corners of the matching pieces. Add additional pins as necessary, securing each pin perpendicular to the sewing line (see Diagram 4).

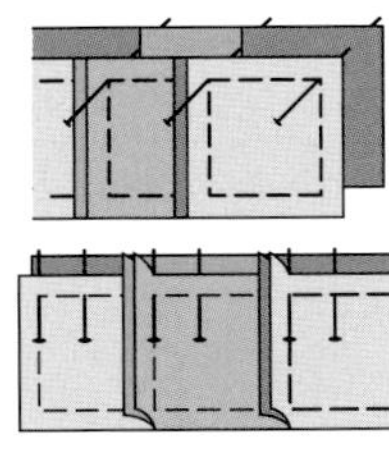

Diagram 4

Stitch the joining seam as before, but do not sew across the seam allowances that join the patches. At each seam allowance, make a backstitch or loop knot, then slide the needle through the seam allowance (see Diagram 5). Knot or backstitch again to give the intersection strength, then sew the remainder of the seam. Press each seam as it is completed.

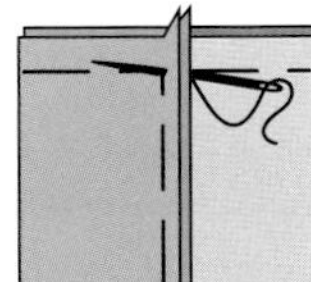

Diagram 5

Machine Piecing

Machine piecing depends on sewing an exact ¼" seam allowance. Some machines have a presser foot that is the proper width, or a ¼" foot is available. To check the width of a machine's presser foot, sew a sample seam with the raw fabric edges aligned with the right edge of the presser foot; measure the resultant seam allowance using graph paper with a ¼" grid.

Using two thread colors—one in the needle and one in the bobbin—can help you to better match your thread color to your fabrics. If your quilt has many fabrics, use a neutral color, such as gray or beige, for both the top and bobbin threads throughout the quilt.

Press for Success

In quilting, almost every seam needs to be pressed before the piece is sewn to another, so keep your iron and ironing board near your sewing area. It's important to remember to press with an up and down motion. Moving the iron around on the fabric can distort seams, especially those sewn on the bias.

Project instructions in this book generally tell you in what direction to press each seam. When in doubt, press the seam allowance toward the darker fabric. When joining rows of blocks, alternate the direction the seam allowances are pressed to ensure flat corners.

Setting in Pieces

The key to sewing angled pieces together is aligning marked matching points carefully. Whether you're stitching by machine or hand, start and stop sewing precisely at the matching points (see dots in Diagram 6, top) and backstitch to secure the ends of the seams. This prepares the angle for the next piece to be set in.

Join two diamond pieces, sewing between matching points to make an angled unit (see Diagram 6).

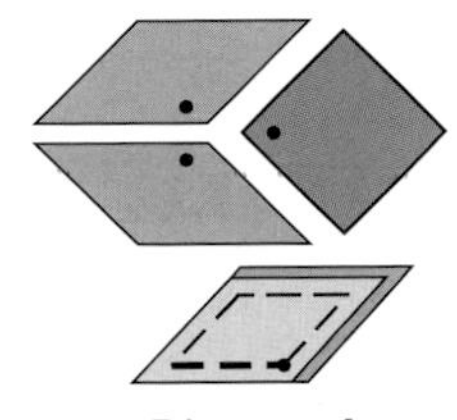

Diagram 6

Follow the specific instructions for either machine or hand piecing to complete the set-in seam.

MACHINE PIECING

With right sides together, pin one piece of the angled unit to one edge of the square (see Diagram 7). Match the seam's matching points by pushing a pin through both fabric layers to check the alignment. Machine-stitch the seam between the matching points. Backstitch to secure the ends of the seam; do not stitch into the ¼" seam allowance. Remove the unit from the sewing machine.

Bring the adjacent edge of the angled unit up and align it with the next edge of the square (see Diagram 8). Insert a pin in each corner to align matching points, then pin the remainder of the seam. Machine-stitch between matching points as before. Press the seam allowances of the set-in piece away from it.

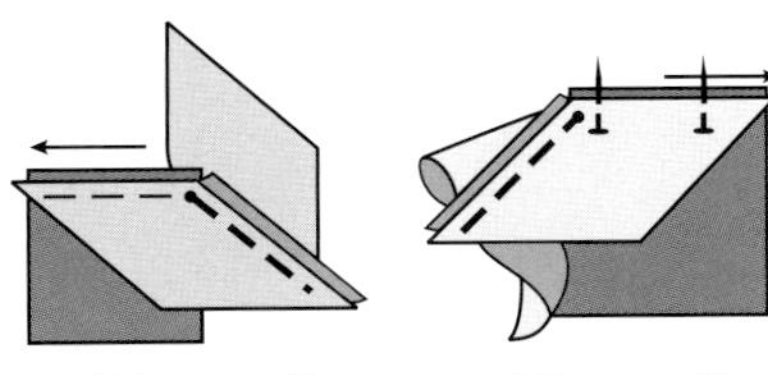

Diagram 7 Diagram 8

HAND PIECING

Pin one piece of the angled unit to one edge of the square with right sides together (see Diagram 9). Use pins to align matching points at the corners.

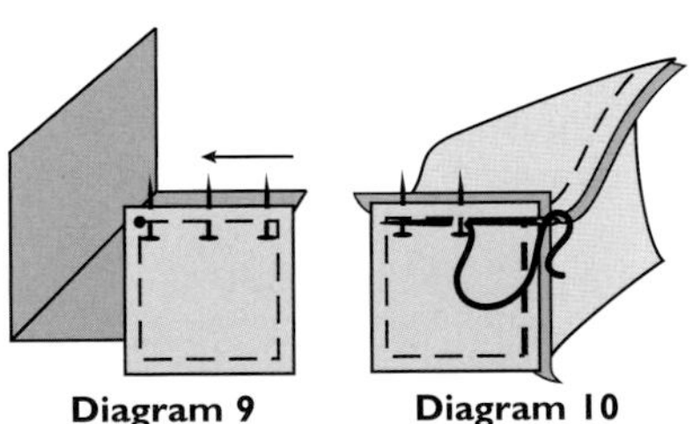

Diagram 9 Diagram 10

Hand-sew the seam from the open end of the angle into the corner. Remove pins as you sew between matching points. Backstitch at the corner to secure stitches. Do not sew into the ¼" seam allowance and do not cut your thread.

Bring the adjacent edge of the square up and align it with the

continued

other edge of the angled unit. Insert a pin in each corner to align matching points, then pin the remainder of the seam (see Diagram 10 on *page 155*). Continuing the thread from the previous seam, hand-sew the seam from the corner to the open end of the angle, removing pins as you sew. Press the seam allowances of the set-in piece away from it.

Mitered Border Corners

A border surrounds the piecework of many quilts. Mitered corners add to a border's framed effect.

To add a border with mitered corners, first pin a border strip to a quilt top edge, matching the center of the strip and the center of the quilt top edge. Allow excess border fabric to extend beyond the edges. Sew together, beginning and ending the seam ¼" from the quilt top corners (see Diagram 11). Repeat with the remaining border strips. Press the seam allowances toward the border strips.

Overlap the border strips at each corner (see Diagram 12). Align the edge of a 90° right triangle with the raw edge of a top border strip so the long edge of the triangle intersects the seam in the corner. With a pencil, draw along the edge of the triangle from the border seam out to the raw edge. Place the bottom border strip on top and repeat the marking process.

With the right sides of adjacent border strips together, match the marked seam lines and pin (see Diagram 13).

Beginning with a backstitch at the inside corner, stitch exactly on the marked lines to the outside edges of the border strips. Check the right side of the corner to see that it lies flat. Then trim the excess fabric, leaving a ¼" seam allowance. Press the seam open. Mark and sew the remaining corners in the same manner.

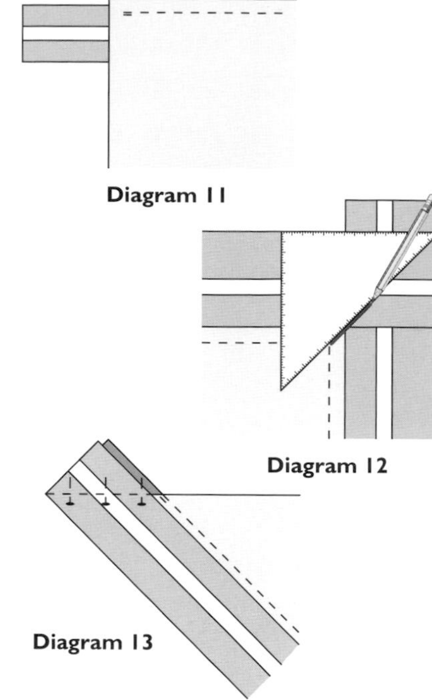

Appliqué

With appliqué, you create a picture by stitching fabric shapes atop a fabric foundation.

Start Simple

We encourage beginners to select an appliqué design with straight lines and gentle curves. Learning to make sharp points and tiny stitches takes practice.

In the following instructions, we've used a stemmed flower motif as the appliqué example.

Baste the Seam Allowances

Begin by turning under the 3⁄16" seam allowances on the appliqué pieces; press. Some quilters like to thread-baste the folded edges to ensure proper placement. Edges that will be covered by other pieces don't need to be turned under.

For sharp points on tips, first trim the seam allowance to within ⅛" of the stitching line (see Photo 1, *opposite*), tapering the sides gradually to 3⁄16". Fold under the seam allowance remaining on the tips. Then turn the seam allowances under on both sides of the tips. The side seam allowances will overlap slightly at the tips, forming sharp points.

Baste the folded edges in place (see Photo 2, *opposite*). The turned seam allowances may form little pleats on the back side that you also should baste in place. Remove the basting stitches after the shapes have been appliquéd to the foundation.

Make Bias Stems

In order to curve gracefully, cut appliqué stems on the bias. The strips for stems can be prepared in various ways. For one method, fold and press the strip in half, then fold the raw edges to meet at the center; press in half again as shown in Photo 3, *opposite*. Or, fold the bias strip in half lengthwise with the wrong side inside; press. Stitch ¼" from the raw edges to keep them aligned. Fold the strip in half again, hiding the raw edges behind the first folded edge; press.

Position and Stitch

Pin the prepared appliqué pieces in place on the foundation (see Photo 4, *opposite*) using the position markings or referring to the appliqué placement diagram. If your pattern suggests it, mark the position for each piece on the foundation before you begin. Overlap the flowers and stems as indicated.

Using thread in colors that match the fabrics, sew each stem and blossom onto the foundation with small slip stitches as shown in Photo 5. (For photographic purposes, thread color does not match fabric color.)

Catch only a few threads of the stem or flower fold with each stitch. Pull the stitches taut, but not so tight that they pucker the fabric. You can use the needle's point to manipulate the appliqué edges as needed. Take an extra slip stitch at the point of a petal to secure it to the foundation.

You can use hand-quilting needles for appliqué stitching, but some quilters prefer a longer milliner's or straw needle. The extra needle length aids in tucking fabric under before taking slip stitches.

If the foundation fabric shows through the appliqué fabrics, cut away the foundation fabric. Trimming the foundation fabric also reduces the bulk of multiple layers when quilting later. Carefully trim the underlying fabric to within ¼" of the appliqué stitches (see Photo 6) and avoid cutting the appliqué fabrics.

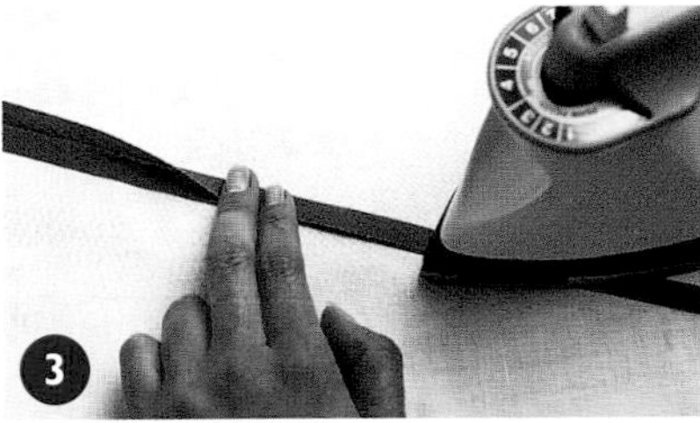

Fusible Appliqué

For quick-finish appliqué, use paper-backed lightweight fusible web. You can iron the shapes onto the foundation and add decorative stitching to the edges. This product consists of two layers, a fusible webbing lightly bonded to paper that peels off. The webbing adds a slight stiffness to appliqué pieces.

When purchasing this product, read the directions on the package to make sure you're buying the right kind for your project. Some are specifically engineered to bond fabrics with no sewing at all. If you try to stitch fabric after it has bonded with one of these products, you may have difficulty. Some paper-backed fusible products are made only for sewn edges; others work with or without stitching.

If you buy paper-backed fusible web from a bolt, be sure fusing instructions are included because the iron temperature and timing varies by brand. This information is usually on the paper backing.

With any of these products, the general procedure is to trace the patterns wrong side up onto the paper side of the fusible web. Then place the fusible-web pieces on the wrong side of the appliqué fabrics, paper side up, and use an iron to fuse the layers together. Cut out the fabric shapes, peel off the paper, turn the fabrics right side up, and fuse them to the foundation fabric.

You also can fuse the fusible web and fabric together before tracing. You'll still need to trace templates wrong side up on the paper backing.

If you've used a no-sew fusible web, your appliqué is done. If not, finish the edges with hand or machine stitching.

Cutting Bias Strips

Strips for curved appliqué pattern pieces, such as meandering vines, and for binding curved edges should be cut on the bias, which runs at a 45° angle to the selvage of a woven fabric and has the most give or stretch.

To cut bias strips, begin with a fabric square or rectangle. Use a large acrylic ruler to square up the left edge of the fabric. Then make a cut at a 45° angle to the left edge (see Bias Strip Diagram). Handle the diagonal edges carefully to avoid distorting the bias. To cut a strip, measure the desired width parallel to the 45° cut edge; cut. Continue cutting enough strips to total the length needed.

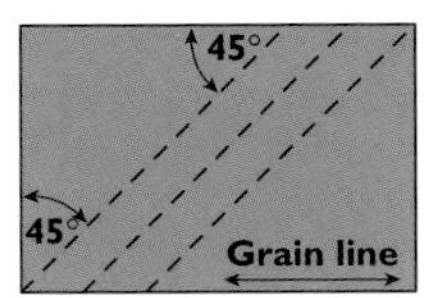

Bias Strip Diagram

Covered Cording

Finish pillows and quilts with easy, tailored cording.

Covered cording is made by sewing a fabric strip around a length of cording. The width of the strip varies according to the diameter of your cording. Refer to the specific project instructions for those measurements. Regardless, the method used to cover the cording is the same.

With the wrong side inside, fold under 1½" at one end of the strip. With the wrong side inside, fold the strip in half lengthwise to make the cording cover. Insert the cording next to the folded edge, placing a cording end 1" from the cording cover folded end. Using a cording foot or zipper foot, sew through the fabric layers right next to the cording (see Diagram 1).

When attaching the cording to your project, begin stitching 1½" from the covered cording's folded end. As you stitch each corner, clip the seam allowance to within a few threads of the stitching line; gently ease the covered cording into place (see Diagram 2).

After going around the entire edge of the project, cut the end of the cording so that it will fit snugly into the folded opening at the beginning (see Diagram 3). The ends of the cording should abut inside the covering. Stitch the ends in place to secure (see Diagram 4).

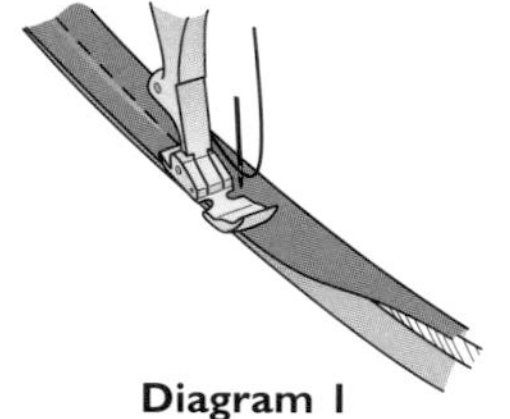

Diagram 1

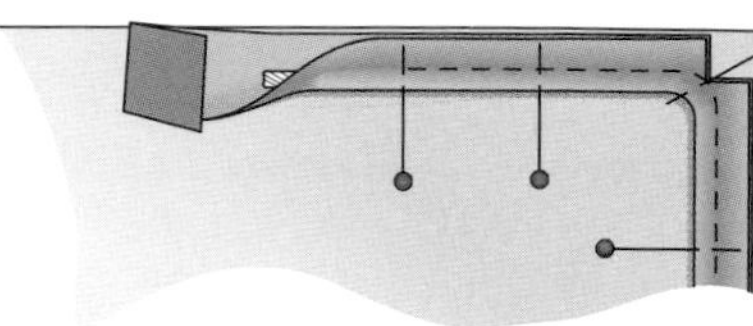

Diagram 2

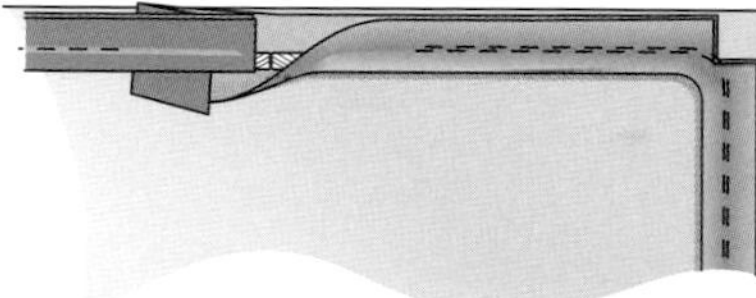

Diagram 3

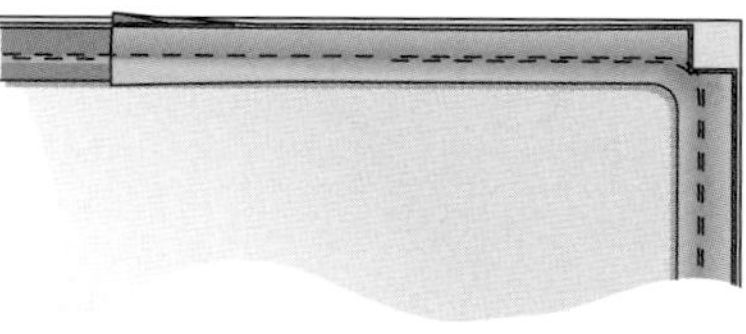

Diagram 4

Hanging Sleeves

When you want a favorite quilt to become wall art,

hang it with care to avoid sagging, tearing, and wavy edges.

Quilts make wonderful pieces of wall art. When treated as museum pieces and hung properly, they won't deteriorate. Let size be your guide when determining how to hang your quilt.

Hang smaller quilts, a 25" square or less, with purchased clips, sewn-on tabs, or pins applied to the corners. Larger quilts require a hanging sleeve attached to the back. It may take a few minutes more to sew on a sleeve, but the effort preserves your hours of work with less distortion and damage.

Make a Hanging Sleeve

1. Measure the quilt's top edge.

2. Cut a 6"- to 10"-wide strip of prewashed fabric 2" longer than the quilt's top edge. For example, if the top edge is 40", cut a 6×42" strip. A 6"-wide strip is sufficient for a dowel or drapery rod. If you're using something bigger in diameter, cut a wider fabric strip. If you're sending your quilt to be displayed at a quilt show, adjust your measurements to

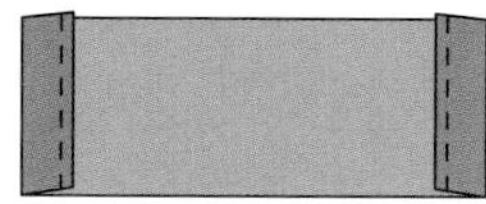

Diagram 1

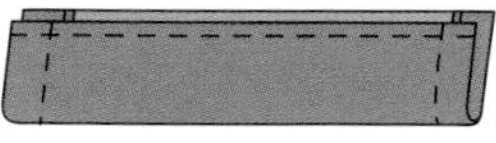

Diagram 2

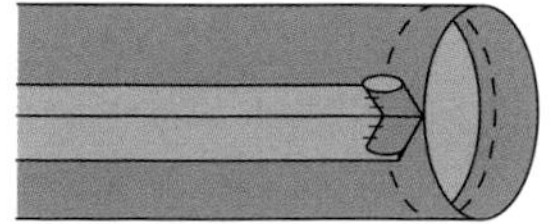

Diagram 3

accommodate the show's requirements.

3. Fold under 1½" on both ends of the fabric strip. Sew ¼" from the raw edges (see Diagram 1).

4. Fold the fabric strip in half lengthwise with the wrong side inside; pin. Stitch together the long edges with a ¼" seam allowance (see Diagram 2) to make the sleeve. Press the seam allowance open and center the seam in the middle of the sleeve (see Diagram 3).

5. Center the sleeve on the quilt back about 1" below the binding with the seam facing the back (see Diagram 4). Slip-stitch the sleeve to the quilt along both long edges and the portions of the short edges that touch the back, stitching through the back and batting.

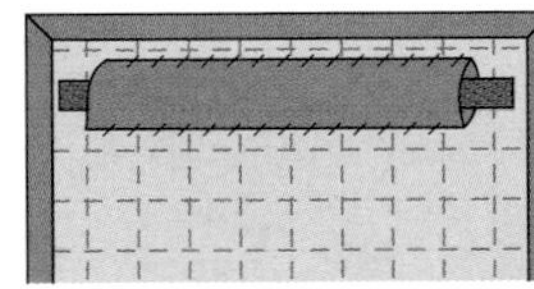
Diagram 4

6. Slide a wooden dowel or slender piece of wood that is 1" longer than the finished sleeve into the sleeve and hang as desired.

FINISHING

The final step in quiltmaking is to bind the edges.

Layering

Cut and piece the backing fabric to measure at least 3" bigger on all sides than the quilt top. Press all seam allowances open. With wrong sides together, layer the quilt top and backing fabric with the batting in between; baste. Quilt as desired.

Binding

The binding for most quilts is cut on the straight grain of the fabric. If your quilt has curved edges, cut the strips on the bias (see *page 157*). The cutting instructions for projects in this book specify the number of binding strips or a total length needed to finish the quilt. The instructions also specify enough width for a French-fold, or double-layer, binding because it's easier to apply and adds durability.

Join the strips with diagonal seams to make one continuous binding strip (see Diagram 1).

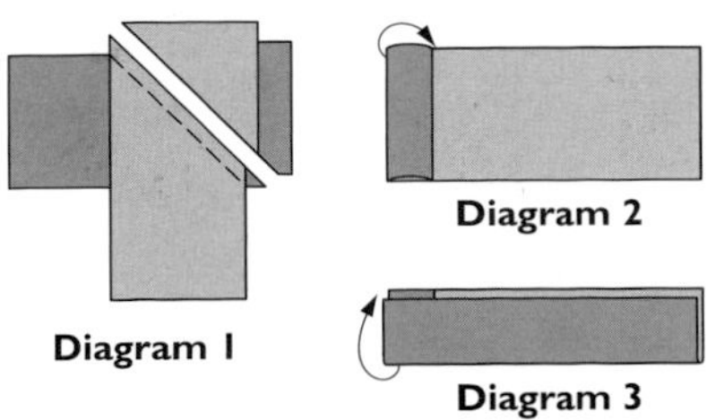

Trim the excess fabric, leaving ¼" seam allowances. Press the seam allowances open. With the wrong sides together, fold under 1" at one binding strip end (see Diagram 2); press. Fold the strip in half lengthwise (see Diagram 3); press.

Beginning in the center of one side, place the binding strip against the right side of the quilt top, aligning the binding strip's raw edges with the quilt top's raw edge (see Diagram 4). Beginning 1½" from the folded edge, sew through all layers, stopping ¼" from the corner. Backstitch, then clip the threads. Remove the quilt from under the presser foot.

Fold the binding strip upward (see Diagram 5), creating a diagonal fold, and finger-press.

Holding the diagonal fold in place with your finger, bring the binding strip down in line with the next edge, making a horizontal fold that aligns with the first edge of the quilt (see Diagram 6).

Start sewing again at the top of the horizontal fold, stitching through all layers. Sew around the quilt, turning each corner in the same manner.

When you return to the starting point, lap the binding strip inside the beginning fold (see Diagram 7). Finish sewing to the starting point (see Diagram 8). Trim the batting and backing fabric even with the quilt top edges.

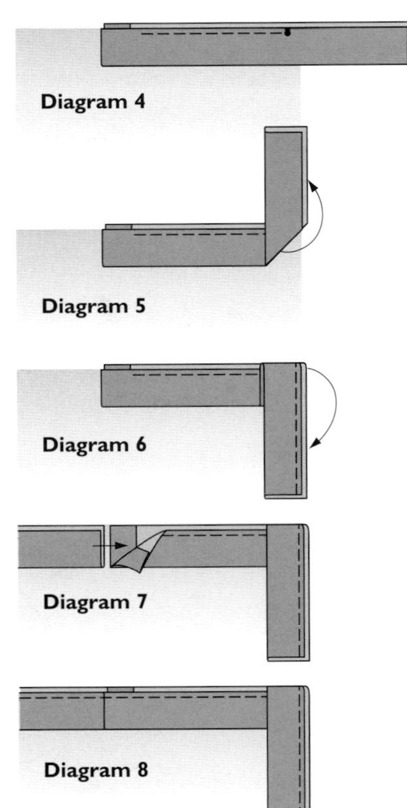

Turn the binding over the edge of the quilt to the back. Hand-stitch the binding to the backing fabric, making sure to cover any machine stitching.

To make mitered corners on the back, hand-stitch the binding up to a corner; fold a miter in the binding. Take a stitch or two in the fold to secure it. Then stitch the binding in place up to the next corner. Finish each corner in the same manner.

CREDITS

Quilt Designers

Alice Berg
Simple Tribute
Alice Berg is one of three quilt and pattern designers at Little Quilts in Marietta, Georgia. She prefers scrap quilts and enjoys replicating antique patterns.

Kim Diehl
Winter Skies
A self-taught quilter, Kim Diehl designs quilts that have homespun charm. She enhances traditional patterns with appliqué accents and other embellishments.

Sandy Gervais
Diamonds Are Forever
Sandy Gervais of Pieces From My Heart creates patterns and fabrics with folksy, primitive designs. Her quilts are casual and scrappy, perfect for a relaxed country cottage.

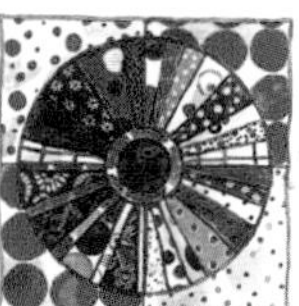

Becky Goldsmith & Linda Jenkins
Completely Dotty
Pattern designers Becky Goldsmith and Linda Jenkins of Piece O'Cake Designs collaborate on intricate appliqué quilts. They also develop innovative methods to accomplish challenging quilting tasks.

Joy Hoffman
Through the Woods
Joy Hoffman bases her original patterns on traditional designs. She experiments with established blocks, challenging herself to use them in innovative ways.

Linda Hohag
Tulip Fancy
Linda Hohag of Brandywine Designs specializes in appliqué patterns and in the techniques to make them simply and quickly. Her liquid-starch method ensures crisp, clean edges in minimal time.

Jo Morton
Prairie Flowers
Quiltmaker Jo Morton continues to prefer hand appliqué and hand quilting. Her passion for appliqué has lead her to develop specialized techniques and to design new quilts that look like antiques.

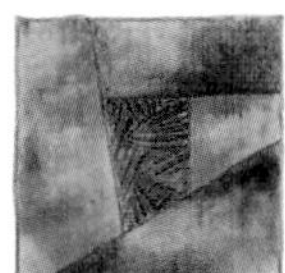

Mabeth Oxenreider
Slice and Dice
Teacher and award-winning quilter Mabeth Oxenreider has worked full-time in the quilting business since 1980. She teaches across the country and uses multiple techniques—from foundation piecing to machine appliqué—to complete projects.

Lila Scott
Pink Spring Fling
Lila Scott loves math and quilts, a perfect combination for her position as technical editor of *American Patchwork & Quilting* magazine and for her orderly quilt designs.

Pat Sloan
Trumpet Blooms
Known for her whimsical appliqué designs, Pat Sloan likes working with quick-to-make projects and large shapes. She loosely bases her patterns on antique quilts.

Laura Boehnke
Quilt Tester
With a keen sense of color and an astute use of fabrics, quilt tester Laura Boehnke gives each project in *American Patchwork & Quilting* magazine an entirely different look from its original as she verifies its pattern, a job she's been doing since the magazine's inception.

Project Quilters and Finishers
Betty Alderman
Jacalyn Bell
Laura Boehnke
Marge Brown
Dorothy Faidley
Karen Gilson
Stephanie Corina Goddard
Linda Turner Griepentrog
Kate Hardy
Roseann Meehan Kermes
Jill Abeloe Mead
Mabeth Oxenreider
Mary Pepper
Janet Pittman
Jill Reber
Pauline Richards
Janelle Swenson
Sue Urich
Kathleen Williams

Materials Suppliers
Andover Fabrics
FreeSpirit
Moda
P&B Textiles
RJR Fabrics
Robert Kaufman Fabrics
Timeless Treasures

Photographers
Craig Anderson: pages 46, 59, 61, 67, 76, 79, 85, 91, 107, 113, 136, 141, 144, 148
Marty Baldwin: page 18
Marcia Cameron: pages 36, 48, 56, 68, 77, 88, 100
Bob Greenspan: page 64
Hopkins Associates: pages 13, 24, 60, 102, 114, 132, 147
Pete Krumhardt: pages 34, 120
Blaine Moats: pages 103, 115
Greg Scheidemann: pages 20, 96
Perry Struse: pages 8, 14, 17, 21, 22, 26, 29, 31, 40, 42, 44, 49, 51, 53, 57, 69, 71, 75, 78, 80, 82, 89, 92, 101, 104, 111, 116, 122, 126, 130, 134, 138, 140, 142, 149
Steve Struse: pages 10, 99
Jay Wilde: pages 15, 22, 23, 30, 41, 49, 50, 72, 81, 93, 123, 131, 133